ON BORROWED TIME

A Mennonite Boy's
High Seas Adventures Aboard
The *Statsraad Lehmkuhl*

The Oceanics School 1972–73

Marlie Smucker

ISBN: 979-8-9946974-0-5

For my grandchildren:

Hannah, Ellamae, Jericho, Westerly, Ophelia, Noah, Arlo, and Rowan

when they come of age

CONTENTS

Statsraad Lehmkuhl

INTRODUCTION

This is a true account of the Oceanics School aboard the *Statsraad Lehmkuhl* commencing with sail training in Bergen, Norway in the fall of 1972, and concluding in Bergen in May of 1973. We sailed to four continents, stopped at multiple ports of entry, and crossed the equator and the Atlantic Ocean twice. Stories and adventures recorded on these pages include an unnerving encounter with a hurricane in the Bay of Biscay, field trip adventures in Tenerife, Gambia, Brazil, Trinidad, the West Indies, the Azores, Spain, and France. They include struggles, emotional pain, and physical hardships induced by community life onboard. We endured clashes with the steward, officers, crewmen, and administrators, with the unpredictable elements of nature, and with each other. We shared celebrations, achievements, humor, and joy. It was a year of education that spawned our coming of age, inspired our grit-in-the-gut determination to survive, developed immeasurable character, and taught us humility. At least some of us. We fought to establish ourselves as individuals, as a community, as a school, and as Norwegian cadets learning the ropes well enough to sail a three-masted, 320-foot square-rigged sailing ship on the high seas.

I journaled faithfully, detailing impressions and perceptions of my experiences, a discipline I had maintained since my fifteenth birthday. Aboard ship, as in the previous few years, my day wasn't complete until I wrote. Some days it was a chore, but most times writing was a way for me to reflect, process, endure, and retreat. My journals remained dormant on my bookshelves for nearly fifty years, three volumes of 586 handwritten pages, unopened, unread, their secrets unshared. Until now.

My perceptions and feelings concerning the accounts and events in this book are my own, as are my relationships and friendships with shipmates, administrators, crew, and folks in port. I don't pretend to speak for anyone else, especially not for the female cadets onboard. My admiration for them and what they endured is unbounded. That said, we each have a story to tell concerning our year with The Oceanics School. Each student-cadet, faculty member, officer, and crewman would tell their stories differently than me. I was a young, naïve, nineteen-year-old Mennonite boy at the time. But this much is true for all of us:

The *Statsraad Lehmkuhl* became our home for the duration of the school year. She thrilled us, transported us, and secured us through calm and storm, cold and warm. She wisely taught us lessons in good times and bad. From the tops of her masts to the depths of her hull, she proudly proved her strength, earned our respect, and proclaimed her might as one of the greatest tall ships on earth. We were and still are some of the luckiest kids in the world to have had the profound opportunity and privilege to call her our home for this wisp of time. She was much more than wood, iron, ropes, and canvas. Somewhere deep in her hull she carried a soul that changed our lives forever.

CHAPTER 1: HOME

I left my home in Bird-in-Hand, Pennsylvania, deep in the heart of the Amish Country, in June of 1971. Community life was all I knew—religious, white, Germanic, hard-working, peace-loving, simple, traditional, nonconforming folks who had separated themselves intentionally from the wiles of the secular world. My early education came from extended family, life on the farm, church folks, and from my three-room Amish-Mennonite school. Life was simple that way, but not necessarily easy.

After my father died suddenly from a tetanus infection when I was three years old, my mother, brother, sister, and I moved into a large farmhouse in Bird-in-Hand with my Grossmommie and several aunts and uncles. Grossdaudy died before I was born. The farm became a place of emotional and spiritual security for my family. The Smuckers had always been on the cutting edge of progressive thinking within the Amish community. So, it was no surprise that when my aunts and uncles desired education beyond eighth grade, my Grossmommie supported their ambitions. She was an unusual Amish matriarch. My father's generation paved the way for me, allowing my siblings and me eventual exposure to a world beyond Lancaster County, Pennsylvania.

Uncle Johnnie moved to New York City to help start a Mennonite Church in the South Bronx. This kind of thing was unheard of for a Bird-in-Hand native. Uncle Marcus spent two years of alternative service in Germany in the early 1950s as a conscientious objector to the military draft. Later, he and three of my aunts attended college and often brought international students home to the farm. I met them all, and my world began expanding. Marcus subscribed to *National Geographic* magazine. I read every page.

After graduating from high school, I was intent on seeing the world, consumed by a desire to travel. I had to start somewhere. Eli and Leamie, my two best friends from school, joined me on a trip to the Midwest and Canada in my 1967 Ford Mustang that I had recently purchased for $550. I bought the car as is, with a smashed front fender, which made it affordable. It ran fine so there was no need to fix anything. I wasn't concerned about impressing anyone, including Nancy, a girl who I had become quite fond of during my senior year. I also allowed my hair to grow with no intentions of cutting it anytime soon.

Eli, Leamie, and I packed enough camping gear and other essentials to survive the trip. In Michigan we worked for a farmer by Lake Huron weeding sugar beets. The wages earned us enough cash to buy food as we crossed into Canada. Odd jobs kept us afloat. Although none of us had much money, two months later we managed to secure flights with Icelandic Airlines to Luxembourg, leaving the States in September of 1971. That's where my real adventures began, where my spirit was given wings, where my worldview created by eighteen years among the Mennonites and Amish was exponentially exposed to the unknowns beyond my safety net.

After an extraordinary experience biking through Europe, working on a farm in Switzerland, falling in love with a Swiss girl, visiting Paris and Rome, surviving three days at the Oktoberfest, and making new friends everywhere, I returned to the States just before Christmas. On January 2, I abruptly moved to Harrison-burg, Virginia on a whim. I spent the next eight months working for a small construction company alongside several back-hills country boys. Hillbillies. My hair was long, often tied back with a leather band. Coworkers thought I was a hippie. Maybe I was. Regardless of our differences, we worked well together after navigating through some initial tough issues of acceptance. And we built several beautiful houses during those eight months.

By August 1972 my time working as a carpenter in rural Virginia had lost its luster. It felt much too normal, boring, and unfulfilling. It was time to move on, time to start a new chapter. So, I decided to move back home to Pennsylvania for a short while to process my next phase of life.

Meanwhile, two female high school friends had invited me to spend a month traveling with them in Florida, ultimately to Key West. One owned a VW Beetle and the other had money. Sounded like a good time. I had already learned to travel and survive on a shoestring, so I wasn't concerned about costs. And who knew what might happen in Florida with two girls? I had always been intrigued by Key West, its proximity to Cuba, and with the American novelist Ernest Hemingway. So I seriously considering joining them.

On my final day of work with the construction crew in Virginia, we framed up a new house. It was fun, fast, and furious as we were all caffeinated, energized, and motivated. A guy named Glen was back on the job for the first time since nearly losing a finger weeks before. And because it was my last day, I treated everyone with all their favorites—Dr Pepper, Coke, peanut butter crackers, chocolates, licorice, twinkies, and Krispy Kreme donuts. It felt sad to say goodbye to those guys, especially to James. He stood close by during our break and wished me all the best, repeatedly. "Come see us agin if yer ever passin' through, and tell us what y'all been up to," he said with a grin. He was serious about that.

During our time together on the job, my stories and perspectives had exposed James to a world he would probably never see for himself. And he might not ever hear about again. He was a simple man, thoughtful and kind, different from the others. But his opportunities aside from carpentry were slim. James didn't do much or get out much except to work.

Aside from me, the entire crew seemed to understand their place and purpose in life—work, cuss, get married, buy a small piece of property for their mobile home, have kids, complain, and worst of all, be proud and feel secure in their lackluster lives.

Daniel, the boss, thanked me for always being on time, for working hard, for my willingness to do whatever he asked, and for paying attention to details. The guys all stood around and nodded their heads in agreement.

Dave, who always had something to say, then rambled on about all sorts of stuff. Mostly about the memories and stories created while working together. Like the day his shirt caught fire from a cigarette while he was lying in the grass during lunch break, forcing him to strip naked while we doused him with water from our jugs. Dave wasn't a handsome boy with his clothes on but was downright uncomely without. After hearing about me being invited to travel with two girls, he responded in typical Dave-like fashion, "Damn, what I wouldn't do fer a chance like that. I needs to find out more 'bout livin' like a hippie. Y'all makes me think different 'bout some stuff," he exclaimed while scratching his head. His tenor voice always raised an octave or so when he was excited. That day he continued his rant in high tenor, "I mean what the hell, maybe I needs to change how I thinks 'bout some things." He explained his rationale for why he might consider voting for the Communist Party in the upcoming election, flashing his rotted teeth and grinning boyishly at the rest of us. His spiel made no sense at all and didn't warrant any response from anyone, except a chuckle from James. But his suggestion of changing how he thinks was as complimentary as anything he had ever said to me. I just smiled.

As I pulled out from the jobsite at the end of the day in my '67 Mustang, Dave yelled, "Y'all be sure to keep yer pants on and don't do nothin' I wouldn't do! YA HEAR ME?!" I sped away with a smile as wide as the Shenandoah Valley.

Back at the apartment I quickly loaded my possessions, turned in the key, then headed north on Route 81 for the last time as a Virginian, reflecting fondly on my experiences there. James and Dave had become significant characters in my everyday life. I had learned to know, love, understand, and care about them in unfathomable ways, realizing that folks at opposite ends of life's spectrum can value each other when we're willing to listen to each other. It was a good life lesson. And secondly, I learned some pretty good carpentry skills, especially from James who was as patient as the day was long.

Four hours later, I was welcomed back home in Bird-in-Hand, Pennsylvania by my family who were all happy to see me, including Dad and Mom. My room in the basement was just as I had left it a year and three months earlier.

Five years after my biological father died in 1956, Mom was introduced to a widower with six children, ages ranging from two to sixteen. I was eight years old at the time. They married three months nearly to the day after they first met. It became easy for me to call my new stepfather "Dad" from the start. He was a good man. Despite the chaotic changes resulting from this new family merger, both Dad and Mom were living examples of perseverance, endurance, survival, and acceptance. So, after my time in Virginia, it felt good to be home.

My brother Merv, who had spent the past two years in Germany with a Mennonite mission organization, had met someone briefly in Amsterdam who told him about an American school ship program sailing out of Bergen, Norway. He wasn't clear about the details but was told the school's main office was in New York City. I received his letter from Europe in late Spring with an address, phone number, and a contact name—Stephanie Gallagher. It sounded interesting, but I realized an opportunity like this would be a long shot. So, I didn't inquire or do anything with his information until months later, at Merv's prodding.

When I eventually received the packet from The Oceanics explaining the program, complete with an application form, it got my full attention. I read with interest the school's intent to provide alternative education for students less inclined to do well in normal classroom settings. Wow! Maybe that was me. I did OK in the classroom, but the thought of sailing and seeing the world by ship sounded adventurous. Money was a problem however, and I imagined the costs involved would surely be prohibitive. So again, I put it on the back burner, trying not to think about it, trying not to become hopeful.

Time passed. It was summer in Lancaster County and I nearly forgot about The Oceanics and the process of applying.

CHAPTER 2: THE INTERVIEW

Finally, one day I called the Oceanics office and set up an interview date with Stephanie Gallagher for late August, then I rode along to New York City with Uncle Johnnie. My brother Merv was already there and hoping to join me for the interview and to help me finalize my application for the school. He and I rode a crowded subway from Southern Boulevard in the Bronx to the Oceanics office on the Upper East Side of Manhattan. I had knots in my stomach from combined fear, hope, and excitement. As we entered the building at 145 E. 74th Street, I nervously rang the buzzer in the vestibule. Within seconds we were greeted by a girl named Tara.

"We've been expecting you." She led us up a flight of stairs into a room that obviously served multiple purposes, then offered us drinks. "Stephanie is on the phone but sit tight. She'll be here momentarily."

I felt anxious when Stephanie entered the room. She was professionally friendly and plainly pretty, wearing no makeup or jewelry. Her dark hair was pulled back smoothly into a small, tight bun at her neck. After brief introductions, she smiled and asked what I knew of the program.

"Very little," I replied, offering nothing more. After a short pause she proceeded to talk for the next ten minutes, first expounding on the history and uniqueness of the ship, then explaining the origin, purpose, requirements, and details of the school itself. I heard every word but couldn't stop my mind from fast-forwarding, already imagining myself as a part of this experience.

She and her husband Chick had become pioneers in experiential education in 1970 after three of Chick's children from a previous marriage struggled continually in formal educational settings. The Gallaghers' concept of a shipboard school developed in response to the problems plaguing their kids. After reading about the tall ships race from England to the Canary Islands in July of 1970, Stephanie became enthusiastic about making their idea of a school ship a reality, and she had Chick's full support. Sixty-three days later they led the first group of students to Norway and boarded the *Statsraad Lehmkuhl*, which at the time sat dormant in the Bergen harbor. There were fifty-five kids total. Stephanie had already signed the contract papers and chartered the ship from Norwegian shipping magnate

Hilmar Reksten after it had been recently abandoned by the Norwegian Merchant Marine as a summer sail trainer.

Chick was forty-five at the time, Stephanie was twenty-four. They had met in New York five years prior, married, and were working jointly as independent producers of educational and documentary films. Chick, the only son of Irish immigrants, was a decorated World War II combat photographer who had served under Generals Eisenhower, Patton, Bradley, and Keyes in Italy. Neither he nor Stephanie were professional educators. So, their desire to start a school aboard a square-rigged sail ship and travel the world was a long shot at best. However, fueled by persistence, creativity, high energy, hard work, connections, and some luck, their dream idea had become a reality in the fall of 1970.

I listened intently, processing every word as Stephanie elaborated briefly on the challenges they faced during their first semester when Hilmar Reksten wanted to cancel the charter contract, furious about one of the students being arrested for smoking marijuana. But the Gallaghers hung tough and finally convinced the ship's owner to follow through with their agreement. Mr. Reksten did not agree to recharter the *Statsraad Lehmkuhl* for a second year, however, forcing them to look elsewhere for a ship.

In time they found another ship in Florida, the *Antarna*, which was registered in Panama. Stephanie signed a more complicated contract with the owners which ended in total disaster for the Oceanics School. Panamanian gunboats eventually surrounded the vessel, arrested Stephanie and held her in custody for a week until Captain Floden surrendered the ship. Students aboard the *Antarna* were then taken to a borrowed farm estate on the south side of Puerto Rico to regroup. That harrowing experience is another story in itself, and not mine to tell.

Stephanie continued talking as I sat quietly, impressed by her confidence, her spirit of fearless optimism, of determination. Of never giving up. She refocused her spiel on the new fall semester and her excitement about rechartering the *Statsraad Lehmkuhl* from Hilmar Reksten. Now it was full bore ahead. I had never met anyone like her in my nineteen years!

"The *Statsraad Lehmkuhl* is a beautiful three-masted barque designed for sailing on the high seas," she said. "For many years she served as a training ship for Norwegian cadets hoping to join the Merchant Marine. This year she'll serve as the floating campus of Oceanics School, again offering students/cadets an alternative to traditional mainstream education, travel, and basic sail training."

Stephanie eyed Merv and me before continuing, "We are firm believers that some teens function better in settings where adventure is at the core." Then she smiled. "Our school provides exactly that, along with physical work, discipline, community, international travel, and onboard classroom studies. The goal is to combine all of that with an experience at sea while maintaining high scholastic expectations for each student. I admit, that's a tall task. We all learn differently. But it's our goal and our resolve." Her words sounded impressively rehearsed. I was sure other kids had heard the same pitch, but I wanted to believe it was formulated just for me.

She then reiterated the fact that this is the third year for the Oceanics School, with the previous two lasting just three months each. "We hope to extend the program for the entire school term," she said with guarded excitement, but with obvious passion concerning community projects and field trip possibilities at various ports of entry. Then she added quickly, "Please understand there are no guarantees of anything. The details of adventure cannot be planned. It's important that everyone who signs on as a student understands he must also sign on as a cadet-in-training and will ultimately be bound by the rules and commands of the ship's officers under Norwegian law. Sail training will be directed by the captain and his crew, not by the school. Students must be committed to both ship and school. No exceptions."

A small crease formed across her forehead. Her lips were terse. I sat slightly forward in my chair as I nodded my understanding. Merv sat erect next to me, listening without comment as she continued, "If anyone cannot complete the sail training program, they'll be sent home, regardless of their scholastic abilities." Then looking directly at me she exclaimed, "No exceptions, no refunds." I suppose she needed to say that, but I wasn't daunted by her words or her tone.

There was a soft side that I sensed in Stephanie as well. A caring side. Like she would do anything to help me succeed if I was accepted into the program. I liked her. And she confirmed my sentiments when she referred to her stepson, Blake, for the sake of whose success she had refocused her career. Like Tara, Blake was part of the previous Oceanics semester.

I found myself becoming increasingly anxious. It was a lot to absorb amid my excitement. I knew in my heart I could survive anything aboard ship, convinced that previous life experiences would serve me well. But how could I convince Stephanie of that? I managed to stay outwardly calm despite difficulty suppressing my innermost feelings. My heart pounded. This whole thing was unimaginable, wild, and crazy!

Finally, she directed personal questions to me concerning home life, family, culture, previous school experiences, skills in getting along with others, anger issues, and my ability to handle disappointments. I found it difficult to answer. I was nervous. Suddenly, the speech impediment I had developed after a difficult tonsillectomy at age fifteen worsened. My vocal cords froze. Merv came to my rescue quickly, exercising his role as the protective big brother. I didn't always appreciate his efforts to take charge of situations, but on this day, he was a godsend.

He explained our Amish cultural history, how we had grown up in the conservative Mennonite Church, about living with Grossmommie Smucker and our close-knit extended family, and about the struggles surrounding the loss of our father when we were young boys. He elaborated on the combined family experience after Mom's remarriage, resulting in eleven of us living together in a small house, and about growing up poor. Although Merv wasn't the interviewee, he held Stephanie's attention. She learned forward, totally interested in every word. He seemed to know the right things to say while presenting me as a nineteen-year-old boy with plenty of innocence, but also with enough personal life experiences to contribute in a positive way to the Oceanics program and community life aboard ship.

In the end, I believe she understood correctly. Merv was looking out for me in a way not often demonstrated by society or by the world around us. Months later she told me she was impressed by his brotherly care and support, and by my family's survival skills.

Tuition was set at $8,500 per student, however, Stephanie determined that just $7,000 was expected from lower income students. The remaining costs would hopefully be raised through fundraising. The Gallaghers had connections with folks in high places. Although actual costs exceeded $8,500 per student, they were committed to keeping tuition affordable for all students. I was already thinking ahead. How could I possibly come up with the $7,000 by mid-October? My parents had nothing, and I had only $2,000 in savings with little time to earn more. I also didn't have time to apply for conventional student loans. I explained that to Stephanie. However, I offered assurance that I'd come up with another $1,500. Then I waited in silence as she made notes on her tablet.

No one said anything for what seemed like a very long time. Finally, she looked up, then without further hesitation, set my terms of acceptance into the program. "You will be responsible for $2,000 total. The Oceanics scholarship fund will take care of the rest."

Wow! Incredible! I was speechless for several seconds, then awkwardly expressed my gratitude, filled with more joy than the moment could hold. Right then and there I determined to prove my worth onboard ship and be an asset to the community. I knew I could do that much.

After a two-hour interview, Stephanie stood to her feet, shook my hand, and officially welcomed me into the Oceanics program. It was a feeling like I'd never experienced before. One of total euphoria! As we left the building, I wanted to shout from the sidewalks of the Upper East Side to the skyscrapers of Midtown Manhattan! This adventure dream was about to come true!

Grossmommie Smucker – the family matriarch

Smucker Homestead - my home as a child

CHAPTER 3: PREPARATION

I had so much to do: acquire my high school transcripts and medical records, get international vaccines for yellow fever and malaria, fill out legal forms with parental permission, purchase accidental death and health insurance, and so much more. The list seemed long. I also needed to earn as much money as possible during my remaining days at home so I had pocket money for incidentals, field trips, and expenses for the year ahead.

I was anxious to share my excitement with friends. Cousin Jerry and I stopped in to see Leamie on Sunday evening after I returned from New York. Leamie and I had been through a lot together during our final two years at Lancaster Mennonite High. We had supported each other emotionally through thick and thin while growing our individual self-esteems, sometimes going on double dates with girls we would've never had the guts to go out with alone. And in the fall of '71, we had traveled together in Europe. Now I couldn't wait to tell him my news, and to brag a bit.

As Jerry and I sat with him at his kitchen table eating cookies and pretzels, telling stories, and catching up, we heard someone coming up the stairs from the family room. Leamie's dad, Toby, wasn't fond of either Jerry or me for reasons of his own. He called us the half-Amish Smucker boys, and it wasn't meant as a compliment. After reaching the top of the stairs, Toby passed through the hallway into the living room, staring straight ahead, then flung open the front door with a bang. He turned and marched to the kitchen table with fire in his eyes. Grabbing my shoulder length hair from behind, he dragged me through the living room to the front door. It happened fast. With one motion he swung me through the opened doorway shouting, "Get this long hair out of my house and don't come back. EVER!"

I offered no resistance but stood stunned in the yard. This was a Mennonite man, the father of my best friend. A Christian. Flashbacks of things Leamie shared with me about his dad raced through my head. I suppose I shouldn't have been surprised. Leamie had been physically and verbally abused for years, especially as a teen. I understood his suppressed feelings, and I always felt his anger was justified. But this was different. This was Toby's first-hand wrath directed at me. This was new and painfully real.

Leamie joined me in the yard, distraught and in tears, quietly mumbling an apology for his father's assault. There wasn't much either of us could say. Jerry stood awkwardly off to the side. The shock sobered us, totally zapping the joy we felt being together. None of us dared challenge Toby. Nor did his wife. She also lived in fear.

I thought aloud, "The world really is an ugly place. Sometimes it sucks, even in peace-loving, God-fearing Lancaster County."

Mom always taught me the importance of forgiveness, with or without an apology from the offender. I suppose it's tougher in some cases than others. Regardless, I had no desire to spend eternity with this man. There were limits in my ability as a teen to offer unconditional forgiveness. God would need to figure that one out and show me more clearly sometime later.

Ω

Uncle Elmer needed assistance landscaping one day, so he called Merv and me, assuming we had nothing better to do. We agreed to help. Elmer suggested we take his wheelbarrow across the road into the neighboring Amishman's hay field and shovel up several loads of good topsoil for his flowerbeds. Not to worry, Elmer said he would pay the guy back sometime. Maybe with compost.

The problem with this sort of work for family members was our pay mostly came by way of food, not cash. And not always from the uncle or family member for whom we worked. If Uncle Elmer's refrigerator had nothing worth eating, we went next door to Uncle Danny's. Or a quarter mile down the road to Uncle Paul's house. There were plenty of family refrigerators in the community from which we randomly indulged. We were teenage boys, and always hungry.

One year prior, Uncle Paul built a new house behind the Bird-in-Hand Restaurant. He needed help picking up stones in preparation to sow grass on his new plot. So, I joined his sons one day to finish the task. We used Paul's new riding mower tractor with a small trailer hitched behind. The work was going well until Cousin Jerry started chasing us with the mower. It was all in fun as we dodged and weaved trying to avoid being hit. I found an old hard rubber ball lying on the ground and fired it at Jerry, hitting him directly on his neck and knocking him off the tractor which was running full throttle!

The out-of-control John Deere ran over Cousin Jeff's foot then continued unmanned across the yard, barely missing a newly planted tree, and on toward the house. We desperately gave chase but couldn't stop the runaway tractor before it crashed into the brick wall. The impact cracked the hood, bent the frame and front axle, and chipped bricks on the house. Uncle Paul was furious, and for good reason. He was a no-nonsense man with little tolerance for reckless play. His free labor that day proved costly.

Despite random boyish behavior, none of us were afraid of hard work. We got things done. And not all reimbursements were paid with food. Several of my uncles owned small businesses and paid cash when we worked for them. I contacted Uncle Joe about the possibility of working at his retail farmers market stand, then stopped to see Great Uncle Jake to inquire about temporary employment at his plant farm in Smoketown. Both responded favorably and offered me all the work I wanted at a decent wage. I was thrilled, needing every penny I could earn before heading off to Norway.

On my first day at the plant farm, I disked downfield stubble with Jake's Ford tractor. Then I learned how to pull pansies from the raised beds. I worked alongside a seventy-something-year-old Amish man named Christian Fisher, also a part-timer. Everyone called him Grishley. His pace was slow but steady in most everything he did, including his speech. Sometimes it took him so long to say what he wanted that coworkers finished his sentences to save time. It took him the entire thirty minutes allotted for break to eat his packed lunch of a half bologna sandwich, small container of canned peaches, one cookie, and a thermos of coffee. He brought the same grub every day. Grishley chewed like an alpaca in slow motion with several teeth missing. Sometimes crumbs fell onto his long gray beard. I soon learned not to ask him questions during lunch break. There wasn't enough time for him to answer and to also finish eating.

Being culturally Amish, he seldom shared feelings or emotions. One day while he and I were working in the field, we happened to be at opposite ends of the pansy patch. Grishley began singing the Amish wedding song, better known as the traditional Lob Song, with each syllable of each word stretching out for an entire stanza. The German lyrics of that song are elongated for the purpose of honoring God, taking more than eight minutes for each verse. Grishley obviously had more time than musical talent and was unaware that anyone could hear him. But I was downwind and heard his singing clear as a whistle. The unusual entertainment continued for nearly fifteen minutes. I chuckled to myself, realizing this unique experience could happen only in Lancaster County, Pennsylvania.

I wasn't privy to the day's tasks at the plant farm before arriving each morning. Great Uncle Aaron, Jake's oldest brother, told Jake one day that he needed me "schloosh" to help harvest sunflowers. The word schloosh was used among the Amish to emphasize the urgency of a point that wasn't negotiable, often with hand gestures indicating finality. Harvesting sunflowers lasted two or three days every fall, and Aaron demanded my assistance for the duration. Jake, being the quiet one of the Glick family, seldom argued with his brothers. It would do no good anyway, in this case, because Aaron always got what he wanted.

Despite his oddities, Great Uncle Aaron was fun to work with. Our past interactions were mostly at Glick family gatherings. He was a great storyteller with plenty of wit, historical knowledge, and humor. He and his brother Dan competed for the spotlight when extended family was together. But during this time of harvesting sunflowers, I felt honored to experience a personal side of Aaron that I never knew.

He was a preacher at Weavertown Amish-Mennonite Church. According to him, he needed an office at the plant farm for daily church work and prayer. Jake, who owned the farm, obliged, allowing him space above the garage by the old airport hangar. It was a rustic setting with an unassuming rickety wooden stairway leading to the upper room. The room itself had an old desk and chair, bookshelf, and a recliner along the wall next to an out of place single bed. A small refrigerator, hot plate, and short dresser sat by the opposite wall, and a faded braided rug covered the center of the floor. During cooler months, a small electric heater removed the chill. The place more resembled a hermit's flat than a preacher's office. But regardless, it was aptly called The Tabernacle. No one was allowed to enter except the high priest himself—Aaron—or those specifically invited by him. The place had a homely appearance but served a special purpose, which only he knew. Preacher Aaron was known to sometimes counsel widows from his church in the Tabernacle—one on one. When anyone asked Jake about his brother's upper room, he just smiled and kept walking.

Jake knew much more about so many things than he ever let on. There was a general sense within the family that as well as Aaron and Dan could tell stories, Jake could keep secrets. The three Glick brothers were unique, each with their own distinct personalities. I often wondered what my grandpa, Dave, would have been like had he lived. He was the oldest of the Glick brothers but died at age 37 from an ether overdose during an appendectomy.

After my father died in 1956, Great Uncle Dan took it upon himself to care for and deepen our spiritual lives. Occasionally he took us out for dinner, individually, with the purpose of engaging in spiritual talk. Merv and I each had one-on-one sessions with Dan. So, when he heard that I was heading to Norway to sign onto a ship as a student/cadet, he scheduled dinner with me at a local restaurant. I enjoyed Dan during my growing up years, especially when I was a child when our interactions were fun and judgment free. But things changed sometime between the ages of twelve and fifteen. That was the age when children became directly accountable to God, according to Dan.

I knew beforehand the purpose of our dinner. After sharing pleasantries about unimportant stuff and reading the menu, he asked if I was ready to order. I had already determined to order the most expensive thing on the menu. If I was expected to endure preaching and questioning, I would at least do it with a happy stomach. Dan eyed me without expression as I ordered a T-bone steak, baked potato with all the fixins, applesauce, and apple pie à la mode.

Midway through the meal, as expected, he asked, "Marlin, how is your relationship with the Lord?" Being a typical, well-taught Lancaster County Mennonite boy, I knew scripture and understood God as only a nineteen-year-old could. But like most kids my age, I wanted to find and know truth. I also sought adventure, love, and experiences beyond what my first nineteen years had provided. And I didn't care to be smothered by someone else's understanding and perceptions of God. I still had things to figure out for sure. I didn't deny that. But I suggested that maybe, just maybe, the Oceanics experience might help me sort out some of those unknowns.

Great Uncle Dan did not agree. "There are no unknowns concerning who God is," he said in a raised voice, then stated in no uncertain terms that this notion of going to Norway to live on a ship was ludicrous. It would not be good for my spiritual life or for my physical well-being. "We become like our surroundings," he exclaimed.

I was quiet for a few moments, not wanting to argue or discuss the subject further. But I was irritated by his condemning spirit, realizing that I needed to say something. Trying to remain calm, I responded matter-of-factly, "Life experiences are different for everyone. One's faith develops from his participation in life, not by what he is told. I must find my own way, and hopefully will stand strong in the midst of storms."

Dan wasn't pleased with my answer and followed with an exhaustive five-minute speech about how good God is. He emphasized the fact that no one is beyond God's goodness, God's love, God's grace, and God's wrath. I had no argument there but chose to disengage from the conversation. That infuriated him. Dan had an agenda, and I wasn't playing along. Of course not. I wasn't about to play into his hand and go on the defensive. I appreciated his concern for me, if indeed that's what this was, but I didn't care for his methodology of manipulation and control over me. And I was appalled by his disregard for my feelings. He wasn't a good listener that night. Maybe he never was, but I hadn't recognized it before.

The evening ended with both of us feeling frustrated, except for the food. He thought I should give him definitive answers concerning my spirituality, and I thought he should just shut up. I felt no need to explain or defend the excitement within my soul concerning my upcoming adventure. Mom always said that wisdom comes with age, and I believed that to be true. But I came to realize after this encounter with Great Uncle Dan that any wisdom we glean from age must also be applied. I could only hope I'd remember that in fifty years when I might have opportunity to treat my own grandnephew to dinner and offer advice before something exciting or adventurous in his life.

Ω

With the additional monies earned at my odd jobs at home, I was able to buy most everything needed for the coming year with Oceanics. Stephanie's list of personal items was detailed but not long. Things like a navy-blue blazer, blue work shirts, dress trousers, new jeans (without holes), high-topped shoes, gloves, a large duffle bag, sleeping bag, toiletries, notebooks, journal, etc. I was told storage space onboard would be minimal.

As the time to leave drew near, I experienced normal pre-trip jitters. Recent comforts of home tugged at my heart strings as questions and unknowns found their way into my psyche. Maybe Great Uncle Dan was right. Maybe Oceanics wasn't such a good idea. The mind games became wearisome. On a positive note, I had one thing left to do: Vote.

The 1972 presidential election was ramping up as the two candidates, George McGovern and Richard Nixon, were in their final months of the campaign. For the first time, I was finally old enough to vote for president. Knowing I'd be out of the country on election day, I acquired an absentee ballot and mailed it in. My candidate of choice was Democrat George McGovern, not that it mattered much. It appeared like Nixon would easily win reelection. And war criminal Henry Kissinger would still be able to maximize his influence in Washington DC and abroad as Secretary of State. But for me, voting was about personal choice, about doing the right thing, about integrity despite the outcome. We were living in difficult times in the USA in which idealism clashed harshly with realism. I was convinced of Nixon's cowardice and untrustworthiness. In my opinion he was clearly not the right person to lead our country. But I dismissed it all when I mailed in my ballot, washing my hands of American politics.

It was time to pack my bags and go. Time to meet up with fellow Oceanics classmates in New York. Dad, Mom, and my three younger sisters escorted me from Bird-in-Hand to Uncle Johnnie's house in the South Bronx on a Sunday afternoon. They stayed in the city only long enough to bid me a proper farewell. The experience was both joyous and sad. Mom hugged me for a long time, trembling with emotion, then whispered, "Goodbye Marlie. I love you," as tears rolled down her cheeks. Everything else had already been said or prayed. I suppose mothers are entitled to feel what they will when sending a son off to the unknown. I remained silent, expressionless on the outside, then waved from the sidewalk as my family disappeared into the traffic heading toward the Cross Bronx Expressway. On the inside I was filled equally with excitement and fear. But I felt loved.

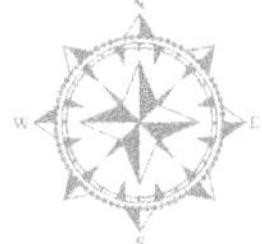

Dusk in Bergen

Dry dock where we boarded ship

CHAPTER 4: BERGEN

I spent two days with Uncle Johnnie's family in the Bronx. Johnnie had a bad case of bursitis and stayed in bed most of that time, but the rest of us heard frequent outbursts and screams from his bedroom as the prescribed pain medication didn't help. He eventually placed a whistle on his nightstand that he blew for assistance. He whistled for food and water, for a throat lozenge, for extra pillows and blankets, and he whistled for help to roll over.

"What time is it?" he yelled from his room. Then before anyone could answer, "Bring me the newspaper." It was disruptive for the entire household. Cousin Woodie complained repeatedly, juggling his playtime between whistle calls. But although he was wary of being scolded, he did manage to laugh at the situation as only an eight-year-old dared.

Aunt Irene drove me to JFK airport along with cousins Dennis and Joy who were excited to see me off and highly motivated to get out of the house. Traffic and horn-honking were more tolerable than the whistleblowing at home. After quick goodbyes at the Scandinavian Airlines terminal, I checked my green army duffel bag and carried a small backpack to the gate. It was then that I saw kids in blue blazers gathered around Mrs. Gallagher, who patiently answered questions while dealing with the logistics of the trip. She was efficient, thorough, and prepared for the challenge of getting sixty students to Norway.

At one point, her assistant Tara commented to me, "This is the easy part. Just wait till we arrive in Bergen after a seven-hour flight and try to get this bunch aboard ship with all their baggage. And I'm not just talking about baggage in luggage form!" Tara had obviously been through this before.

I nodded with a smile, knowing only too well the demands of international travel from my time in Europe the prior year. Some kids appeared to come from affluence, but not all. Ages ranged from 15 to 20, with more guys than girls, but it was difficult to know how many of each.

I sat in the middle seat between two female students on the night flight to Bergen. Jane was talkative, obviously excited about the opportunity to sail. Through research she had familiarized herself with the *Statsraad Lehmkuhl* and was anxious to set foot on her deck. Mary was engaging but kept her comments short.

Upon arrival in Bergen at 6:20 a.m. local time, buses transported all of us to the docks at Laksevag where we formally signed onto the ship as Norwegian merchant cadets. At the time, the *Statsraad Lehmkuhl* was temporarily in dry dock for last minute repairs to the hull. We were greeted by several officers as we reached the main deck. It felt surreal. I was now accountable to the captain and his crew, subject to Norwegian law, without any sort of emotional transition. It all happened quickly.

Yards: Large horizontal steel spars attached to the masts that hold square sails

As I walked onboard, I stared in awe at the ship's masts and yards towering majestically above everything else by the pier. My mind raced wildly as the reality of this long-anticipated adventure began sinking in. Goose bumps covered my arms. This massive sailing structure was now home. As directed, I found my sleeping quarters, known by the Norwegian term banjers, one level down from the main deck.

The rooms were small and basic with two sets of bunks positioned perpendicular to the outside walls of the ship. Upright lockers, one for each cadet, stood at the foot of the beds and opened into the hallway. There was a glass porthole 10" in diameter allowing daylight into my room from port-side, and a lamp centered between the bunks by the exterior wall. A long curtain hung from ceiling to floor at the entrance. There were no doors. Rooms in the banjers were all laid out basically the same, separated only by thin plywood which extended almost from floor to the ceiling. Luxuries were few.

Two hallways running fore and aft divided the banjers. Room assignments were made by the school administration prior to boarding—four cadets per room. Although guys and girls didn't share rooms, there wasn't much separation between gender quarters. Names posted on each locker corresponded with room assignments. No one was permitted to switch without authorization from the administration. But with sixty teenagers aboard ship, that was the first policy to be challenged.

I met each of my roommates as we unloaded our stuff. Eric was tall and thin with long straight hair that hung below his shoulders. He was quiet and soft spoken, obviously an introvert, but well-read and knowledgeable about birds and plants. On that first day, he acquired the nickname "Birdman" after sharing about his week-long survival experience in the forest several months earlier. He took with him only a sleeping bag, a small tent, a pocket-knife, and a few other essentials, and survived on berries, mushrooms, lichens, frogs, and small critters while camped next to a mountain stream. "The best part," he said flatly, "I saw lots of birds and no humans." Birdman's story was impressive but didn't appeal to me at all. Regardless, we became instant friends.

Todd, from upstate New York, was a solid boy, tall and pudgy with wavy light brown hair, friendly but embarrassingly loud. He was as transparent as a clean single glass pane, speaking first before thinking. That tendency forced him to explain and apologize often. But to his credit, Todd was honest, decisive, inquisitive, and eager to learn. I enjoyed his wit and humor. He made me laugh from the first day I met him. More importantly, we shared several things in common. We both valued fairness for victims of injustice, even as it applied to small things aboard ship, and we both were competitive by nature—I more quietly so, Todd in a fierce, in-your-face way.

Jones, the fourth bunkmate, was more serious than the others and carried himself with an air of subtle arrogance. Unnecessary humor wasn't his bag. He expeditiously judged and formed opinions about folks and told us that a person must prove himself worthy of acceptance, friendship, and trust. "That goes for you guys here in this room," he monotoned.

His responses came across as smart-alecky, like he presumably had more common sense than the rest of us. I was initially taken aback by his attitude but joined Todd and Eric in welcoming him as our roommate. Jones was cordially considerate of most folks, and it became evident that if treated respectfully, he'd reciprocate with the same. But I found it more comfortable to discuss functional stuff with him rather than engage him philosophically.

Each personality found its place as the four of us developed an unusual sort of friendship. We didn't necessarily hang out onboard but showed support and respect for each other during our daily activities. However, after several nights onboard, we all got on Todd's case for snoring and talking in his sleep.

After unpacking and organizing what few possessions I had on day one, I invited Todd to go for a walk onshore. Nothing was formally scheduled on our first day except to acclimate to our new surroundings. We were strongly encouraged not to sleep until nightfall. As the two of us headed down the gangway, we met several crewmen loading supplies onto the ship from the dock—canned foods, flour, sugar, condensed milk, and lots of unmarked boxes. We were too tired to offer assistance, but I later volunteered to help serve the evening meal and clean up, along with seven other students.

The cooks, Burgo, Johnnie, and Joe, were a lively bunch, and anxious to practice their English. Jane, my friend from the plane, was also on mess duty. She thought it wise to befriend the cooks, noting smilingly, "The galley crew can set the tone and mood onboard, especially at sea, so let's keep them happy." I agreed and did everything they instructed with enthusiasm. But by the time cleanup was finished, I was experiencing serious fatigue. It felt like a week had passed since we left New York.

An all-aboard meeting was scheduled after dinner in the mess hall. Timing for that seemed unreasonable. Those of us who arrived from the States early morning tried desperately to stay awake and attentive as the ship's crew was introduced by Chief Mate Gronningen, starting with Captain Fossa, then First Mate Schnitler, Second Mate Kjemtrup, Bosun, chief engineer, the quartermaster, several ordinary seamen, the carpenter, and the cooks, all totaling more than 25 crew members. Several of them appeared to be thick-skinned salty seadogs, right out of the pages of Moby Dick. Quite a contrast from us hippie wannabe sailors.

Chief Mate: Officer 2nd in command to the captain

Chief Mate then explained his expectations onboard, emphasizing zero tolerance for illegal drug usage, including marijuana. Anyone caught smoking weed would immediately be removed from the ship and punished to the fullest extent of the law. Absolute compliance with all commands from the officers was imperative, including all ship's work and punctuality for scheduled watches. Cadet responsibilities could not be undermined or compromised. In addition, Chief emphasized the importance of each watch.

"The lookout watchman is stationed on the bow, watching for other ships, foreign objects, land, or trouble ahead." Glancing around the mess hall as our heads bobbed, he continued, "Buoy watch is positioned at the stern. He is the last person to spot a fallen fellow sailor or any unusual sightings from the rear of the ship." At that a few heads jerked up. Falling overboard sounded serious! "There is a lifebuoy and a long rope hanging by the aft railing to be used during a rescue attempt," he added.

Seconds later, heads again began nodding as Mr. Gronningen continued, "The fire watchman is expected to move about covering the deck, banjers, galley, and public areas of the ship. His job

Chief Mate Gronningen

is to report fire, hazardous spills, and anything unusual or out of place, including reckless behavior. He or she must assist the deck officer as requested and be sure the next scheduled watchmen are ready for duty. This is especially important during the nighttime hours between 22 hundred and 06 hundred."

Gangway watch seemed simple enough. Stationed at the top of the gangway, the person on duty oversees the clipboard used to register each person who comes and goes. All visitors need documentation and written consent from the attending officer before boarding.

Chief Mate's spiel drug out with details that couldn't possibly be absorbed by all the sleepy bobble-heads. Like the fact that the 24-hour clock would be implemented starting immediately. And that all sea schedules, watches, meals, musters, ship's work, and curfews in port would be posted accordingly. He again reminded us of the importance of punctuality before describing the duties of wheel watch, "The cadet at the helm is driving the ship."

Between intermittent nod-outs, I heard something about maintaining precision and accurate headings at all times, especially during the challenges of rough seas. I was too tired to care.

He finished by welcoming everyone on board the *Statsraad Lehmkuhl* and wishing us a good year of sailing. "It will take teamwork and effort to navigate this ship. Everyone must work hard. Insubordination will not be tolerated. This isn't a ride of leisure. Tomorrow we will begin sail training starting with Norwegian language classes. Ship's orders will often be communicated in Norwegian. You must learn and understand all instructions from the officers and crewmen in charge. It could be a matter of life and death."

We all heard him say that before we hauled our tired butts off to bed. But even the words concerning "a matter of life and death" didn't seem as important to me as sleep.

I huddled down into my sleeping bag on the bunk below Jones, happy to finally be in bed. I managed a short prayer of thanksgiving to God for this amazingly unnerving experience. And for my new home aboard ship. Todd was already snoring loudly on the bunk above Birdman. It didn't matter.

My bunk

Everyone aloft

Furling the stay sails

Bending sails

Bergen Harbor at dusk

Morning muster on deck

Furling the merse sail

Yard arm work

CHAPTER 5: SAIL TRAINING

The next morning at precisely 06:30, someone walked through the banjers blowing a ridiculously loud, shrill whistle, shouting in a heavy Scandinavian accent, "Wake up, wake up, it's time to get up—the birds are singing, the sun is shining!" (neither of which was true).

The whistle and verbal alarm continued while the sailor walked fore and aft through the banjers, ending all possibility of continued sleep. I was up in a flash as a small orchestra of cadets, the Florida boys, yelled obscenities in response from their bunks: "Holy shit!" "What the fuck!" "Asshole!" "Who's blowing that goddamn whistle?" This daily morning routine continued throughout our training. I couldn't determine which was most offensive, the whistle or the obscenities. But the cursing and the use of vulgarities wasn't just done in anger. I realized that normal conversations onboard included references to "the beautiful fuckin' wheel" or "the tall fuckin' mast" or "the goddamn stay sails," both in English and Norwegian.

At home, Mom washed our mouths out with soap when we used 'bad words,' as she called them, like "gee-whiz," "shucks," "darn-it," or "heck." But there wasn't enough soap onboard to cleanse these vulgar mouths. Adjusting to and accepting the language of shipmates was one of my early challenges. I developed linguistic immunities quickly for the sake of my ears, not for my tongue, however. I wasn't about to become like my surroundings at this early juncture.

On that first morning aboard I dressed quickly, brushed my teeth, and reported to the main deck. Sail training had begun.

Muster was at exactly 07:00 that day, and every day thereafter. We lined up on deck and counted off. Going forward, we were identified by our numbers which were permanently marked on the shoulders of our rain gear. Number 45 was my new ID. We, the cadets, were expected to stand in a straight line at attention, in numerical order. Anyone late for muster, out of line, or not at attention, was disciplined. Punishments varied from an hour of polishing brass to scrubbing the deck, cleaning toilets, or anything involving ship's work. Countless tasks and

Muster:
Organized roll call of cadets on deck

procedures were taught during training sessions. The work was tough enough without additional chores resulting from an infraction.

This style of training was a new experience for me. My childhood teaching didn't resemble any of the tactics used during sail training. It felt unsettling at first as my individuality was lost. I was now just a number, a mere cog in the big wheel. No cadet was more important than another.

The work and discipline became easier with each passing day as our individual wills melted, like horses being broken. We were constantly reminded that sailing a large ship like the *Statsraad Lehmkuhl* demands selfless teamwork to overcome the challenges of wind, rain, cold, rough seas, storms, and unforeseen troubles. Todd and I discussed our training at the end of each day. It was a good way to reflect and summarize what we were taught from dual perspectives. Like verbal journaling. But before retiring for the night, I still pulled out the notebook binder from under my pillow and wrote. There was so much to record.

♌

"When orders are given," Chief Gronningen accentuated, "each cadet must respond quickly without questioning." I understood the necessity of discipline aboard ship. This was our ticket to travel the world. But I had serious questions whether this motley bunch would be able to sail the ship and meet the inevitable provocations of the sea. Regardless, it was exciting for sure. I felt like a character in a storybook adventure with the novel opportunity of helping to create the story itself.

After our first muster, six groups were formed: A, B, C, D, E, F. The groups were scheduled to cover all designated shifts, both on-duty and standby, 24/7. At least one group was on duty throughout the entire Oceanics School experience, even while in port. Groups self-organized their tasks of galley duty, serving meals, clean up, ship watches, setting and taking in sails, and all ship's work. While on duty, group members were responsible to the officers and crew, not to school administrators.

Ideally, the six-group concept allowed for relaxation and sleep time, class and study time, and ship duties. But when the command was given, "Alle mann pa dekk" (all hands on deck), every able-bodied cadet was required to report immediately to the main deck, regardless of schedule. Chief Mate made it quite clear that the ship came first. Everything else was secondary. "There is nothing more important than the safety and performance of this ship," he exclaimed emphatically. "None of you as individuals are more important than the ship."

Silence followed as we processed his words. This ship was like God. I had my own thoughts regarding the ship being more important than people but I kept them to myself. The Chief's words didn't match what I was taught at home. This wasn't the world I knew. However, I was committed to obeying the rules onboard. I determined to follow all officers' orders, apply myself, cooperate, and work hard. I would even hold high the value and absolute importance of maintaining the physical aspect of this amazing ship. But I could not compromise my beliefs concerning the value of fellow cadets, faculty, and crew. In my heart, humans would always be more important than wood, iron, and canvas. I knew where I stood on that.

Aside from sail training and the physical aspects of the ship, there was also the educational component of the school to consider. Stephanie called a school meeting several days into sail training to share insights and express her scholastic goals for this adventure. She had a way of offering us encouragement. "Sail training will improve your communication skills, build character, and better prepare you for life's future challenges. As you learn the technical details of sailing, some of you will be motivated by desire, others will learn out of obligation. But once on the high seas, you'll learn from the innate survival instincts within. You'll experience a spawning of bravery and confidence to conquer the unknowns, one challenge at a time. You'll learn valuable lessons in teamwork, acceptance of hierarchical structures, and the need for accountability at all levels. What appears to be loss of freedom now will become an even deeper sense of freedom as the benefits of this adventure play out. Freedom knows no borders, nor does sail training. This is truly an opportunity that most of you will never see again. Make the most of it."

Her speech was inspirational, even for the few disgruntled kids. Sail training suddenly took on a more serious tone. Efforts were stepped up by many to learn Norwegian, learn the ropes, and accept the regimented schedule. At least for now.

Ω

The *Statsraad Lehmkuhl* remains one of the largest square-rigged ships still in operation, and the most environmentally friendly tall ship in the world. She was built in Bremerhaven, Germany in 1914 for the purpose of training German merchant marines under the original name *Grossherzog Friedrich August*. During World War I she was used by the German Navy, but eventually became a war prize for England in 1920, well after the war ended. One year later a shipping company out of Bergen, Norway bought her for the sake of training its own merchant marines. Cabinet Minister Kristofer Lehmkuhl was instrumental in helping acquire her for that purpose; thus, the name *Statsraad Lehmkuhl* (Minister Lehmkuhl). From 1923 to 1967 the ship continued serving as a Norwegian training ship except during a five-year period from 1940 to 1945 when she was confiscated by the Nazis, painted black, and renamed *Westwarts*.

Costs and declining interest in traditional sail training finally caused the merchant marine to abort their program aboard the *Statsraad Lehmkuhl*. So, in 1967 Hilmar Reksten, a wealthy Norwegian ship owner, bought the ship to prevent the possibility of losing her abroad. He stationed her in the Bergen Harbor while continuing his efforts to involve her operationally as a cadet training vessel. In the summer of 1970, the Gallaghers came on the scene, seriously exploring the possibility of leasing her to promote their ideas of creative education combined with sail training. A school ship.

The ship has always been an impressive structure, measuring 321 feet in length from the end of the bowsprit to the aft rail—notably longer than a football field. Its actual hull length is 277 feet, with a width of 41 feet across at center. It was difficult for me to appreciate her size while in dry-dock, but my first view of the ship docked alone in the harbor was impressive, majestically towering above the Bryggen wharf as an icon of this picturesque Nordic city. She was beautiful by anyone's description.

Mesan Sails: Sails attached to the aft mast used for steering and stability
Square Sails: Large rectangular sails set on horizontal yards attached perpendicular to the mast
Stay Sails: Triangular sails set on a support wire between the masts used to balance the ship and provide sail area in various wind conditions

The height of her main mast is 157 feet. I quickly calculated the top of the mast to be more than two times higher than the silo at the Smucker Homestead in Bird-in-Hand, which stands at 65 feet. That had previously been my highest vertical climb. Under full sail, we were told, the *Statsraad Lehmkuhl* can reach speeds of 17 knots (approximately 20 mph). By comparison, an Amish horse and buggy in Lancaster County travels at an average speed of 10-15 miles per hour. The diesel engine, located in the lower backside of the hull, is used mostly for docking, maneuvering in harbor, and for providing stability in rough seas. But in calm waters the engine can propel the vessel up to 11 knots.

Although the ship's total weight is 1,516 tons, the most impressive characteristic is its canvas with ten square sails on the fore and main masts, two mesan sails aft, and ten staysails—a grand total of twenty-two sails.

As for me personally, I felt honored to be a cadet onboard this remarkable ship in the fall of 1972. The moment I first saw her, I couldn't wait to climb her masts.

Ω

The paid crew proved to be an interesting bunch of characters. First Mate Schnitler was tall, slender, and proud with a peculiar snarl when he spoke. It was he who taught us the ropes in Norwegian with the help of a posted diagram of the entire deck. The detailed drawing named each belaying pin and the corresponding ropes they secured from each of the twenty-two sails. That felt overwhelming initially, until the actual hands-on training began. But in time, it began to make sense. Schnitler covered a lot of material quickly, with high expectations of cadet comprehension.

He also taught a brief conversational Norwegian language class during which time his demeanor was noticeably kinder. When not on officer duty, the first mate was more expressive, cordial, and personable. Eyeing the informal appearance of the American cadets, he explained local traditions and culture, the do's and don'ts when going into town. "Wear your blazers and nice trousers," he said. "Clean up and be on your best behavior."

Although encouraged by the friendlier side of Schnitler, we knew better than to test his authority during sail training. We were only numbers then, not people, and there were consequences for crossing him up or pissing him off.

Second Mate Peter Kjemtrup was a big strapping Dane with a teddy bear personality who had been sailing since he was fifteen years old. His English was far from perfect, and his accent and choice of words were sometimes comical. He often said one word when meaning another. Peter laughed at his own verbal blunders but when giving orders or supervising ship's work, he demanded obedience and respect. He oversaw the daily workstations, which involved him interacting directly with us, the cadets. I enjoyed his work ethic, his ability to laugh, and his efforts to engage. Kjemtrup detected my willingness to do what he asked, and we got along just fine.

Sometimes while we were doing mundane, mindless work, like polishing brass on a cool day, or washing the deck in the rain, Peter entertained us with funny stories. The hilarity came from his presentation rather than from the stories themselves. When he determined something not to be important, he said repeatedly, "That's a never mind." The expression caught on. Soon cadets all over the ship were saying it when referring to something of little significance. But some kids pushed the limits, using the term loosely for things of absolute importance, like curfew, being late for muster, missing scheduled watches, or breaking ship's rules.

Kjemtrup misused the expression as well, like when we complained about the working conditions in freezing rain and driving wind during training sessions. Peter set his jaw and responded in a booming voice, "That's a never mind!" No one dared argue with the big Dane. After all, he was the author of the term.

Able-bodied seaman Peter Poulsen, another Dane, also played an integral role in sail training. He had the appearance of a picture-perfect Scandinavian sailor with thick skin, blonde hair, hefty build, and a square chin. He could do the work of a giant. Poulsen was gung-ho when it came to ship's work, with little patience for slackers. If ever there was a custom-made sailor fit for a square-rigged sail ship, surely it was he. I mused quietly one day as I compared this guy to my old neighbor, Dick Hubbs. Dick, who was a bully in our neighborhood, eventually became an able-bodied seaman on a US Navy ship, but he mysteriously fell overboard and died at sea, chopped up by the prop. "Poor Dick never had a chance," I mumbled to myself as I watched Poulsen climb impressively fast to the mesan beam like a windup toy.

After a few days onboard, we came to realize that Poulsen was the morning whistle-blower. It was he who blew that rude, dream-shattering, heart-stopping wakeup whistle in the banjers—the sound every cadet came to dread, and the rhythm we all unintentionally memorized. In time, Peter became more gracious. Without a doubt he was good for the ship and good for anyone serious about learning to sail—a great teacher by example with a "git 'er done" personality.

Jacobsen, also an able-bodied seaman, was as hard-nosed and rock-headed as they come. But he was a funny guy as well. Moderately short and stocky in stature with wavy reddish hair, he was built like a gymnast, moved with quick, jerky agility, and worked like a mule. Some thought he had the mind of one as well. His boisterous, outspoken character made him stand out among the crewmen. He definitely wasn't a behind-the-scenes guy. Often seen with a cigarette hanging from his mouth, he epitomized the terms "salty dog" and "drunken sailor." Jacobsen drank excessively. He had been a sixteen-year-old cadet aboard the *Statsraad Lehmkuhl* in 1952 when the ship sailed to New York City. So, in 1972, as a thirty-six-year-old, he had already been sailing for twenty years.

Despite being crazy at times, he was fearless in the rigging, impressively knowledgeable regarding the ship, and played a major role in the details of sail training. The only thing that really mattered and the only thing he took seriously onboard, was sailing. However, those priorities shifted to booze and women while on shore, where he pulled all stops on responsible drinking and reckless behavior. In his mind, women had their place and purpose but should not be aboard a sail ship. I was thankful to be a guy, not a girl, when under his authority. Contrary to his convictions, however, he made a few exceptions, especially for my friend Jane who proved her worthiness among the cadets as a qualified sailor.

When Jacobsen was ill-tempered, I did my best to steer clear. Aside from those times, however, I liked the guy. Maybe it was his ability to entertain or the confidence with which he performed his tasks, but there was never a dull moment when he was on duty. His earthy laugh and devilish eyes were beguiling and sometimes strangely stirring.

Arne was a twenty-year-old sailor—another able-bodied seaman. His long, unkempt blonde hair was fine and straggly, like that of a runaway orphan. He wasn't bothered by being at the low end of the crew's pecking order. Being just a kid himself, he shared commonality with many of us and eagerly imparted what he knew about sailing. It was he who helped ease my initial apprehensions of walking out the yards and working high in the rigging.

Bernes and the Bosun (or Boatswain) were the two oldest crewmen. I never knew the Bosun's name, but it didn't matter. Everyone just called him Bosun. He was responsible for the ship's hull, rigging, anchors, cables, sails, and miscellaneous equipment, and determined the condition of the deck and its gadgets. It was he who assigned the daily maintenance tasks. Knowing little English, he shouted orders in deep, booming, clacking Norwegian. His commands could be heard above the sounds of pelting rain, howling wind, whipping sails, and thunder, bellowing from his lungs as if from a megaphone. While on duty, he wore a black, gold-embroidered officer's cap that framed his thick-skinned weathered face.

Bernes was much quieter but not less knowledgeable. Thought by some to be even more qualified than the captain, he was often seen sitting somewhere on deck chatting with the crew. His role as sail master put him in charge of caring for, mending, and replacing the canvas as needed. Bernes was a seasoned sailor who spent many years at sea and who played an active role in determining the ship's course. He also bore navigational responsibilities in the chart room.

Timberman (the ship's carpenter) was a quiet crewman who spent little time with the cadets unless we were assigned to work with him directly. He assisted Bosun with the specific duties of maintaining the wooden deck, masts, yards, officer cabins, and crew quarters. He also managed all repairs in the banjers, galley, and supply closets. Rather awkwardly built with small shoulders, Timberman was tall and thin and leaned slightly forward when he walked. Unlike the others, he appeared more like an 8-hour-a-day assembly-line factory worker and family man than a sailor.

Other crew members included Chief Engineer, Sargent, Radio Officer Stein, Evenson, Johannsen (known also as Morgan Kane), the Steward, able-bodied seaman Egil, and the crew cabin boy, supposedly a nephew of the steward. There were also three cooks—Johnnie, Burgo, and Joe, an engine room supervisor, messman Stormark (who acquired the nickname Lotion), and of course Chief Mate Gronningen. All total, there were between 25 and 28 crewmen.

Last but certainly not least was Captain Od Fossa. He wasn't an impressive man in stature or tone. I saw him on our first day in Bergen but didn't realize who he was. Of moderate height, a bit stout, and soft-chinned with a doughboy face, he stood passively just outside the officer's quarters on the main deck as we checked in. Captain mingled only with the crew that day.

Calm and mild-mannered in public, Captain Fossa was often seen nodding and smiling for no apparent reason at no one in particular. He appeared to be mentally slow and didn't fit anyone's image of a valiant sea captain. I thought he more resembled a church parishioner whose task was to find seats for the elderly. Communications from him were directed mostly through Chief Mate and his officers. I was told he spent a lot of time sailing and had been involved with the *Statsraad Lehmkuhl* for many years. In 1952 he served as second mate aboard ship and was chief mate in 1956 when the Lehmkuhl visited NYC. Obviously, the officers and crew respected him. I had no reason not to do the same. But more than a few cadets were convinced he had earned his first name—Od.

Ω

Rigging: System of ropes, cables, chains and pulleys that support the masts & yards and control the sails, including climbing ladders and platforms.

As a nineteen-year-old cadet seeing the ship for the first time, I was most fascinated by its rigging supported by three masts—fore, stor (main), and mesan. The fore and the stor masts hoisted five yards each: royl, bram, merse, stumpe, and fokke, from top to bottom. Square sails hung from each yard with corresponding names. A maze of ropes, each with a specific purpose, were attached to the sails, strung through pulleys, then extended down to belaying pins on the side walls of the deck. A series of thick cables (shrouds) ran from the outer walls of the deck, port side and starboard, upward to the first platform about forty feet up. The shrouds were spread wider at the bottom, narrower at the top, with rope ratlines stretched horizontally between, spaced approximately twelve inches apart, top to bottom, forming a structure known as Jacob's ladder. From the side rail, sailors climbed up Jacob's ladder to enter the rigging for any reason, like setting and furling sails or performing maintenance tasks in the rig. Climbing required both leg and arm strength. Sometimes a ratline snapped during the climb—always an unsettling experience. The first time it happened to me was traumatic, arguably the best situational lesson for always keeping a good handgrip.

Another steeper ladder extended from the outer perimeter of the first platform upwards to the second landing, another 40 feet up. From there a third ladder, very narrow by comparison, went skyward to the upper yards 35 feet higher still. I was scared stiff the first time I climbed to the royl yard and walked out the thin foot cable to the end. It was a windy day, and I didn't enjoy it for even a moment, aside from the ungodly thrill of being scared out of my skin! Each sectional climb possessed its own risk and danger, always requiring more caution than speed, especially while the ship was in motion.

The most challenging part of the climb was hoisting up from Jacob's ladder to the platforms. Ropes stretched under the 4-foot landing for handhold assistance while the climber first maneuvered horizontally with his back facing the deck, then pulled himself up and over. It was demanding for even the best climbers to master. I was pumped with fright and adrenaline the first several times I did it. There were no safety nets. But of course, that was a never mind!

Checking and replacing torn ratlines became a daily task. Early in sail training, we had a two-session class learning the essential knots. Some were more important than others for safety reasons, like when replacing ratlines, securing the safety rope and clip around one's waist, or stabilizing the Bosun's chair in the rigging.

We did numerous drills during training that tested our comprehension of what we'd learned. When an order was given, immediate actions were expected. For instance, when an officer gave the command to set the fore bram sail, six cadets climbed quickly above both platforms to the bram yard on the fore mast to release sizings. Others found the corresponding ropes on the belay pins on deck to pull the yard upwards and tighten the sail. The procedure required coordination between cadets in the rigging and cadets on deck each time a sail was set or taken in.

The lower square sails (fokke and stumpe) were massive, weighing approximately 2 tons each. Although the bram and royl sails were smaller, they still required numerous cadets spaced along the yards to furl and tie them atop the arm. Setting sails was easier, requiring 15–20 cadets. Furling them required the manpower of 30–35 cadets. During training, however, everyone was involved, regardless of the numbers. Practice drills in port and in the harbor became routine. Mate Schnitler reminded us often, "You can't make mistakes when at sea. It could be fatal." I cringed every time he said it.

The weather created additional challenges to sail training. Some days were balmy and mild but as the fall of 1972 progressed, the elements worsened. All-day rains were common, sometimes with bone-chilling winds that whipped our exposed skin. Twice we had hail. Training sessions were never postponed or delayed by weather, and our daily routines seldom changed: muster at 07:00 followed by breakfast, then ship's work and sail training all day with an hour break for lunch. At times the schedule felt brutal. And by day's end I was exhausted, cold, grimy, and sometimes grumpy. I especially despised the cold, which had a numbing effect on my hands and feet.

Jacobsen showed me a technique one day to keep blood circulating in my hands and fingers. While standing upright with plenty of clearance, he swung his arms swiftly from the crucifix position inward, passing each other across his chest, slapping both hands around the sides of both shoulders in rapid repetitive succession until the blood rushed to his fingertips. He seldom wore gloves, claiming it was too dangerous. This simple exercise, done periodically, kept his hands warm and free. It worked for me as well. So, I quickly adopted his technique and aptly called it "The Norwegian." I used it often during my time aboard ship, and for many years after. Like Jacobsen, I also disliked wearing gloves while on duty. They negatively affected my grip.

Each cadet was given protective rain gear when we signed on—a hooded, canary-colored, plastic water-proof jacket with matching pants. In addition, we received dark blue mid-shin rubber boots. Our gear proved to be valuable many times over, but it didn't sugarcoat the work nor ease the dangers. In fact, climbing with boots felt clumsy. We were continually reminded of the consequences of a slip or misstep in the rigging and the fact that there was zero chance of surviving a fall.

Jacobsen once described in detail the splat of a cadet hitting the deck. His insensitive narration sent chills up and down our spines. No one said anything in response, but "the splat" became a humorous term we sometimes used while in the rig. We figured if we talked about it often enough, it was less likely to happen.

The crewmen eventually learned which cadets climbed well, and which did not. However, we all were pushed beyond our comfort zones initially to sort out fears from laziness. I slowly became comfortable in the rigging. As my confidence increased, so did my agility. It felt just like climbing tall trees as a kid on the farm in Bird-in-Hand. But that wasn't the case for everyone. Some kids never climbed beyond the first platform. No one was forced to climb against their will. There was plenty to do on deck during the sail setting process.

One day several crewmen hung a set of gymnastic rings from a cross-cable above the main deck. Working out on the rings was a great way to build upper body strength for cadets and crewmen alike. And a good way to show off. I spent time there daily with noticeable results. My time working construction in Virginia was a good start, but training aboard the *Statsraad Lehmkuhl* developed muscle tone like never before. I was able to do pull-ups, shoulder stands, dips, and muscle-ups with ease. It felt great to knock off 25 pull-ups. However, none of us matched Jacobsen's upper body strength. He even perfected the iron cross.

Ω

As sail training continued, I developed a true desire to work in the rigging daily. It motivated me, humbled me, and completed me. Nothing was more exhilarating than climbing high into the maze of ropes, sails, and yards on good weather days. The physical challenge was rewarding, views from aloft were great, and feeling the wind in my face standing at the end of the royl yard was an experience beyond compare.

In time, conflicts developed between crewmen and cadets. There was chaos in the banjers as well. Emil, one of only two black cadets onboard, and my roommate Jones went at it one day—a full-fledged fight resulting from a racial slur. Although normally mild-mannered, Emil felt forced to defend his dignity. I couldn't blame him. Then there was Richie, an outspoken kid who had a knack for finding his way into the middle of squabbles. He thrived on mayhem. If there was none, he created it. But amidst the increasing complexities within this diverse community onboard ship, I found my place of retreat high in the rigging. It was the best place to clear my head and experience solitude. It was where I felt closest to God.

Me on the royl yard

Looking down from aloft

CHAPTER 6: STUDENT-CADETS

We came from various places and backgrounds. No matter what efforts were made to level the playing field for the student-cadets, it was an impossible task. First, the student body ranged in age from 15 to 20 years old, with many kids enrolled in high school curriculum according to their grade while others were taking college courses. Secondly, the economic status of the students varied drastically. Although bank accounts onboard were supposedly managed by the administration, available cash for individuals proved to be impossible to control. Several of the more affluent kids seemed to have secret cash stashes when going ashore.

The social dynamics onboard were continually changing as kids sought to find their places within the community during the first several weeks after arriving in Bergen. Leaders emerged, as did antagonists. Several students isolated themselves for emotional protection. Others became vocal for the same reasons. Survival techniques varied, but we all desired acceptance into this new communal conglomerate. Several cliques formed for the sake of small group security. Male-female relationships developed as well. Couples. Jones hooked up with Nancy, a quiet, fair-skinned girl from Minnesota who became an unofficial part-time roommate of ours. The original banjer room structure broke down within the first few weeks. Kids traded bunks. Others just moved to another room. These changes sometimes made it difficult to find cadets for scheduled watch posts at night. Eventually, groups on duty self-organized and took responsibility for each other, despite the shuffling. Authorities needed not be involved.

Many of us guys arrived in Bergen with long hair in the fall of 1972, but the formal look of navy-blue blazers and white trousers cleaned up even the roughest looking kids, at least enough to ensure entry into Hotel Norge and other high-end restaurants in town. In time, local folks recognized us for who we were—American cadets training aboard the famed *Statsraad Lehmkuhl.*

Steve and Debbie Hilbert were the administrators who oversaw each student's onboard bank account. We were supposed to carry small amounts of cash when going ashore, for good reason. Limited spending was an intentional part of the

Oceanics educational plan of discipline and self-control. Those limitations didn't bother me. I didn't have much money from the start. And budgets forced us to be creative. Although bus routes were affordable and easy, hitchhiking became my most common means of transportation.

On numerous occasions several shipmates and I hung out with locals in town. The Bergenese were fascinated by our stories, and often paid for our food and drinks in exchange for stories and dialogue and sometimes even an accompanied visit aboard the ship. Fair trades were fair game as we learned the value of giving, receiving, compromise, storytelling, and manipulation as ways to manage our lives on and off the ship.

During the first week, three Norwegian boys signed on as cadets—Tor, Fredrik, and Robert. Tor's home was in Bergen, so he was familiar with all the important things the rest of us wanted to know about the city, like the pop culture, good restaurants and bars, and the best places to meet local kids. One night, Tor and Fredrik invited me to a party in the suburbs. Most kids there spoke English. Although conversations varied, the Norwegian teens seemed eager to discuss American politics and the reelection of President Nixon. They asked interesting questions. Music blared from the stereo as beer flowed from the bottles. I nursed two beers during the evening. I still was not a fan of beer.

Most notably, the girls were all picture perfect. They appeared confident, well-adjusted, and seemingly knew their place in society. Norway had no slums in 1972. Taxes were high but as one guy explained, "Everything is included—education, medical coverage, five weeks paid vacation for workers, full care for retired and elderly folks." I quietly compared life here to my parents' long struggle to make ends meet back in the States. It was no wonder these kids felt secure. They had endless opportunities, including good education without financial worries.

As the party continued, intellectual discussions digressed into laughter and noise. Teenagers, no matter where they're from, enjoy being teenagers. I was learning that as well. Not everything was about hard work, responsibility, and religion, the things I was taught. So, on this night, I enjoyed being one of the teens.

When we returned to the ship, fellow cadet David Lashefer was roaming the banjers in a daze, claiming not to have slept since arriving in Norway. If looks were true, I should have believed him. Some thought he was on some kind of dope. He didn't involve himself in real conversations with anyone, but his eyes became fixated on whoever tried to engage him. Eventually his eerie, almost demonic behavior caused him to be sent home.

Late one night several cadets made a rope swing and hung it from a ceiling hook in the banjer hallway. Mattresses were then thrown onto the floor as kids swung and jumped. It was a cheap thrill, simple entertainment, and harmless except for those trying to sleep. But the night had just begun. Crewmen and cadets alike routinely went into town on Friday night to celebrate the end of another week of sail training. Although we had a midnight curfew, bars stayed opened until 02:00. After the swinging in the banjers subsided, a handful of kids came back to the ship drunk.

Tom was a short guy with long red hair, usually tied back into a ponytail. That night he boarded the ship puking his brains out. The gangway watchman helped him across deck to the center hatch leading to the banjers. From there he was on his own. The steep metal stairway from the deck to the banjers had handrails on both sides. However, the steps were unforgiving in the event of a fall. Finding it impossible to sleep, I was in the dayroom just a few yards forward of the stairs, writing in my journal. As the commotion commenced at the hatch, I turned just in time to see Tom sliding and bumping down the stairs on his ass before landing in a heap at the bottom. Moaning and cursing, he managed to get up twice, then collapsed onto the floor both times. His white pants were totally trashed with dirt, grime, puke, and red wine. Another cadet, Pisacano, helped him to his bunk where he passed out for the night. One down, with still more to come.

A few minutes later, Todd staggered into the banjers drunk. He was like a wind-up motor-mouth as he and Richie were laughing, yelling, belching, farting, and comparing stories from their night in town. Suddenly Chief Gronningen appeared in the banjers, like a ghost in the night, totally appalled by what he saw. The swing was still hanging in the hallway, girls were in guys' cabins, drunken underwear-clad cadets ran aimlessly in the corridors. There was pure, or better said, impure bedlam in the banjers. Chief stood quietly assessing the situation as another wave of inebriated kids came onboard. Now fire-faced angry, he ordered everyone to their rooms immediately, demanding that the noise stop. But the damage was already done. Trust was breached and his respect for the cadets was now in question. I felt sad about that.

Chief Gronningen was a good man, and a fair man. I crawled into bed feeling conflicted. Most times I was able to find humor in life situations, but I'd never seen anything like this. Then I remembered the words of caution from Uncle Dan regarding influences of the secular world. Of the weak and ungodly. "We become like our surroundings."

I lay in bed wide awake for a very long time. Todd was in a semi-conscious state on the opposite bunk, mumbling in his drunken stupor, repeating one-liners from the book *Stranger in a Strange Land*, and recent quotes from Chief Mate. Therein was the humor I so badly needed, bringing a hilarious ending to a not so funny night, allowing me to fall asleep smiling. I thanked Todd for unintentionally being a great roommate.

The following night while I was on Gangway watch, Willy approached me with a sly grin. He was a friendly chap, even-tempered, and casually cooperative, also in Group C. Since he wasn't scheduled for any of the remaining watches that evening, nor for ship's work, he decided to go ashore, convinced there was no legitimate reason to stay onboard. Only a skeleton crew remained. But Schnitler denied him shore leave. Rules were rules. Disgruntled, Willy discussed the matter with me.

I explained my responsibility as watchman, reminding him that I couldn't sign off a cadet who was officially on duty. But he wasn't asking for that. Smiling devilishly, he shared his plan to jump ship by way of the aft mooring line. All he needed from me was a clear signal to hoist himself over the railing when the deck officer made his rounds on the opposite side of the ship. He then chuckled, "See nothing, say nothing, know nothing." There would be no registry sign-out, and no record of anything.

Willy waited aft until I gave the signal, then he jumped over the rail, and slid down the rope to the dock. I wasn't concerned about his return. By then I'd no longer be gangway watchman and wouldn't need to deal with the hassles of signing on a cadet who was officially still on board.

Next morning Willy and I sat across from each other at breakfast, bundled up in warm clothing, eating fried eggs and bacon. I asked no questions, and he said nothing at all, but gave me a nod of thanks and a thumbs up. The ship was frigid cold that morning due to a boiler failure during the night—no heat and no hot water. Aside from that, all was well aboard, and for sure with Willy and me.

It was Sunday, a day for sightseeing. I joined a group of cadets and walked from the docks to the base of Mount Floyen. From there we rode the funicular to the top of the mountain, beautifully covered with snow. The fun, furious snowball battle paled in comparison to the breathtaking views of the city below. Later, we rode a public bus to the village of Paradise, then hiked to the 800-year-old Fantoft Stave Church situated in a nearby pine forest. The church's old wooden structure and architecture were magnificent, and the grounds emitted a hallow spirit of tranquility—800 years' worth.

With each passing day, Bergen's beauty became more evident. Old town was a nice destination easily accessible from the docks. It hosted the library, interesting shops, wonderful bakeries, bookstores, and timeless cafés where a person could spend hours if he had the time. The city was becoming a place of comfort for me, an emotionally healthy place to break from the ship. After dark, it took on a more formal appeal, folks dressed in fashionable attire as restaurants and bars buzzed with activity. By now there was increasing social interaction between students and faculty.

Stave Church: A uniquely designed, wooden, medieval Christian church building once common in Norway.

One night Professor Soja invited Bill Bacon and me to Hotel Norge for dinner. Bill and I were fast becoming friends. I enjoyed his upbeat, positive spirit, communicative skills, spontaneity, and humor. He was fun to work with, hang out with, and engage in any type of conversation. I came to realize he could hold his own in most any situation, unafraid of the unknowns, a risk taker, and willing to do whatever needed to be done. And he was gifted at countering the negativity of others. Some of his comments were hilarious. Most in fact.

At Hotel Norge, Soja, Bill, and I were joined by two Norwegian graduate students, Venka and Alisa, plus Oceanics profs Frank and Arturo, for an intellectually inspiring evening. Venka was a student of British and European history. Alisa was an anthropologist. Both girls were fascinated with the Amish culture which became my ticket to engage them and share personal stories about my family back in PA. By evening's end, they all knew who Grossmommie Smucker was. Better still, I didn't pay for any food or drinks that night.

The Engen Cinema became a frequent destination for student entertainment. Most movies were in English with Norwegian subtitles. One evening I joined Professor Frank and several shipmates to see the new release, *Fiddler on the Roof*, which quickly became my favorite movie. As we entered the theater, I casually struck up conversation with Lucy, one of the female cadets onboard. Except for shared kitchen duty, she and I had very little prior interaction. She seemed self-assured, unpretentious, sometimes outspoken, and possessed a calloused disposition, appearing to have a deeper understanding of life than most kids onboard. I found her a bit intimidating.

As we stood in the lobby together sipping sodas, Lucy invited me to sit with her. So, I did. Our conversation continued intermittently during the movie. At one point I casually mentioned that the Jewish traditions and culture in the film reminded me of my home community in Lancaster County. She turned and looked at me with big eyes, then threw her arms around my neck and hugged me exclaiming, "You've gotta be kidding! I'm from Morgantown, Pennsylvania!" (Morgantown is just 25 miles northeast of Bird-in-Hand, beyond the town of New Holland.) We couldn't stop talking after that.

Both of us were patients of the same dentist in New Holland, Dr. Williams, whose fingers always smelled like tobacco when he worked on our teeth. She frequented the Way-In Youth Center near Leola, the same place I hung out with high school buddies back in the day. We shared several common acquaintances as well, including some random Lancaster Mennonite High School kids. Suddenly, Lucy and I felt like old friends as we cozied up and enjoyed each other's company with flashbacks from home.

Although Lucy and I remained friends throughout the next months, our personalities were drastically different, as were our interests and expectations of life. She told me about her two-year-old son at home as the pieces of her story began falling into place. She was searching for something more than her life back home could provide. Joining the Oceanics program was the beginning of her do-over.

As the days passed, I enjoyed interacting with many of my fellow students, especially those in Group C, but I found it difficult to get close to anyone. There were reasons for that. Besides harsh schedules, trust was an issue as well. Some kids stood out as being genuinely nice. Others, not so much. I enjoyed the group from Minnesota from the start—Jim and Janet Johnson (brother and sister) were both tall, blonde, fair-skinned, Scandinavian-looking kids. Katie, Sue, Jill, and George were upbeat, sensible, hardworking, and even-keeled. Katie could've passed for a Mennonite girl from back home. Sue reminded me of Chava, Tevye's third daughter in *Fiddler on The Roof*. But I was in a different group than those kids and unfortunately had little interaction with them. I also developed cordial friendships with several of the younger kids onboard, like Sam, Kevin, Zoe, Amor, Mitch, and Tim, who were never in the spotlight but did as they were told, obeyed orders and rules, and learned survival skills within the sometimes-tough confines of the community onboard.

Sail training didn't necessarily complement our individuality or do justice to our personalities. I believe too many judgments were made during those first few weeks, unfairly labeling us for the remainder of our time aboard. We all were guilty of that. Although some cadets were better at functional tasks, others had better minds. There was a place and special purpose for everyone onboard. Jane became my friend on deck and in the rigging. Her work ethic matched the Germanic diligence and familiarity of my cultural community back home. Nevertheless, we all were students aboard the *Statsraad Lehmkuhl* for the 1972–1973 school term regardless of background, ethnicity, economic status, culture, or reason for being aboard. Theoretically, the deck wasn't leveled; however, the cracks and crevices were reduced concerning our individual opportunities onboard as well as in port. Who could know our future or what we'd glean from these shared experiences? Or even if any of us would live long enough to apply anything we learned. In that sense, I suppose we all were living on borrowed time.

Susan and me hauling up sails from below

Mike Kemp (left), School Director/English Prof; Eiji Imamura, World Religion/Marine Biology Prof

Barry North, Science Prof

Steve Hilbert, Admin. Director

CHAPTER 7: ADMINISTRATION

The faculty members were officially cadets in training, like us, and were expected to learn the ropes. They were encouraged to participate in sailing operations alongside the students. However, they didn't participate in watch schedules or basic daily ship's work, at least not initially. Academics were their priority. In time, their undefined working relationship with the Norwegian officers aboard caused conflicts.

Both faculty and crew made efforts to demonstrate mutual respect publicly, but not always willfully, as each served vital roles in the overall success or potential failure of the Oceanics program. Throwing a group of sailors and a group of educators into the same community aboard ship, each in positions of authority, was a stretch from the start. Their methodologies in accomplishing specific tasks were as different as land and sea. One couldn't always read the minds of Chick and Stephanie Gallagher, but at times it appeared as though they were more brave than smart.

Several of the faculty avoided unnecessary conflict by limiting their contact with crewmen during and after sail training. Despite their differences, others stayed engaged. The strengths of the sailors didn't necessarily encourage the weaknesses of the educators, or vice versa. So, they learned to coexist. The biggest challenge for us as student-cadets was to determine whose authority we were under, and when. While on ship's duty, of course, we answered solely to the officers. In class and on shore, we were accountable to the administration. I suppose in theory it was all well-defined. But things weren't categorically black and white, especially while at sea. Sometimes both chains of command were in play, and sometimes there was overreach of authority.

Classes started after the first two weeks of sail training. Between school and training, we had little time for anything else. The administration seemed to recognize that from the start and eased into classroom requirements. But in time it felt like the administration was intentionally overwhelming us. From their perspective, too much free time was the devil's playground.

Mike Kemp, the twenty-six-year-old school director and English professor, communicated his expectations to the students with confidence, applying a no-nonsense approach from day one. A graduate of San Francisco State, he taught classes such as English Literature and Myth, Dream and Identity. He was a strong man, both physically and mentally. With a deep voice and uncompromising eyes, he sarcastically challenged us to defy him. "There will be consequences for breaking the rules," he barked. "I'll personally see to that."

Early on, I avoided him whenever possible, intimidated by his demanding tone. He had done background checks on each of us with help from Stephanie, of course, and knew us by name before boarding ship. This was his second stint with Oceanics. In the classroom however, Mike's tone changed. His ability to articulate thoughts into words, and his proficiency in mastering two distinctively different positions, was admirable. He loved talking about dreams and encouraged us to record them whenever possible. My negative first impressions soon passed as he exercised fair treatment in exchange for hard work, application, obedience, and cooperation.

He initiated the school newspaper, which was aptly named *The Daily Muster*. I was encouraged when he invited me to join the staff. Printings were done periodically, depending on stories, humor, editorials, newsworthy events, and time. I wrote articles for each edition—mostly positive stuff about community life onboard.

Professor Jim Soja, who had a B.A. in US History and an M.A. from Georgetown University, taught world history. He proved to be thoughtfully analytical, an intentional listener, and a man who enjoyed intellectual debate while engaging us onboard and off. He encouraged dialogue regardless of opinions, depth, and beliefs. I loved that about him. He taught lessons from history as applications to present-day situations, especially pertaining to world powers and politics. And he expressed his displeasure at how often history repeats itself. Soja had the mind of a man who could articulate a revolution but lacked the ability and motivation to do it. In fairness, however, he was a great educator and made an unforgettably good first impression on me.

Frank Twiggs graduated from Boston College with a B.A. in Philosophy, the subject he taught on the ship. He had spent time studying at a Jesuit Seminary, which credited him with a background in Greek and Latin, along with world religions. Frank was slightly overweight, soft-spoken, friendly, sometimes abstract, and often played the devil's advocate in philosophical dialogue for the sake of debate. He asked crazy questions while shooting holes in solid facts. "Know who you are," he chirped. "Know what you believe, and why." Frank laughed well and became popular among the kids. He was often found in the center of group discussions concerning horoscopes, once commenting that I didn't fit the profile of a Gemini. His claim was that most Geminis lose their temper. I didn't know anything about horoscopes, nor the wisdom gleaned from astrology, but I enjoyed discussing life's inconsistencies with him. We humored each other by debating without basis.

Barry North, professor of science, was a certified scuba diver with considerable sailing experience prior to coming aboard. His strong background in biology, chemistry, physics, astronomy, and celestial navigation, nearly qualified him as a sailor on those merits alone. And he seemingly had the ability to apply his knowledge of mathematics to oceanography and sailing. Barry did his undergraduate studies at Johns Hopkins University, received a Ph.D. in Organic Chemistry from Brandeis University, then later did post-doctoral research in Haifa. He was a small-featured guy, a bit socially awkward, believed in absolutes, and was probably too calculated for a bunch of teenagers aboard the *Statsraad Lehmkuhl*. His efforts to be friendly were genuine but were undermined by his less exciting, tenor-toned, mind-numbing conversations. I enjoyed Barry's spirit but found it difficult initially to engage him in discussions of interest. Our chats sometimes became too long and boring. In time, however, that changed as I better learned to know and understand his personality. Unfortunately, his sincerity made him a laughingstock among Florida boys Perry, Tom, and Pisacano, who characterized him unfairly as a cartoonish loser, sometimes impersonating him in the banjers before a small audience. Their role playing was entertaining and funny, but also insensitive and cruel, ridiculing and victimizing him personally.

Arturo Rivera was one of the most interesting members of the staff. A native Puerto Rican, he was impressively well-educated in language studies, psychology, and sociology, with degrees from Georgetown University and the University of Puerto Rico and continued studies at Columbia University. His kinky black hair formed a miniature afro atop his Pillsbury Doughboy physique. When he spoke, his words flowed like music on a warm summer breeze. Arturo enjoyed the finer things in life: gourmet foods, exotic pastries, fine wines and liqueurs, music, theatre, and good conversations. He was a social buff, often found in the center of discussions about the arts. Along with being a talented musician (piano and classical guitar), he did most everything with stylish flair, whether eating, drinking wine, telling a story, explaining logic, or simply wearing a scarf. Someone suggested that he must have been trained in butler school because of his table manners. Like the way he wore a napkin, held his fork, cut his food, chewed, and lifted a wine glass with his left pinky curled slightly outward. Charm and pizzazz were his persona, but none of that benefited him in the rigging.

Arturo's personality appealed to many students, but not necessarily to the crew. No part of him remotely fit the mold of a sailor. He was softer than a feather pillow, theoretically too soft to splat if he fell from the rigging, if indeed he could climb that high. I enjoyed him, especially when he played guitar or piano. Nothing was more relaxing after a day of fighting the outside elements than to retreat two levels down to the music room for a mini concert. The heavenly sounds that flowed from his guitar were mesmerizing, temporarily extinguishing from my memory the effects of cold rain and the day's hard work above deck.

One evening Jane and I were in the music room, stretched out on cushioned benches after a particularly difficult day in the rigging. As Arturo played the piano, my mind drifted back to childhood days at the Smucker Homestead. To the small record player in Uncle Marc's room that piped out classic tunes from Germany. Those same feelings of peace and security were replicated, only now as a 19-year-old aboard a Norwegian sail ship. That night I gained a deeper understanding of the importance of music as it pertained to my emotional survival. No one said a word while Arturo played, but the feelings deep within my soul were ones of spiritual and cerebral completion. It was a time of recharging my courage and my soul energy for the unknowns ahead.

Ω

Joe Feinblatt was a well-rounded educator with training in physical sciences, mythology, photography, and calligraphy, a B.A. in Chemistry from Reed College, and an M.A. in Folklore from UCLA. Onboard ship he taught calligraphy and photography, his obvious passions. Not surprisingly, he brought a lot of expensive equipment onboard. Joe was soft-featured with a head of thick brown curly hair, a full beard, and a mustache, none of which were well groomed, and was of average build but not athletic in appearance. He was also well-spoken, idealistic, and intelligent with seemingly unrealistic expectations of this conglomerate community as he appeared unprepared for the teenage antics aboard ship. His kind demeanor, patience, sensitivity, and friendly spirit didn't rub off on those around him. Joe smiled often for reasons unknown, especially when he was surprised by something. Like a crewman cursing a cadet. Although analytical, he seldom expressed verbal anger, staying mostly behind the scenes. I found him broadly knowledgeable and enjoyed his company. But sadly, few students engaged with him enough to realize that.

I'm not sure why, but Joe liked me from the start. Despite our differences, we seemed destined to become friends. He wasn't necessarily comfortable with the physical ship's work, lacked arm strength for the rigging, and wasn't thrilled with heights. The opposite of me. However, our commonalities included love for hiking, culture, people, music, and the beauty of the outdoors. He enjoyed fine dining and specialty foods. I did as well, but mostly when he paid. I sometimes found a secluded perch aft where I played my recorder while Joe sat quietly by and listened. We developed a nice friendship.

Eiji Imamura, of Japanese origin, grew up in California before traveling the world. His assigned role onboard was to teach World Religion and Marine Biology, but he could've taught almost anything. With a B.A. and an M.A. from the University of California at Berkeley and San Francisco State respectively, his expertise was in plant ecology and marine sciences. Eiji spoke five languages and was blessed with a brilliant mind. Also, with humility. He seldom found cause to raise his voice. I sensed an unusual aura about him that had a calming effect on me. He possessed enviable self-discipline. The most interesting class he taught, in my opinion, was Eastern Theology. After he introduced the concept of Zen as a personal meditation experience, not reliant on scripture, doctrine, or ritual, I signed up. He described four principles that illustrate the Zen spirit: no dependency on words (I wasn't well-spoken anyway), a special communication outside the scriptures, pointing directly to the human mind, seeing into one's own nature and attaining Buddhahood (awakened one). Having grown up Mennonite, but still seeking, I found his introduction appealing. Eiji never included more than three students in any of his sessions. And he scheduled one-on-one training with each understudy. My time with him felt special as we shared things from our cultural past and from deep within. Like me, Eiji was a pacifist. But unlike me, he understood who he was.

David Freedman was the youngest prof onboard at twenty-two years of age, and the only one with whom I had no classes. He graduated from Occidental College with a degree in Anthropology, then studied in Japan as well as Jerusalem where he attended Hebrew Union College. David was thin with shoulder-length hair combed to one side and appeared to be in good physical shape. He could climb. I was impressed with his conscious effort to involve himself in ship's work and sail training, never shying away from hard work. That rightfully earned him respect from the crew. Although politically progressive, he was socially opinionated concerning fairness, political correctness, and gender equality. And like Arturo, he was musically talented in guitar, piano, and singing.

Dr. Abbott served as the ship's doctor. A graduate of Indiana University and Indiana University's School of Medicine, he was a quiet man of twenty-eight years, serious and professionally knowledgeable, and he quickly earned the confidence of our community. Doc taught classes in general health, sex education, and human anatomy, and willingly answered questions concerning anything health related, without judgment. He administered my prescribed weekly allergy injections. Before joining The Oceanics staff, Doc bicycled across the USA from San Francisco to Philadelphia. He also broke some sort of bicycle world speed record traveling behind a car. Although not a participant in sail training, he treated many injuries of those who were. And he provided condoms indiscriminately to anyone who asked, guys or girls, with complete confidentiality. That was arguably one of his most important tasks onboard, according to some. Doc remained very private.

Mid-year, however, Dr. Payne, who brought his wife, Kat, onboard, replaced Doc Abbott. That change was scheduled from the start because of prior commitments for both doctors. So, Dr. Payne joined us in early March in Trinidad and resumed the same responsibilities as Dr. Abbott. From the start he had more social interaction with the students.

Steve and Debbie Hilbert, husband and wife, hailed from Lake Tahoe, Nevada. Steve earned a B.S. in Finance and Business Administration from the University of Oregon and served as Administrative Director onboard. His official duties included giving oversight to all student activities and school policies as well as being the purser, bookkeeper, and distributor of funds onboard. Debbie, who had a degree in Sociology, also from University of Oregon, assisted Steve in operating the school office and ship store. Being the only female member on staff, her position was well-served for the girls onboard. She was more vocal than Steve as it pertained to student behavior, which sometimes set her up as a target for unfair ridicule. Steve, on the other hand, maintained a calmer, quieter disposition when dealing with student challenges and too often found himself in the center of conflict between his wife and the students. I suppose it boiled down to their personalities, but also to their different expectations of the students as it pertained to the Oceanics experience. Although that probably could be said for many onboard.

Jaime (Hai-may) was in a category of his own, not an official part of the faculty, nor of the crew. But no matter, most everyone liked him. Jaime understood diesel engines. He spent much of his time in the engine room at the bottom of the hull with Blake Gallagher. Some days I forgot he was onboard.

But when he surfaced, I'd see him standing under the half-deck or by the railing, smiling, enjoying the outdoors away from the grease and grime. Ethnically Mexican, his English was mediocre at best, but language didn't hinder his relationship with us, nor with the crew. Jaime was humble, kind, mild-tempered, notoriously happy, positive-spirited, and willing to befriend most anyone. His acceptance of life was remarkable. At least that was my perception. However, I found later that Jaime was not necessarily trusted by several female cadets who experienced him differently than me.

The entire Oceanics staff, despite notable differences, appeared to understand their purpose with initial optimism, setting the educational tone from the start. But their tasks proved to be much more difficult than anyone could have expected. We, the students, were a diverse bunch from varying economic and social backgrounds, and with less understanding of our place and purpose aboard the *Statsraad Lehmkuhl* in the fall of 1972. Plus, we were subjected to two sets of commands, rules, and discipline, first to the captain and his crew, but also to the educators of the Oceanics program, including Chick and Stephanie Gallagher. Stephanie stayed with us for a short while in Norway, then showed up at various ports throughout the year to organize field trips and to address concerns within the administration and officers. Although Chick stayed mostly behind the scenes concerning operational details, his encouraging influence was felt more than seen.

Some days I was too tired to study or read, finding it nearly impossible to secure a quiet place to complete assignments with proficiency. Fatigue was a serious obstacle to scholastic achievement. It affected us all. Some kids gave up on their classroom education in the first month. Others' efforts were severely compromised. I was determined to do well but was forced to change my expectations and redefine the meaning of "do well." My most difficult challenges came early on. In time I adjusted to the demands onboard and stayed abreast of my course work. However, I recognized the fact that the education I was receiving from this experience far surpassed any classroom, books, or standard requirements of land-bound universities anywhere in the world.

Chick Gallagher

Anchored in the fjord by the town of Odda

Lifeboat drills

CHAPTER 8: ODDA

A s weeks passed, we all became increasingly anxious to leave Bergen. Cold freezing rains were now as old as the sail training itself. Despite daily complaints, we were told Captain Fossa was pleased with our progress. The sails had all been hoisted and attached properly to their respective yards. On calm days we continued setting and furling them, just for practice. The process became noticeably easier with time.

In preparation to sail, supplies were hand-loaded from the dock daily. Cadets and crew worked together forming human chains, passing cargo from the dock, up the gangplank and to its final place of storage. Sometimes the chain of hands wasn't long enough, so the stuff was temporarily stacked on deck. One day a large quantity of beer was brought aboard, for the officers and crew of course, but we helped load and stack it on deck. After the beer was left on deck temporarily, several students—Todd, Randy, Gary, and Mark—secretly hauled two cases into the banjers as a joke. But the situation became serious when several bottles were opened. It was duty-free and sealed, forbidden to be opened until at sea, at least ten miles from shore, according to standard international law. No one in authority witnessed the beer snatching, but the customs agent's final inventory was found to be two cartons short. He immediately summoned Captain Fossa.

The issue could've been resolved quickly had it been up to the captain. However, aside from finding the culprits, this episode was out of his hands and under the jurisdiction of customs officials. A supervisor from the maritime customs office was immediately called onboard to deal with the issue and the four beer burglars were questioned individually. Fortunately, their stories matched, and the spontaneous act was found to be a joke and nothing more. But the three empty bottles in the returned cases created further complications. The agents eventually departed without finding who drank the beer, as nervous chuckles and quiet laughter were shared among the crew and cadets. Captain Fossa was embarrassed and returned to his quarters red-faced and without comment. But that was a never mind. He never said much anyway.

Ω

A new chief mate, Mr. Kavanvik, came onboard to replace Chief Gronningen, who we were told had prior commitments. Kavanvik looked like a military man—tall, thin, square-jawed, tight-lipped, with nerves of steel. He didn't mince words but spoke with stern, seasoned authority, giving the appearance of a man not to be questioned. Bill Bacon made a comment under his breath at muster on that first morning suggesting the new chief probably ate razor blades for breakfast. I quickly agreed, adding in a whisper that his gums probably didn't bleed either.

Chief Kavanvik was serious about discipline and reemphasized the importance of punctuality for watch posts, efficiency in the rigging, obedience to all the officer's commands, and respect for the ship itself. Although he made a frightful first impression, in time he proved to be thoughtful, fair, approachable, and good for the ship. It was he who made the long-awaited announcement at muster one cold, crisp morning as we stood on deck. "We will leave Bergen tomorrow," he said flatly without emotion. Immediately, handclapping, hooting, and hollering erupted from the line of cadets. "We will do more training and maneuvering of sails in the North Sea, then relocate to the Hardangerfjord by the town of Ulvik." More cheers and shouts followed. He then explained that everyone should be on deck for our departure from Bergen Harbor the following day regardless of shift schedules.

After his announcement, I decided to strike out on my own for the day, realizing it might be my last opportunity to enjoy any solitude for a while. Group C was officially scheduled for liberty, with no scheduled class time. I left after a brief clothing auction onboard. Whenever jackets, sweatshirts, gloves, shoes, pocket knives, or anything was found in any of the common areas of the ship, they were stashed in the lost and found closet then sold at a monthly auction. Sometimes we had to buy back our own things. But the stuff sold that day was all junk. After signing out, I hitched a ride from the docks to the University.

Happy to be alone, I hummed songs from *Fiddler on the Roof* while walking the streets of Bergen. "If I Were a Rich Man" played over and over again in my head. I chowed down a cream-filled pastry from a small bakery, then wrote letters to friends back home. During my search for the post office, I approached a pretty girl browsing casually in front of a clothing shop to ask directions.

She responded in perfect English, "The post office is across town." Smiling, she added, "I'm going there also. Would you like to walk along?"

My desire for solitude suddenly vanished. Emilie was better than any quiet time. So, we headed across town, talking as we went, sharing things about our families. She took hold of my arm and suggested we visit several places of interest along the way. It was nice to have the attention of an attractive young female again. And the arm thing was nice.

She showed me the site of a brutal murder just several months prior. A deranged man attacked a fourteen-year-old girl from behind a bush as she was walking home from school, then stabbed her to death. Emilie clung tighter to my arm and shuddered as we passed the spot.

"Violence here in Bergen is unusual. Normally this is a safe city," she exclaimed with a sideways glance, "except by the docks." Then smiling broadly, she continued, "Sailors cannot always be trusted, you know."

I wasn't sure how to respond to her comment. She knew I was a sailor-in-training, but the twinkle in her eye said it all. After a second's hesitation, I grinned, squeezed her hand, and said matter-of-factly, "Yes, you need to be careful who you hang out with these days." Obviously, she wasn't threatened by any potential bad boy behavior from me.

We arrived at the post office after a joyous hour together. Sadly, it was time to say goodbye. Emilie paused on the sidewalk, gave me a warm hug, and wished me safe and exciting travels. I offered her school blessings as well—she was just starting college. We didn't exchange contact information, both aware of our realities. I was leaving town the next day on a ship to explore the world. She was staying in Bergen to study. And who knew, maybe she already had a boyfriend. But that was a never mind.

Alone again, I walked on, putting quality miles on my black, ankle-high army boots. The sun shone brightly, adding a blessing to my last day in town. I enjoyed a hot dog with ketchup, relish, and onions at a small café, and by early evening I had done a full circle back to the university. I stuck out my thumb and within thirty seconds, a clean, navy-blue Mercedes Benz stopped by the side of the road. The thirtyish-year-old man eyed me as I hopped into the front seat, then reached out with a strong arm, and offered his hand. "My name is Victor," he said with a heavy accent. "Are you one of the American cadets?"

During the next few minutes, he shared about his opportunity ten years earlier to become a cadet aboard the *Statsraad Lehmkuhl*. But he had a girlfriend at the time who convinced him otherwise. They eventually married. Looking over at me he shook his head and said emphatically, "Don't get married when you are young."

Life for him didn't go as planned. After fathering two children, he and his wife divorced. He expressed deep regrets about not sailing and about losing the opportunity to see the world. Obviously, he had done well for himself financially, but perceived his life as unfulfilling. "I wish I was you," he exclaimed. His tone and words spoke volumes as he continued offering advice. "The world is for you to explore. Make the most of your opportunities. Life changes very quickly." It was difficult to know how to respond. From the street he drove all the way along the dock and dropped me off at the bottom of the gangway. I thanked him and wished him well, but my words felt inadequate. Victor sat in his car for another ten minutes looking up at the ship after I boarded. God only knows what he was thinking.

As I quietly stood on deck, Clark, a fellow cadet, invited me to have dinner with him in town. He had just completed eight hours on duty and was feeling stir crazy. Clark and I didn't know each other well, mostly because of his introversion. He was extraordinarily quiet, but also bright, well-read, and wisely slow to respond or comment to anyone or anything. Kids who hung out with him had to deal with extended periods of silence. For me, that was a stretch. I sometimes forced conversations just to ease my own discomfort.

Although I had considered my day complete, I agreed to join him. He was uncharacteristically talkative as we hitched a ride with an ex-sailor. After having a beer and ice cream at a small café, we joined up with several shipmates at Hotel Norge. They were already in celebration mode, recognizing the start of our new chapter.

Ω

As the ship pulled away from the docks the next morning, everyone was on deck as ordered by Chief Mate, including the captain. We didn't hide our jubilation. Several of us wanted to climb the rigging and position ourselves along the top yards during our departure, but it was disallowed for safety reasons. Unfortunately, there was no wind that day as the diesel engine powered us through the harbor. Our disappointment was short-lived, however, as the thrill of finally leaving Bergen trumped everything else.

The new two-lane Sotra suspension bridge had opened the previous year, crossing the narrows of the harbor from Bergen to Litlesotra. It was more than a kilometer long, 325 feet high, and had a vertical clearance of nearly 160 feet on the underside during low tide. Tides played an important role in scheduling departure times for the *Statsraad Lehmkuhl*, whose main mast towered skyward at more than 150 feet. After we cleared the bridge, mountains rose majestically from the calm fjord waters as we headed west toward the North Sea, gazing at the breathtaking views of the rugged coastline. I was scheduled for buoy watch during the first hour, so my enjoyment of the scenic beauty was from aft as the mid-November sun slowly disappeared below the horizon and as the mountains became mere silhouettes. It was quiet. This magical setting itself proclaimed our right-of-passage through the fjord.

As we entered the North Sea, rolling swells caused pitching and rocking. I struggled to maintain balance. Meanwhile, normal ship activities resumed. Group C was on duty, Group A had classes, a newspaper staff meeting was scheduled in the mess hall, and mealtimes remained the same. The only notable change was the constant motion of the ship. But it was like being rocked to sleep after I went to bed. And the only sounds came from the sea slapping the hull and portholes. Oh, yes, and the groans of seasick kids. Pisacano, who was overly sensitive to motion, became the first victim.

I reported for lookout watch at 06:00 on a very dark, frigid morning. By then the ship had steered eastward from the North Sea into the Hardangerfjord. Destination Ulvik. Deck lights disallowed views of the landscape. It felt strange and eerie as the mountains loomed quietly unseen on both sides. Most everyone was asleep below except the cadets and crew on duty. Aside from the dull hum of the diesel engine, all was quiet on deck. I stood motionless on the bow enduring the cold.

Suddenly there was a loud terrifying noise, a crunching sound that pierced the early morning air. Something had hit the hull! The ship slowed to a crawl, then stopped completely. Chills of panic numbed my spine. "Oh my God," I exclaimed, "What just happened?" My heart pounded through my chest! "I'm the watchman," I said aloud. "I'm responsible for sighting danger ahead!" Leaning over the railing, peering straight down from my perch, my eyes widened—large chunks of broken ice were pinching the hull. "You gotta be kidding," I shouted in disbelief. "We hit a large hunk of ice!"

Frantically I rang the bell just as Poulsen rushed up from behind with a handheld floodlight, yelling something in Danish. I heard shouts of response from crewmen on the main deck followed by a scurrying around like I'd not seen before. Multiple floodlights soon shone across the frozen fjord.

Ulvik was still several kilometers away, but it was evident we couldn't continue forward. Captain ordered the ship to reverse course. As the diesel engine revved, we slowly propelled backward creating space enough to maneuver an awkward turnaround—not an easy task for a 300-foot ship in frozen waters. Cadets swarmed up on deck from the banjers. Crewmen manned the wheel and watch posts, but I stayed at lookout with Poulsen, feeding my curiosity while experiencing the unheralded adventure of navigating a ship in a frozen fjord. I suppose it really wasn't as big of a deal as I first thought.

After the maneuver, we headed south for 50 kilometers to the small town of Odda in the southern dogleg of Hardangerfjord. We encountered no more ice and dropped anchor fifty yards clear of the dock upon arrival. The rest of the day was spent in training—lifeboat drills. It was no easy task dropping the heavy wooden boats from their perches above the outer perimeter of the main deck. We crawled into the lifeboats at deck level before being lowered to the water by cadets and crew still onboard. Rowing back and forth across the fjord for several hours was also more difficult and more physically exhausting than I expected. And rowing properly in sync with fellow cadets was a huge challenge. There was definitely a right way and a wrong way to row. Although we eventually caught on, we hardly perfected it.

Mate Kjemtrup oversaw the training from a small, motorized runabout while shouting orders and teaching technique. He was in his glory, like a little kid on Christmas morning. When he grinned, his face lit up, eyes twinkled, ears wiggled, and his entire body took on movements unbefitting of his strapping physique. Despite the physical challenge of rowing, watching the big Dane was pure entertainment. By day's end, my arms felt disconnected from my body. Kjemtrup reminded us however, that fatigue, aches, and pains are a never mind. And that tomorrow is another day. "We will do it again," he said with a grin.

For dinner we were rewarded with hamburgers, french fries, and ice cream. Then two films were shown in the dayroom to commemorate Thanksgiving Day back in the States. The first one was about the tall ships race from England to the Canary Islands several years prior, in which the *Statsraad Lehmkuhl* participated. It was an incredible morale boost to see our ship under full sail and realize the things we had to look forward to in the coming weeks.

Our second day anchored by Odda included more lifeboat drills, bracing on deck, lowering and taking in sails, etc. We finally docked at 14:00 and Chief Mate declared a liberty muster for Groups B and C. Plenty of smiles circulated among the cadets as he announced the official completion of sail training. Captain Fossa stamped his approval for the ship to sail as soon as weather in the North Sea was cooperative.

Suddenly a unified sense of accomplishment rose from within the community. Dreams of warm weather in the Canary Islands consumed us. No more cold toilet seats under the half deck, no more polishing brass or climbing the rigging in freezing rain, no more chilling night watches under the black arctic sky. Finally, we had something to count on as renewed spirits of anticipation and hope filled our souls. It was as exciting as the day we first arrived in Norway.

Ω

The population of Odda and its nearby communities topped more than 3,500 in 1972. Although surrounded by mountains, waterfalls, and breathtaking natural beauty, the town itself had little charm. Its working-class community was centered on smelteries for carbide production, which had been established in 1913. A local man invented the world-famous process of three-component NPK fertilizers, now known as the Odda process.

Local teens curiously gathered by the gangway as we docked. It was now late November. A small town like this hosting a large sail ship with American students onboard was a big deal. Some of my shipmates were eager to socialize with the dock huggers. And it was no surprise that cadets and crewmen visited the local bars that first night. So, the ship was again blessed with late night noise and ruckus in the banjers. Yelling, screaming, running through the corridors, banging on lockers, and incessant laughter continued into the wee hours. During all that, an alcohol-fueled fight broke out between Bill Snare (who was eventually sent home) and Bill Bacon.

Hopes for sailing were put on hold as weather in the North Sea proved to be stubbornly defiant. So, we waited. Classes were in full swing for all students as each group divided their time between school and ship's work. For me personally, it was a time of patience testing and soul searching. Several Zen sessions with Eiji and Mark Kaiser helped improve my perspective despite the tiring, ongoing ship's work and long days of rain. One night I went out drinking with fellow shipmates, bored with reading and studying, and disappointed by being stranded in a small town. The few good days in port were swallowed up by time. Even journaling had become a chore. My entries were short with so little to say.

One day, after hearing First Mate's grim forecast concerning our inability to sail, I was told that Chuck shimmied through the porthole in his room and dropped into the fjord for an icy swim. He did it on a dare. Foolish? Of course, it was. But he claimed there was nothing better to do. I understood. As he swam to the dock, onlookers hooted and hollered from the deck. We were all restless and the town wasn't big enough to hold our interest after a week. Several guys hooked up with local girls. Some of us formed intentional interaction groups with which we shared our innermost thoughts and feelings. Amid the disappointment of not sailing, several students and profs made concerted efforts to initiate positive vibes.

Kjemtrup engaged with students socially in the music room one night. His humor and stories were always entertaining. However, this time he went off on a fictional tale describing an imaginary storm that our ship would encounter in the North Sea after setting sail from Norway. "The winds will be strong, and the waves will be big," he said with wide eyes, "so the ship will not be able to float and will turn upside-down and fall apart." Peter's facial expressions, hand motions, Danish accent, and booming voice brought the story to life. Then his narrative ended suddenly and dramatically, "And EVERYONE WILL DIE!!!"

We all became alarmingly quiet. After pausing momentarily, he looked around the room, grinned broadly and said in a quieter tone, "But that's a never mind. A hundred people less on the world is a never mind." I was stunned. But Linda, who was superstitious and fearful by nature, was completely taken aback by Peter's prophetic narration. She had gone to the music room to relax and clear her head. Not to fill it with anxiety!

Ω

Latefossen Waterfall is a place of amazing natural beauty situated in the mountains ten kilometers from Odda. One day the school administrators planned a field trip and hired several buses to transport us there. From Country Road 13, a narrow, winding path led to the top of the falls. During our ascent we self-entertained with snowball fights, then Kjemtrup entertained Jane and me with tales from his school days in Denmark. I loved Peter's stories, especially his animated presentation of one tale in particular.

Several bigger kids at his school were picking on the smaller kids during recess. They did it every day. Peter claimed he was one of the little kids at the time—hard for me to imagine. Finally, he and two of his friends, tired of being harassed, ganged up on the bullies one at a time and beat them up—three against one. Their euphoria was short-lived, however. The bullies corralled Peter and his friends and smashed their heads into the concrete. He paused for a moment, lowered his head and showed Jane and me the scars on his forehead from that incident.

On our return from the top of the falls, we crawled, slid, and jumped across slippery rocks and boulders alongside the falls, clambering our way down the steep 500-foot drop to the six-arched stone bridge below. The setting was a spectacular natural playground, and the perfect antidote for a bunch of stir-crazy cadets cooped up on a ship docked in a small town. It felt good to live without the constraints of discipline, sail training, musters, ship's work, watches, and officers (except Kjemtrup, who had become one of us for the day). Being carefree kids again, even for just several hours, felt like a slice of heaven.

Finally, the second long-awaited announcement came after breakfast on the morning of December 2nd. We would leave Odda the next day! That, of course, triggered an immediate festive response. Group C creatively decorated the mess hall with toilet paper before dinner. Several officers reserved a local bar and dance hall for the evening and invited everyone to join the celebration, including recent acquaintances from town.

Bill Wright had hooked up with a girl named Venka on the first night after we docked. They hung out often between his schedule onboard and her school schedule on shore. Venka brought her friend, Chastie, along to the party that night. Both girls were sixteen years old. On Venka's prompting, Bill asked me to hang out with Chastie for the evening, like a blind date. I agreed to the arrangement without giving it much thought, mostly for Bill's sake.

The party was lively from the start with great dance music and free beer. Some of the old sailors even made their way to the dance floor. And Chastie wasn't the least bit shy while dancing and drinking beer. That somehow made up for her poor English, but I wasn't prepared for her forwardness. Although our time together was fun, it wasn't intellectually stimulating. Nor did we learn anything important about each other aside from our shared energy and a few romantic sparks. With Schnitler's permission, Bill and I brought the girls back to the ship. He stretched the midnight curfew to 01:00—the perfect time for a last kiss. Although eleven days was too long to stay in Odda, the time suddenly seemed short. I felt a twinge of sadness at the thought of leaving, knowing that Chastie would need to wait for her next ship to come in.

The next morning as the ship pulled away from the dock, all the lights on the pier and on Odda's main street blinked continuously until we were out of sight. It was a nice send-off from a town that received us well. The local newspaper printed numerous photos and articles during our stay, including interviews with cadets and faculty. Sail training, especially work in the rigging, provided entertainment for town folks. And their presence kept us focused while performing tasks, like a dress rehearsal before the big show. I must admit, there were times I experienced showmanship pride. The *Statsraad Lehmkuhl* now felt very much like my ship and my home. It's where I belonged.

We headed west toward the North Sea, and by 16:00, the sea schedule was fully operational. My group was on duty until midnight. As we motored from the calm waters of the Hardangerfjord into the choppy North Sea, I was perched on buoy watch. The ship rocked and pitched, again creating excitement onboard, but also taking its physical toll on all of us. And on the same unfortunate seasick cadets as before.

Group C was ordered to remain on deck for the duration of our shift. We were then scheduled for eight hours of standby watch. That meant staying awake, ready to report on deck if needed. At one point I dozed off but was rudely awakened by Chief Mate who made his below-deck rounds. Consumed by exhaustion, I staggered up on deck periodically for fresh air and to peer out into the sea. This vast, powerful, mysterious, mesmerizing ocean was about to become my ticket to see the world. That night during standby watch, I developed a deep respect for the sea, rooted in both fear and awe. It was a small taste of what was to come. Morning muster, workstations, and breakfast were an indescribable chaotic blur. We had not slept for the past twenty-four hours. And now, a new day was dawning.

Because the winds weren't good enough to continue south toward the Canary Islands, Captain ordered the ship to dock in the old coastal city of Stavanger in the south of Norway.

The bow at sunset

CHAPTER 9: STAVANGER

We were again met by curiosity seekers at the pier. Within the first hour, journalists and photographers from the local media came onboard. We felt like young celebrities while giving interviews and posing for photos. Four of us were selected to stand with Captain Fossa on deck by the wheel—a photo that was displayed on the front page of the *Stavanger News* the next day. My sleep-deprived group was reenergized from all the activity. While climbing high to assist one of the crewmen in the rigging, I enjoyed an amazing view of the city. "Wow, what a cool town," I thought to myself. I endured the morning work and several afternoon classes before an evening on the town with Professor Soja and others. What started out as casual drinks and quiet philosophical discussions at a café-dance hall turned into a welcome to Stavanger celebration initiated by several local enthusiasts. None of my shipmates nor I paid for any food or drinks. It was a great first impression of the town.

Our stop in Stavanger was expected to be just a layover before gearing up for the high seas. But, as in Odda, the unexpected happened, and the ship stayed docked for thirteen days. Luckily, unlike Odda, this beautiful old Nordic town established in 1125 provided lots to see and do. Our time there proved to be wonderful with educational visits to the old cathedral from the 1100s, museums, Viking ship memorabilia, and the King's Palace. Bars and restaurants reflected the city's social culture, while schools and universities embodied its educational values. Most young folks spoke perfect English, and as much as the town was a gift to us, our presence was also a gift to the town. The *Statsraad Lehmkuhl* stole the show by the waterfront. No matter where we strolled on any given day, it was always a proud moment to walk up the gangway and board ship amidst crowds of onlookers.

The American High School of Stavanger challenged the Oceanics School to a basketball game. We had no time to practice in advance as a team. In fact, we had no team, until now. Emil, Perry, Randy, Pisacano, Jack, Martin, Todd, Alec, and I pulled together quickly without knowing each other's ability. Despite our efforts to play hard and develop teamwork, we got off to a pathetically slow start, trailing 25–4 at the half. But Emil's basketball skills and leadership eventually turned things around. We began finding an open teammate, making good passes, and hitting our shots. Perry became like an animal under the basket, snatching most of the offensive and defensive rebounds. His and Emil's bullish play inspired confidence in the rest of us, and the second half belonged to the cadets. We stormed from behind to pull the game out by two points in the final thirty seconds, 43–41.

Winning wasn't as important as the spirit with which we played. A cohesive bond developed on the court that day beyond anything I had experienced thus far aboard ship. Interestingly, our individual competitiveness had turned into unselfish team effort. After the game, I walked home with Alec as he shared personal stuff from his heart. He told me about his ongoing struggle with anger that he'd been addressing in counseling for the past year. Although unwilling to enlist in the military, as several folks had suggested to him, he joined Oceanics with hopes of becoming more disciplined in this structured setting. He desperately desired to become a better person from the inside out but lacked the skillset to do it. I was impressed with his candor and willingness to share personal stuff with me. It set a new tone for our relationship going forward, shifting my previous perceptions of Alec as being selfish, arrogant, and ill-tempered, to someone who was caring, sensitive, and searching for the same things in life as me.

The Stavanger team, still in disbelief about their loss, challenged us to a rematch. We eagerly obliged as Chief Mate Kavanvik showed up to watch, inspiring us to play well. Jim Johnson, Rufus, and Jeff joined ranks this time as we achieved a decisive 68–44 victory, stunning the locals. Chief Mate, pleased with our performance, gave each team member an additional hour of liberty onshore to celebrate.

I believe our time in Stavanger established value for our community. Suddenly, I felt more connected with shipmates. Classes continued in full swing, and although sail training was officially over, we fine-tuned our tasks onboard. Most of us were now in better physical shape than before, and the crew seemed to be gaining confidence in our abilities on deck and in the rig.

Weekends were fun. We frequented dancing joints and hung out with local teens expending an abundance of energy. Some nights after returning to the ship, we were hungry. Grilled cheese sandwiches became a midnight hit in the small mess kitchen. I made and sold sandwiches to my friends, capitalizing on their late-night appetites—anything to make a few bucks. Lucy was one of my regular customers, eagerly paying three Kroner (50 cents) for a grilled cheese sandwich.

Front page - Stavanger News: (L to R) me, Martin, Captain, Jack, Tara

We attended concerts in town. Joe Feinblatt and I once went to a Norwegian folk music gathering for an evening of pure enjoyment. The music hall was decorated in unique fashion resembling an old town square and featured highly talented local performers. It was one of those nights that could've lasted forever.

Other evenings were spent in the music room listening to records or live music performed by shipmate musicians. Loggins & Messina's album *Sittin' In* was popular among the students. "Danny's Song" played daily, over and again from the balancing turntable. Onshore, the American School opened its doors for us to use their facilities on weekends. We frequented the gym to shoot hoops, work out on the equipment, kick soccer balls around, and climb ropes. Every Friday night, a movie was shown in the union mess as an alternative to going ashore. We had plenty to do while developing positive community life onboard and off.

Norwegian newspaper article

Views from aloft

CHAPTER 10: THE SEA

Late afternoon on Sunday, December 17, the *Statsraad Lehmkuhl* pulled away from the docks of Stavanger into the North Sea, heading south toward the English Channel. There was excitement in the air. Finally, we were heading out to sea! My watch shift started at midnight, allowing four hours of sleep after dinner. I was surprised to see staysails already set, majestically rising high above the deck when I reported for duty. This was the first time I witnessed the sails functioning with purpose, beautifully and proudly catching wind in their bellies. I stared in awe at the large white canvas from the bow under moonlit skies. Except for that, my eight-hour shift passed quickly and uneventfully.

After a hearty breakfast, it was time for classes—never mind sleeping. During our first two days at sea, we had little ship's work except to set sails. The seas were calm, nearly as calm as the water in the fjords. Everything seemed unbelievably easy.

Our third day was more of the same, highlighted by three of nature's best: sun, sky, and sea. It was amazing to stand on deck and look in all directions, absorbing the vastness of each. I suppose nothing compares with first impressions. And there in the middle of it all was the *Statsraad Lehmkuhl* carrying this unique floating community, far from the security of land. Suddenly we were small, seemingly powerless, and vulnerable, totally at the mercy of our environment as the ocean's mysteries began revealing themselves to me as a first-time sailor.

The school administration capitalized on the fact there was little to do on deck. Several faculty members hammered out extra assignments—classwork consumed large chunks of our time in those first few days. Advantage faculty. But we knew the reverse could and would be true without a moment's notice. We were aware that ship's care trumped everything else.

The mood onboard remained good throughout day four. Students, crew, and faculty interacted well, laughing, joking, and singing on deck. Dave Freedman strummed his guitar and sang songs, "Sloop John B" and "Blowin' in the Wind," as we gathered around and sang along. I finished my credo for English class, then wrote an article for the second issue of *The Daily Muster*. Life couldn't have been much better as we sailed through the narrowest section of the English Channel past the White Cliffs of Dover. Winds still weren't strong, and our sea schedule routine remained easy. Training details of the past months made good sense and, naively, we felt like full-fledged sailors.

On day five, all the square sails were set at sunrise. It took most everyone to coordinate and complete the task. But still, winds were weak. Mate Schnitler commented that he had never seen such quiet seas and lazy winds at this location before. Sometimes the sails flapped unproductively from the yards as we continued motoring just south of Southampton, England. At sunset, however, the square sails were taken in, supposedly for safety reasons. Kjemtrup explained to several of us in his best bad English, "You never know when might the winds get strong."

Next morning the sea woke up. Large swells caused the ship to roll and pitch. While on lookout watch I experienced an incredible joy ride as we headed into the waves. The bow lifted high as the crest of each swell passed underneath, only to drop quickly into the trough before the next one approached, shifting my body weight from heavy to light, repeatedly. It felt strange. Several cadets got sick again. I developed a headache for the first time at sea, like the kind you get after back-to-back roller-coaster rides at an amusement park. But onboard there was no escape. I crawled into bed with a knot directly behind my eyeballs, listening to Pisacano moaning and dry-heaving in the next room. I felt strangely fortunate.

At midnight we entered the Bay of Biscay off the west coast of France. It was a place I previously knew little about. That was about to change.

On our seventh day, Group C went on standby watch at 08:00. I had mess duty for both breakfast and lunch but was summoned to lookout watch at noon to cover for a sick cadet. That was surely better than lunch cleanup. I stood on the bow with the bright sun and warm breeze caressing my face while the upper yard swayed amazingly far side to side. Later I climbed to the royl yard—the highest place to safely perch and ride the ship's slow rhythmic movement. It was a thrill beyond compare, peering down from the furthest point of sway and seeing nothing but sea more than a hundred feet below, waiting to swallow me up if given the chance.

Most everyone was on deck enjoying the sun and surf on this glorious afternoon. But as evening approached, the ocean became noticeably agitated. It was difficult for anyone to sleep. Pisacano could no longer perform any of his duties, so the rest of our group covered his watches, extending our own shifts from one hour to an hour and twenty minutes. I was asked to assist Schnitler in the chart room between watches as he set the ship's course. He was unusually quiet and focused, seemingly aware of something beyond what he shared, keeping his eyes fixed on the radar screen.

I took my turn at the helm at 04:00 as it began raining. Temperatures dropped considerably. I stood for a full hour and twenty minutes with both hands grasping the wheel, making every effort to keep the ship on course as we battled rough seas. Except for my face and hands, the hooded rain gear provided protection from the cold pelting rain. Poulsen stood nearby shouting orders to the sailors on deck. It was December 24, the day before Christmas.

As Group C's shift came to an end, I quickly took a washbowl bath and shampooed my greasy hair. There was no hot water, and no explanation why. Breakfast was good, complete with bacon, fried eggs, plenty of bread, and corn flakes, followed immediately by the call, "All hands on deck." The ship was about to change course, so we reported to bracing stations. As always, a ship as large as the *Statsraad Lehmkuhl* requires lots of hands to complete a directional change maneuver. On this day, the task was accomplished surprisingly well as officers barked commands over the harsh sounds of the wind. I suddenly began realizing how much fun it is to sail this ship! But also, how challenging.

There were no more calls to assist on deck after my group went off duty. After dinner the ship began rocking and pitching beyond anything we'd yet experienced during our week-long journey. The winds howled eerily through the rigging, and by midnight had increased from gale to storm, making verbal communication on deck nearly impossible. While Group A was on duty, all hell broke loose. Sea swells grew to eye-popping size. Waves crashed onto the deck. For several hours all cadets were asked to stay below except those on scheduled watches. Both lookout and buoy watch were harnessed to the railing. Rescue of an overboard comrade wouldn't have been possible under these conditions.

Suddenly I heard an enormous CRACK as the wind exploded one of the top stay sails, ripping one end loose from the cable and shredding it like a worn cloth. I stayed below deck as ordered but heard pounding feet and shouting just above. Loudest of all, even above the whistling wind, was the sound of the torn sail, cracking like a whip in the night. Then came the call, "ALLE MANN PA DEKK!" Bosun's voice could be heard penetrating the sounds of the storm repeatedly, "ALLE MANN PA DEKK! ALLE MANN PA DEKK!"

Assuming the ship was in trouble, I staggered from my room just as it lurched strongly to starboard, throwing me headlong into the large ventilator pipe. After taking a moment to gather myself, I got up and slowly made my way up the metal stairs to the deck. Outside the hatch, I looked up and saw the untamed sail fiercely

whipping the rigging with unprovoked fury. It was an unforgettable sight as
I stared in fear. Then suddenly, I saw dark figures climbing toward the unleashed
sail—crewmen for sure. Were they crazy? No one else dared climb in these conditions. Chills shot up and down my spine as I processed the unfathomable risks. By
now the ship was rocking wildly out of control. Several waves washed completely
across the deck, soaking everyone in their path. I saw the entire side of the ship
disappear into the sea as the deck stood at a jaw-dropping 50 degrees! The masts
protruded what seemed like a mile out over the sea.

Before every cadet could respond to Bosun's call, a second order was given to
clear the deck as water sloshed dangerously side to side. Without footing, there
was little good any of us could do. Crewmen commanded all watch posts for the
remainder of the night as the gale-force winds continued to howl and batter every
exposed part of the ship.

Being below deck was also an adventure. Lockers flung open, spewing deodor-
ant, shampoo, toothpaste, clothing, shoes, and anything not secured, into the
corridors. Broken glass rattled across the floor. Kids screamed in excited fear.
Pisacano continued moaning and vomiting. Chairs, desks, and books were tossed
randomly from rooms. Lifelines were strung from the banjers to the day room. As
I made my way forward toward the day room, I experienced more mayhem—furniture and cadets literally went airborne as the ship rocked ferociously. Benches
smashed together, dishes broke on impact as they flew from cupboards, while
clanging pots and pans added random percussion to the storm music.

Water penetrated through several portholes in the banjers. At one point,
I headed through the hallway toward the union mess and was thrown into a
locker. Before regaining my balance, I was smashed into the opposite wall, all the
while hearing cursed moans from Pisacano's room.

Suddenly, another fierce CRACK cut through the night air from above—another
staysail had blown apart, followed by loud voices and stomping feet as the crew
responded. Hatches were closed to the main deck. No one could go outside who
wasn't already there. I felt only a mild security in the fact that I was below deck.
The storm raged on throughout the night as most of us hunkered down in our
bunks, wide-eyed and scared. No one slept. It just wasn't possible.

Kjemtrup later told me he went below and crawled around the bottom of
the hull checking that the ballast was properly secured without mentioning his
concern to the captain or the other officers. The ballast consisted of paver-size
rocks piled in wooden compartments on both sides of the lowest section of the

hull, totaling 750 tons with the purpose of keeping the ship upright. Had the ballast shifted, the ship would surely have rolled over!

The next morning Group C went on duty at 08:00. Breakfast could not be prepared in the galley so the cooks handed out finger food and fruit instead. I chomped down an apple and a hard-boiled egg, then reported for lookout watch to start our shift. Lookout was moved back from the bow to the halfdeck. Even still, I got soaked from the cold sea mist thrust skyward from the crests. After sunrise the wind tamed considerably, and the storm began to subside, but the seas remained strong, punishing the ship with angry swells and breaks of mindboggling size.

I relieved Todd on buoy watch, clipped onto the aft railing, then suddenly remembered it was Christmas Day. My mind drifted back home to where the Glick side of my family would surely be gathered for its traditional turkey dinner, children's gift exchange, and Christmas carols. My aunts and uncles would be singing "Beautiful Star of Bethlehem"—Grossmommie's favorite carol. Despite fleeting moments of homesickness, I realized I wouldn't exchange this experience for anything in Pennsylvania—not even for a minute.

That evening, a nice Christmas dinner became a reality onboard. The cooks did a phenomenal job of rebounding from the chaos in the galley and proceeded to make plenty of turkey and potatoes for all onboard. With peaches for dessert. After dinner, Emil and I stood on deck peering toward the ever-moving horizon, each sharing what Christmas would've been like at home. Our conversation was interrupted by a roving group of cadets who began singing on deck. As the group size grew, the singing got louder. Kids belted out Christmas carols at the top of their lungs. The crazy cadet choir eventually relocated to the union mess where volume and lunacy continued, maximizing the decibels of undecipherable sounds. It was a wild, unusual Christmas Day from start to finish.

Ω

The winds shifted by late evening, allowing four square sails and two additional stay sails to be set, not just to stabilize the ship, but also to increase speed toward the Canary Islands. There was rumor of another storm heading our direction. I wasn't capable of processing news like that. Finally, I crawled into bed at midnight, totally exhausted. The banjers were unusually quiet, and within minutes I was rocked to sleep by the ship's steady cradling.

December 26 started with a good breakfast after eight hours of solid sleep. Although we didn't know it at the time, it would be our last good meal for several days. Feeling rested and energized, I was greeted by warm sunshine as I climbed up on deck. Cadet Sue Nelson was quietly celebrating her eighteenth birthday. The winds were perfect and the sails full as the ship cut through swells at an impressive speed, listing heavily to port side. It was the best sailing weather we had experienced since leaving Norway.

But within half an hour the command went out for all hands on deck. We were puzzled as to why. Schnitler answered our questions quickly and matter-of-factly, "There is another storm close by which we cannot avoid. We must bring in all the sails except the stumpes and two staysails."

We worked hard and fast to do just that, chattering nervously amongst ourselves. The crew entertained every plausible possibility to skirt around the west side of the advancing storm, but Kjemtrup said it would take a miracle to avoid. We didn't have enough time. Again, the ship appeared to be in trouble, evidenced by several terse-faced crewmen who knew more than we did, and who understood the ill-fated challenge of another battle ahead.

By noon the sea became highly agitated, unleashing its power with impressive swells upwards of forty feet. The winds picked up simultaneously, progressing quickly from gale to storm—force ten. The *Statsraad Lehmkuhl* tossed dangerously, like a plastic toy in a wave pool. Although nearly powerless in a storm of this magnitude, the diesel engine ran to help steady the ship's heading. Several times the stern came completely out of the water, including the prop, as the crests of the swells flowed under the ship, front to back. It was an incredible thrill for anyone manning the fore and aft watch posts. Our reality had become a live performance of our most imaginative sea adventure! Luckily, the ship stayed afloat during the next few hours. Turning sideways or hitting swells broadside could've caused us to capsize; the heavy rigging and steel masts would have surely challenged the ship's ballasts to the point of not being able to right itself.

Again, cadets were relieved of the wheel, allowing crewmen the responsibility of steering the ship. For a period, the winds reached force twelve—hurricane force! It was absolutely crazy. No sail training in the world could have prepared us for this. We were hundreds of miles from the closest landfall when in a flash, I remembered Kjemtrup's imaginary description of being shipwrecked. Suddenly the feared realness of his story came to life.

Some kids hunkered down in the banjers, strapping themselves to their bunks. Others gathered in the music room several tiers down and lay on the floor in the lower section of the hull, riding and rolling, pitching, and rising with every toss of the ship. There was no safe place. I couldn't imagine anyone sleeping through this and was reminded of the Biblical story of Jonah.

At 05:00 hours I heard the dreaded command, "ALLE MANN PA DEKK!" I knew the importance of heeding the call, scared or not. I jumped into my rain gear and struggled to the deck. The situation presented by First Mate was one of life and death. Our best chance of survival was to save the ship. And the best way to save the ship was to change course 100 degrees. That seemed like a tall order, knowing the danger of such a maneuver in these conditions, but imagining our fate if we didn't, gave us the motivation to do it anyway. Radar showed the center of the storm directly ahead and coming our way.

The entire crew was already on deck when I exited through the hatch—Jacobsen, Kjemtrup, Poulsen, Arne, Bosun, Evanson, Timberman, Morgan Kane, Eigl, everyone including the cooks. Apprehension and fear were written in the eyes of even the saltiest sailors that night as the winds howled mercilessly. We had a job to do despite the difficulty of our task. Hearing officers' detailed commands was nearly impossible because of the horrific sounds of the winds raging through the rig. The ship continued rocking ferociously. Sometimes the entire side railing was totally immersed into the sea as water poured onto the deck. We hung onto the lifeline strung on deck, or to whatever we could to stay upright as our scared, cold faces reflected our fright.

Darkness was thick beyond the perimeter of the ship. Flood lights from the first platform partially illuminated the deck, casting eerie shadows on a scene likened to an artist's depiction of a ship and crew out of control. The sea mist water-blasted our exposed skin like a pressure washer. Twice I was knocked off my feet and thrust sideways into the railing. Surviving the elements on deck was of utmost importance, but we also had to complete the maneuver, according to Schnitler, "if any of us has serious hopes of seeing the light of day."

Lines were formed for bracing as everyone held tight to the ropes with a two-fold purpose: first, to hang on for our own security, and secondly, to move the yards for directional change. It wasn't possible to maintain a solid foothold. Several times the entire line of cadets was thrust into the port side rail, only to be thrown the opposite way moments later when the ship lurched starboard. The deck stood at fifty degrees in each direction repeatedly, challenging our ability to perform the task. We were not sure-footed mountain goats! It was later confirmed that at

Bracing: The task of changing the angle of the yard arms to accomodate wind direction when changing course

one point during the storm we rocked fifty-two degrees twice, a number beyond what the indicator gauge could even show!

At the most critical point in the maneuver, the ship rode sideways down a huge swell into the trough, with walls of water towering on both sides. The three masts angled sideways as the ship rode up and over the approaching swell. I was screaming inside, "Where is the point of no return?!" But the incredible *Stats-raad Lehmkuhl*, the ship that survived World War I, overcame Hitler's capture in World War II, trained thousands of cadets since 1914, and weathered many storms—that same ship again showed her character, exercised stamina, demonstrated strength, and proved her seaworthiness amid yet another challenge. Most everyone onboard gained a new level of respect for our ship that night. We also gained a new level of respect for ourselves as we accomplished the dangerous and difficult challenge of changing course—a credit to our knowledgeable crew as well as cadet perseverance through the technical details of what we had learned during sail training. That in itself was a tactical miracle!

Although we crossed a major hurdle, we still weren't out of trouble, as the seas and force twelve winds continued to batter and pound the ship's hull and rigging. Captain Fossa eventually ordered the black flag to be raised on the main mast, signaling that the ship was out of control. It wasn't a reflection on the crew or cadets, nor a sign of surrender. Rather, an act of humble submission to the powers of nature. Under Captain's orders, Stein radioed our location to any merchant vessel that might happen to be within range. A French tanker, twenty-five miles away, responded. Then a second ship about forty miles further north also answered the call. Both stayed in touch by radio throughout the night.

After the miracle maneuver, we all sat tight and rode out the storm. There was nothing more to do but survive. Incredibly, both square storm sails held fast. One developed a small hole but didn't come apart or tear loose from the yard. Kjemtrup told me that if the storm sails had exploded, it would've been difficult to keep the ship upright. This whole experience was beyond anything I could've imagined, even in my worst nightmares.

I spent most of the following afternoon on deck staring in amazement at what was unfolding before my eyes. Although officially off duty, I didn't want to miss a minute of this wild escapade. Journaling was difficult. There was no way I could articulate the emotions of this experience into words anyway. So, I decided to just feel it for as long as I could and write another day. Surely, I would relive this adventure in my mind for weeks and months to come.

The crew continued to man the wheel when Group C went on duty at 16:00, but we were responsible for all other watches. It was frigid cold on buoy watch as I sat at the stern facing fierce winds from behind. It was there that I finally thanked God for His protection and mercy—no one had fallen overboard, and no one was seriously hurt. So far, we all had survived.

At midnight we were ordered to set two more sails. My shift was just ending but I volunteered to go up and unleash sizings. By then most of us were exhausted, with little expendable energy. Even those just coming on duty were sluggish and not eager to climb. The ship continued rocking a total of 80–90 degrees side to side as the winds stayed strong. Climbing was not a task for the weak of heart or for the godless. Honestly, I was scared to death!

Ω

From the first day of sail training, Jane was a highly motivated, full-hearted cadet beyond the rest of us. She willingly did all necessary tasks enthusiastically and never shied away from ship's work. Her upbeat spirit was remarkable, and although not the strongest cadet onboard, she could do anything she set her mind to. She was an inspiration to me. That night, at midnight, several cadets had reluctantly agreed to climb to the fokke sail—the closest yard to the deck. Poulsen looked at Jane and me without saying a word, trying to read our minds. Jane responded to his unspoken request with a smile. "We'll go high," she said, glancing at me. I was all in, sort of, but not smiling. As we prepared to go aloft, Poulsen quickly explained the obvious danger, then finished his short spiel by adding, "You must have good hand grips at all times. Do you understand?!" I had used a safety clip several times before but found it most useful when I remained stationary for an extended period, not while climbing. It was much too cumbersome to attach and detach every few feet. Neither Jane nor I used them that night.

The wind was at our backs as we started our ascent from port side. Maneuvering up and over the first platform was a challenge as we fought the elements. Time wasn't as important as safety. When we reached the merse sail level, Jane moved toward port side, and I shifted from Jacob's ladder toward the mast and starboard side. Under normal circumstances the maneuver around the mast required focus but wasn't difficult. And it was quick. But this night was different. As I reached the slippery wet mast, I stepped onto the short foot cable and moved toward the other side without a good handhold for only a second. I had done it many times before. But fate had its way as the ship dipped violently during that moment, and I lost my balance backwards. There were no ropes or cables within reach, only the mast itself. And it was much too large and too slippery to get a good grip. I flung my arms around its sides in desperation, but my hands couldn't hold. During that cold, anxious moment I anticipated the worst—going airborne, then SPLAT—realizing that I couldn't save myself. Two seconds felt like forever as I cried out to God. A million pictures reeled through my mind...

Suddenly, as the dipping motion of the ship was causing me to lose my balance, there was a steep pitch downward in the opposite direction, thrusting me upward and forward—a miraculous display of power beyond my control—like from a guardian angel! I responded quickly, lunged around the mast, and grabbed onto the first available handhold. There I stood, frozen in place for a full fifteen seconds, unable to release my grip from the cable. It was a defining moment.

My heart pounded as the wind continued to howl through the maze of ropes and cables, making communication difficult. Jane was already out on the yard port side when she turned to make sure I was ready to unleash the sail, totally oblivious to what had just happened. Suddenly full of adrenaline, I slid to the end of the yardarm, but the excitement wasn't over. I looked down at the raging waters below as I rode the arm completely out over the waves on the starboard side, appearing to head straight into the sea. The sway slowed however, rebounded, and swung the other way, pointing the massive yards straight up into the night sky. The ride was an unbelievable thrill from my position. Cadets pulling on the skotes eighty feet below appeared small from my place in the rig. It was surreal. I knew with certainty there was nowhere in the world that I could experience this combination of fear, excitement, and duty except aboard this ship in a storm. And there was no way to articulate what I felt to anyone who wasn't there beside me.

Refocusing my attention, I hung on with one hand and worked with the other, completing the task of unleashing the sail. When the heavy canvas dropped from the yard, the wind immediately blew it full toward the bow with a horrendous popping sound. Below, the crew struggled to control the sail, pulling frantically to tighten the skotes—like a tug-o-war with the wind. I heard Kjemtrup shouting, "PULL... PULL... PULL," as the cadets on deck battled to maintain their balance. Again, the hours of training in the cold driving rains of Norway paid dividends. This was our true test of endurance, courage, and of knowing the ropes.

Skotes: (sheets in English) Ropes attached to the lower corners of a sail used to control its angle and tension

Finally, after the sails were set and the necessary ropes were secured to the belay pins on the side walls, I retired to the floor of the guest saloon. I told no one what had happened in the rigging. How could I even begin explaining it before I had fully processed it myself? After returning to my cabin, sleep was slow in coming. I lay awake, wide-eyed, face up in my bunk, blood still pumping hard through every vein in my body, realizing I had just experienced the most adventurous day of my life, and thankful it was not my day to die.

Ω

The next morning, December 28, evolved into emotional hell for the cadets. We were all physically exhausted from several days of battling storms. The Norwegian crew was exhausted as well. During the mandatory 07:00 muster on deck, Kjemtrup was in an unusually sour mood. The fallout from two storms had taken its toll on him. I suppose we all responded in our own way. Jacobsen drank, Kjemtrup got extremely pissed off, and a lot of us were sorely confused. Kjemtrup took roll call twice that morning because of the chaos during his first attempt. When the ship pitched and rolled, some of us lost balance and stepped out of line. Peter screamed, demanding that we maintain our positions. In a fit of untamed anger, he lost his cool and yelled, "No one will eat breakfast until the whole ship is cleaned up!" His eyes were fiery red, only partly from fatigue. "Do it NOW!" he bellowed. His disposition was troubling. I had never seen him like this.

We offered no resistance to his demands as we went about the business of cleaning up the ship. Other crewmen joined him in shouting unreasonable commands, sometimes contradicting each other. Kjemtrup said one thing, the Sargent another, and Poulsen still another. There was no way to know who was supposed to do what as the crew wreaked emotional havoc on us. It was insane. I stood on deck in disbelief, barely able to move, feeling like a slave, a peon, less than human, like one of a herd of cattle being loaded onto the back of a truck without a ramp. The crew's behavior was completely unnecessary. Somehow, I was able to swallow my pride and dignity, maybe only because I was hungry. Then I worked like a freaking horse alongside my comrades to clean up the entire ship—the deck, day room, bathrooms, and banjers. By the time I finished, most everyone else had already gone for breakfast. And when I arrived in the mess hall, there was little food left. Without a word to anyone, I ate two scrawny hardboiled eggs and went to bed.

Ten minutes later Bosun's dreaded call bellowed down through the hatch into the banjers like a megaphone, "ALLE MANN PA DEKK!" I hesitated for a moment, then remembered my commitment to duty when the call went out. I also rationalized that this morning was unusual. I needed to forgive the crew for their ridiculous ranting two hours earlier. I now felt like a bona fide sailor aboard the *Statsraad Lehmkuhl.* I had obligations to the captain, to his officers and crew, to the ship, and to myself. I remembered my determined resolve to the program during my interview with Stephanie in New York. I was serious then, and I must remain serious now. Sleep would have to wait.

The entire remainder of the morning was spent setting and trimming sails. I climbed high into the rigging and joined fellow cadets along with Arne and Poulsen, two of my favorite crewmen. By then the crew's mood had improved. Although the winds had weakened, the sea was still tempestuous, and the thrills were still alive. No challenge seemed insurmountable anymore—the higher the better! With all the square sails set, the ship looked absolutely beautiful both from the top and from the deck.

Mark and I stood by the rail on deck after the work was completed, enjoying the bright sunshine for the first time in days. He was a great guy, soft spoken but not soft-minded. His ideas and thoughts were always worth hearing, especially when we engaged in creative dialogue. That day he told me about an outfit that organizes camel cruises on the Sahara Desert and suggested it might be something we should consider after returning to Norway in the spring. He also suggested the idea of hitchhiking from Norway to India. Adventure was now ingrained in both of us. At lunch we scarfed up more than our share of Swedish meatballs to replenish our depleted bodies. But after lunch I began fading fast. I couldn't remember the last time I had slept in my bed. Totally exhausted, I lay back in my bunk, too tired to take off my clothes.

I shouldn't have been surprised that within minutes of stretching out, the call went out again, "All hands on deck!" I woke with a start, jumped up again, threw on my jacket and boots and hit the deck. We set the few remaining sails. Although the work wasn't as urgent as before, it required lots of manpower. And because we again changed course, there was bracing to do. Thank God for pulleys! I never appreciated their value until living on this ship. After an hour we finished, but I was afraid to go back to bed. Instead, I joined friends in the dayroom, dreaming about Tenerife, our first scheduled stop in the Canary Islands.

Things improved as the day progressed. Sunshine after a storm isn't just a figure of speech. And I finally slept three full hours before dinner. We headed due South under full sail at ten knots, 150 miles west of Portugal. It was just our thirteenth day at sea but it felt like we had been through a year's worth of adventure.

Ω

Tables in the mess hall still couldn't be set up because of rough seas, but the cooks dished up food from big pots as we lined up. We were, however, able to sit on benches at tables for the first time in days and eat hot food from bowls with spoons. That was nice. Christmas dinner had been our last previous sit-down meal. During the storm, we survived on apples, oranges, hard boiled eggs, and snack foods, if we ate anything at all.

Not that it mattered much, but I had my first bowel movement in six days. Todd laughed hysterically when I shared that fact, then sobered up quickly, realizing he couldn't remember his last time. For certain, anyone who sat on the toilet during the storm remembered it well. Several kids were thrown off the pot into the stall walls. They said as much. But humbled victims were reluctant to divulge further details. It was also an adventure to pee, whether standing or sitting. I guessed the hit/miss ratio to be about 50%.

After dinner freshwater showers were turned on. I made a dash for the shower room behind Todd and Jack as soon as it was announced. Freshwater was always limited at sea. Some days the showers weren't turned on at all. But when they were, we were instructed to soak for one minute, turn the water off, lather up, then rinse for a minute. Total time in the shower was supposed to be three minutes or less.

When at sea for more than a week, fresh water was saved for brushing teeth, hand and face washing, cooking, drinking, and washing dishes. The other shower option was primitive—a metal bucket with multiple holes in the bottom hung from a cross cable on the main deck. The same saltwater hydrants used for scrubbing the deck and washing hatches and lifeboats were also used to fill the sea shower buckets. Gravity took care of the rest. Sea showers weren't great, but they served a purpose.

As we sailed past the Strait of Gibraltar and the northwest coast of Morocco, I was perched on the bowsprit watching dolphins swimming and diving on starboard side. The warm breeze was heavenly. Spring weather had finally arrived on the *Statsraad Lehmkuhl*. That night there were impromptu piano performances by Frank, Arturo, and Dave Freedman. The depths of the hull had never heard sweeter sounds.

It seemed fitting that on the last day of the year and our fifteenth day at sea, the lookout watchman spotted land at 11:00 hours. Tenerife was on the horizon! But there wasn't a pilot available to escort the ship to dock until the following day. Bummer. So, we took in all the sails and quietly drifted toward the island in calm seas. The weather was gorgeous. Kids hung out on deck all afternoon in shorts, shirtless and shoeless.

Dinner was great: chicken, rice, potatoes with gravy, green beans, cake, and plenty of everything. Then at 19:30 the New Year's Eve celebration began with an apple bobbing contest on deck, followed by a chewing gum competition between profs Frank and Arturo. Each contestant was given five packs of gum, five pieces per pack. They had to open and chew all twenty-five pieces until the wad was soft enough to blow a bubble. The first to blow a bubble an inch or more in diameter was the winner. Frank won. Arturo was just too proper.

The evening noise decibels were high and getting louder. Although alcohol was supposedly not available to the cadets, there was some serious drinking going on among the crew which somehow spilled into the banjers. And there was an abundance of food. Emil and I scarfed up anything edible on deck and in the mess hall. We found eggs in the galley and made omelets, then French toast. We ate fruit, cookies, and cake. It had been a very long time since we had even seen that much food. As pots and pans banged and the ship's horn blasted, Captain Od Fossa walked around the deck smiling and shaking hands with everyone. A rarity. All I wanted was a big bag of hard pretzels to finish out this remarkably unusual year. But it wasn't to be.

CHAPTER 11: TENERIFE

The Canary Islands, located off the coast of northern Africa, belong to Spain. With warm tropical climate year-round, bright sandy beaches, lush green mountains, and friendly people, the islands have been a popular vacation spot for mainland Europeans for many years. Especially Germans. Tenerife is the largest of the islands, the most populated, and boasts the third largest volcano in the world. Mt. Teide can be seen towering more than 11,000 feet in the center of the island, displaying its prominent snow-capped peak. Terraced farms and lush lowlands produce an abundance of fresh fruits and vegetables, supplementing an economy that is mostly reliant on tourism.

Our ship docked in Santa Cruz at 08:30, and for the first time in more than two weeks, we walked on solid ground. It felt awkward. In the same way we had to acquire our sea legs after leaving Norway, we now had to find our land legs.

The town itself was gorgeous with small sidewalk cafés, restaurants, palm-lined plazas, lush vegetation, and a relaxed atmosphere. After going ashore, Emil and I met a Spaniard from the mainland who was traveling alone on a personal sabbatical. Antonio was a Berkeley graduate who spoke perfect English. Fascinated by the fact that we had just come off the sail ship, he offered to show us around. We spent several hours together, then he treated us to pastries and tropical drinks in a shaded plaza by the town center. Antonio loved the stories concerning our recent sea adventures.

"Ah, the Bay of Biscay," he mused. "Seamen have long feared passing through those waters, for good reason. Thousands of ships have been lost there. Many just disappeared, never to be found or heard from again. The ocean floor is more than 5,000 feet deep," he noted with historic certainty.

I was familiar with the Bermuda Triangle but knew nothing about the Bay of Biscay prior to our recent experience. Being with Antonio was like taking a crash course in history, geography, and anthropology. Without flaunting his education, he shared experiential knowledge from his years of travel. In exchange for his kind hospitality, we invited him aboard the ship. It was the best we could offer. He was thrilled with the opportunity, having seen the world but never set foot aboard a square-rigged sail ship. Crowds of onlookers, including local media, were gathered by the pier to get a better look at the ship, when we proudly escorted Antonio up the gangway. Beholding a tall ship of this magnitude on a tropical island is no doubt a coveted experience.

Antonio was in awe of the rigging and the tall masts. Gazing upwards, he asked nervously, "Do you go up there?" Emil and I smiled at each other and nodded. Without redirecting his eyes, he responded in a low whisper, "Wow!"

Ω

Each group of cadets was given the opportunity to plan an overnight field trip somewhere on the island. It was up to us to self-organize and go where we'd like, with or without faculty members. Willy, Eric, and I made tentative plans to search for the Cave of the Guanches where evidence pointed to an ancient settlement dating back to 200 BC. So, I was conflicted when Joe Feinblatt invited me to join him. I knew his trip would also be educational, and I knew we'd eat well. He was both a generous guy and well-learned. I decided to go with Joe.

As we headed out from the docks, my pack was light, carrying only the necessary stuff for the overnighter. Joe carried a heavy, fully loaded aluminum-framed backpack with enough supplies to last several days, plus his camera equipment. We boarded a bus from Santa Cruz to the small town of La Laguna, considered to be one of the most beautiful inland villages on the island.

The old town center surrounded by colorful colonial-style houses was a scene right out of a picture book. Joe took gobs of photos. Since all his photography equipment was in his pack, each shot became an ordeal of dismantling and repacking. He documented each photo in a small notebook as well: date, time, place, and short description. I offered to help, but still, the process was slow. One photo, start to finish, could consume five to ten minutes. In time, the process tested my patience.

We strolled through La Laguna in the late afternoon. The island was quiet during its traditional siesta, but by 19:00 everything reopened and the town came to life. Joe and I had a nice dinner at an outdoor cafe near the square, then lingered for an hour sipping wine and listening to live music. A diverse crowd meandered about. Interestingly, the holiday festivities were still in full swing. One of my personal highlights was a live performance of "The Little Drummer Boy" in Spanish.

At 21:30 Joe and I hopped a bus to nearby Mercedes, then started walking from there. Our plan was to camp on Mt. Mercedes for the night, but neither of us had thought to bring a flashlight. The night became thick black as we ascended into the forest. I led the way, feeling the road with my feet, barely able to see my hands in front of my face. We trudged several kilometers, then stumbled onto a rock pile near a clearing overlook by a sharp bend in the road. From there we could see lights from a town far below. We chose to set up camp by the rocks on a crushed gravel surface. It was not the most comfortable spot, but we each enjoyed a juicy orange before crawling into our sleeping bags. Joe carried a real pillow in his pack. Mine was a sweatshirt wrapped around my high-top shoes.

The next morning Joe woke with a stomachache. The air was cold and dense as wet mist rolled inland from the sea. He got up early hoping to photograph the sunrise. I suppose it would've been a great shot if not for the fog. But with no reason to hang around, we continued our trek up the mountain. I was energized by the cool mist and a new day on this beautiful island. Joe was bogged down by everything, including the fact that he wasn't feeling well. I carried his pack to give him a break and quicken the pace. Within an hour we happened upon a small mountain restaurant where we met up with several shipmates. Bill Wright, Pisacano, Katie, and Sue had camped on the same mountain.

After the break, it became evident that Joe couldn't continue on foot. He was feeling worse. I suggested we try hitchhiking, but Joe didn't respond. Then within minutes, a German couple in a yellow VW Beetle stopped and offered us a ride while we stood by the side of the road, before I even stuck out my thumb! We were in luck. Without a moment's hesitation Joe and I jumped into the back seat with our stuff.

Gretchen was friendly, pretty, and talkative. Hans was less expressive, calculated, and heady but cordial. Both were in their forties. Our conversations were a mix of German, Pennsylvania Dutch, and English. They explained their plan to visit a town on the northeast side of Tenerife, Taganana, then circle around to the north and eventually make their way back to Santa Cruz by late afternoon. They invited us to spend the entire day with them. It was the perfect solution to our situation.

Taganana was an interesting little hamlet, rather isolated from the rest of the island, and nestled between the sea and the tall, jagged mountains just beyond town. As we descended downward toward the sea on the narrow road with hairpin turns, the views were spectacular. Joe didn't say much but kept his camera ready, out of the pack. Traveling through the countryside visiting small villages with the Germans was an unexpected gift. Sheep, goats, and donkeys meandered along the way. Women carried filled baskets on their heads while men worked the terraced fields. It appeared that life hadn't changed much in the past few hundred years. This primitive culture and landscape was something I'd never seen before.

We sat for an hour by a black sand beach watching waves crash over volcanic rocks, shooting water high into the air. As luck would have it, we found a small restaurant close by with outside patio chairs and a table facing the sea. And ice cream. Hans and Gretchen were great traveling companions—a nice addition to our island exploration.

Upon our return to Santa Cruz, we invited them onboard for a tour of the ship, of course. They felt as lucky to find us as we did them. Gretchen ooh-ed and aah-ed from the deck below as I demonstrated climbing aloft, then scooted out the stumpe yard.

After dinner, Mike announced that a large bundle of mail had arrived from the Oceanics office in New York. That was our system for receiving letters from home. Stephanie bundled all the mail in NYC then forwarded it to the next scheduled port of entry. The mail that day made up for the disgusting dinner of mutton stew, which I more accurately renamed "bones, fat, and gristle." Brother Donnie sent me a picture of his beautiful baby daughter, Chrissy. And the aerogram from Ruth Ducrey in Switzerland was special, confirming that she hadn't forgotten me. Suddenly I felt homesick, insecure, and sad. I just wanted to cry.

Sensing my quiet tone, Sam invited me out for the evening, away from the ship. After a game of miniature golf, he bought me two glasses of Rum & Coke as we sat at a café trying to figure out the meaning of life. Jaime, the Mexican, joined us. He was forever the encourager, and his even-keeled demeanor never seemed to change no matter the circumstance. His broken Spanglish always made me smile, and his realistic nature seldom allowed conversations to become too abstract. Jaime had a knack for avoiding sadness and conflict. I believe that was a conscious choice. Regardless, during his time with Sam and me, Jaime refused to entertain any depressing vibes. His remedy of positivity worked for me.

CHAPTER 12: FILM CREW

S tephanie joined the ship briefly in Tenerife to plan details for our next stop in The Gambia, West Africa. On the morning of January 5, she also brought a Hollywood film crew on board along with actor David Wayne, just before we prepared to sail. Their purpose was to produce a narrated documentary of the school ship experience. "Seriously?" I questioned. "They're going to sail with us?"

As the *Statsraad Lehmkuhl* pulled away from Santa Cruz in the early afternoon, filming began. Cameras rolled most of the day with random shots of cadets climbing the rigging, setting sails, and doing routine ship's work. It felt irreverent to have photographers walking around wherever they pleased with no under-standing of positioning or protocol while the ship's structured tasks, work, and discipline continued. Jacobsen made sure the work didn't suffer because of the filming.

Our first day at sea was sunny, warm, and relatively calm as we headed east toward Africa. Several cadets hung the sea shower bucket on deck, which pleased the film crew—girls in bikinis and guys in shorts showering together on the main deck of this novelty ship. Who wouldn't enjoy that?

Several crewmen were not thrilled about having film producers onboard, in part because of the ambiguity it created concerning the chain of command. Who were the Hollywooders accountable to? When was it okay for them to interrupt daily musters, cleanings stations, ship's work, and essential activities for the sake of filming? The idea of uppity, unseaworthy folks roaming the deck with pricey equipment seemed counterproductive to sailing.

Loren, the film director, was an arrogant cuss. And quite demanding. Students, faculty, and crewmen were each asked to sign a consent form before the cameras rolled. Blake, Chick's son, refused. It wasn't so much out of defiance as it was about his "leave-me-alone" attitude. Blake was very private and shied away from large crowds and hoopla concerning anything. He served mostly in the engine room during the two months of sail training. And since this was his second year in the program, his role was different from the rest of us. He chose to be stationed in the engine room for the entire trip. And honestly, few of us would've traded places with him. It was he whose unfulfillment in traditional schools had inspired Stephanie and Chick to create the Oceanics School in the first place.

After two days at sea, frustrations between the film director and the established community onboard became evident. In response to Blake not signing the consent form, Loren went on a cursing tirade one evening, venting his anger to a small mixed group including Blake, Mike, Ellie, Todd, the chief engineer, several others, and me. He belittled Blake unsparingly, but his rant also showed his displeasure with Captain Fossa, his crew, and essentially all of us, claiming intentional lack of cooperation with him as film director. It all boiled down to Loren and his selfish agenda, with little regard for anyone else.

At the end of his fiery tirade, Mike suggested that he and his crew should adjust to the community onboard rather than the other way around. "Change your expectations," Mike challenged him calmly, looking him directly in the eye. His words carried weight.

Within ten minutes Loren broke open several packs of cookies and shared them with us. His tone changed. Then he sat with me and a few other cadets on watch duty, informally interviewing us—without running the cameras—concerning our perceptions of the program and why we were here. He and his crew made efforts to join the students for every meal in the union mess. They listened and dialogued with us about everything under the sun—things that interested us.

The following night David Freedman began singing and strumming his guitar on deck and was soon joined by a crowd of students and the entire film crew. The harmony was heavenly. Those Hollywood guys could sing. During a pause David Wayne told a John Wayne joke, triggering hoots of laughter. It was an extraordinary experience under moonlit skies, squelching any remaining tensions between the students and filmmakers. But cookies, jokes, songs, and lunar rays didn't change the opinions of crewmen who were hell-bent on their feelings that sail ships were meant for sailing, not for singing, filming, or romancing the sea. In time, those same crewmen became increasingly more irritated. They avoided interaction with the Hollywood crew while becoming more demanding of the cadets. Classes were often held on deck during good weather, which appealed to Loren. It felt to me like the more engaged we became with educational activities and filming, the more disgruntled several crewmen became. Tensions mounted.

Food from the galley was noticeably better after the Hollywood boys came aboard. Someone suggested that Stephanie must have stretched the budget and ordered the steward to improve the quality of the menu. Regardless, during the seven-day trip to West Africa, breakfast included eggs, bacon, cereals, and plenty of fresh fruit daily. Dinners consisted of roast beef, chicken, fish, potatoes, soups, and fresh vegetables. Best of all, the disgusting mutton stew wasn't served even once. I hung out longer at the dinner table, enjoying seconds and thirds with Bill Bacon and Eiji on several occasions. We unapologetically consumed more than our share, making up for previously lean times. None of us were hoarders by nature, so our uncharacteristic responses to good food created humor. I laughed hysterically watching Eiji, the Zen Tsar, shovel his mouth full of roast beef one night.

The weather was great during the entire trip to Africa. So were the sunsets which drove most everyone up on deck every evening to "ooh," "aah," and gasp. One sunset in particular was absolutely spectacular. I gazed, quietly amazed, realizing that human hands could never create anything like what was displayed in the sky that night. It calmed all of us, even the toughest crewmen, like a blanket of spiritual tranquility was thrown completely over the ship for those few minutes of time.

All the square sails were set every day, adding purpose to our voyage. I suppose it was the picture we'd all imagined in our minds before arriving in Norway. Winds were moderately good, and the ship listed only slightly as it cut through calm seas. A sailor's dream.

Loren asked me one day if I'd be willing to do a live interview in front of the camera. I felt honored, but quickly declined, feeling self-conscious and not trusting my voice in that situation. My answer was too difficult to explain to Loren or to Steve Hilbert, who also encouraged me to do it. I sadly retreated to my room, numbed by my own disappointment, wishing I could do the interview with confidence, wishing I had speaking skills like so many of my shipmates. I had exciting things to share and stories to tell. Some days my voice was better than others, but I had no assurance of when that might be, and I couldn't take the chance in front of live cameras. I shied away from Loren and his crew after declining the interview, except while doing ship's work.

Like many celebrities, David Wayne was selectively engaging and proud. But his rendition of "Sea Fever" by John Masefield was impressive. As cameras rolled, he stood by the fore railing on deck and recited the poem from memory with a professional flair:

I must go down to the seas again, to the lonely sea and the sky,

And all I ask is a tall ship and a star to steer her by;

Although his performance was staged, the sky, the sea, and the full-sail backdrops were abundantly real, authenticating John Masefield's poetic portrayal of a sailor's relationship with the sea.

Ω

On one occasion I had Captain's mess duty. I assisted the officer's mess boy, Lotion, in serving dinner to the captain and his brass. Their dining room and quarters were aft under the poop deck. The setting was much more formal than ours, including china plates and dishes, real silverware, wine goblets, linen napkins, and tablecloths. The crewmen were served custom-ordered meals, prepared like in a hotel. And, I was told, it was an honor to serve them.

Formal attire was required for the task. I wore white trousers, a blue shirt, and a navy-blue blazer. Proper etiquette was expected as well. Although not officially trained, I was supposed to just follow the mess boy's lead. But he sometimes did crazy things. Once there was a fly on the captain's butter. Smiling deviously at me, he tossed the butter, fancy dish and all, into the sea. Later, for reasons unknown, he threw another dish and server's towel overboard. The kid said nothing at all as he watched me, measuring my reaction. I returned nothing more than a neutral grin and resumed my duties.

It felt strange working in the officers' quarters. I felt invisible, serving the crew without acknowledgment from anyone. Conversations around the table were in Norwegian, of course. That made it easier to stay focused on my task without paying any mind to what was being said. But I wasn't convinced these guys, including the captain, deserved more special attention than anyone else onboard. So, when I accidentally dropped Captain Fossa's fork on the galley floor while setting up, I didn't bother exchanging it for a clean one. That was a never mind. I also carried the captain's water glass with my thumb partially inside the rim. It was easier that way.

He always drank a cup of black coffee with sugar after dessert. When I left the galley with his coffee, I took two sips then popped a sugar lump from his saucer into my mouth before serving. I suppose it was my insignificant way of keeping myself and the captain on a level playing field. And it confirmed my brother Donnie's notion, when we were still kids at home, that what folks don't know won't hurt them. But I did chuckle, remembering what Principal J. Lester Brubaker once told us during chapel at Lancaster Mennonite High, "Integrity is doing the right thing when no one else is watching."

So, my question was this: "What is the right thing?" According to our discussion in Professor Frank's philosophy class, knowing the right thing is up for debate. "It's a matter of perception, and is most times circumstantial," Frank said with a smug grin. I couldn't have agreed more as I served the captain, with the taste of his coffee and sugar lump still on my lips.

Lotion was perfect for the job of mess boy. It was common knowledge that he didn't get paid to think. Rather, he responded to commands and submitted to the ship's hierarchy without question. Stories circulated among the cadets about his role onboard beyond mess duty, and about him supposedly being gullible and a bit crazy.

During the storm in the Bay of Biscay while the ship was being tossed violently, Lotion had become deathly afraid and went completely crazy, screaming in terror and heading for the cadet banjers. Several crewmen tried to quiet him. The last thing they wanted was panic among the cadets. It took three able-bodied seamen to hold him down. Actually, they knocked him unconscious and tied him to his bunk. (This story was confirmed by Poulsen fifty years later at an Oceanics reunion in Minnesota.)

Tor and Robert explained one day just how gullible Lotion really was. They convinced him that the ship rolled completely over three times in the storm. Since he was tied up in his bunk, unconscious, he had no recollection of his own. They also told him a conjured-up story explaining the equator crossing process for our ship that went something like this: A crewman stands on the bowsprit and cuts the equator cable with large shears as the ship passes through. Another crewman stands aft and quickly splices the line back together again after crossing. If the equator crossing happens during low tide, the cutting and splicing must be done from the rigging. Lotion's gullibility fed well into cadet humor.

Ω

As we sailed closer to The Gambia, Loren joined a gathering of students on deck and shared experiences from his previous trip to Africa. Aside from the intense heat, he mostly talked about the wildlife—crocodiles, spitting cobras, army ants, rhinos, and elephants—and things to watch out for. He was a great storyteller, and over-dramatized things for sure, but kept our attention. Then for some reason, in the middle of all that, several cadets began discussing the idea of cutting their hair. I listened without comment but had no reason to consider cutting my shoulder length locks. They were just fine. However, the haircut conversation continued in earnest. Lilly offered free cuts to anyone who desired, as long as she didn't need to clean up afterward. I was surprised at the number of instant volunteers. A stool was placed near the foredeck where she went to work with the scissors. More cadets followed.

While lying in bed that night I reconsidered. Maybe I was crazy, but the next day I asked Lilly if her offer was still good. "Of course," she smiled. Without thinking twice I sat my butt down on the stool. She finished one side completely as I watched in a hand mirror, then she asked what I think. Honestly, it felt better than it looked. But I instructed her to do the same on the other side and the back. Mom and both Grossmommies would've been proud. It was my shortest cut since the fall of 1970, two years prior. And cleanup was easy—my hair was swept into a dustpan then tossed overboard. I felt a twinge of momentary sadness as I watched it disappear into the wake, swallowed by the sea and gone forever. It was a new day.

My haircut with Lilly

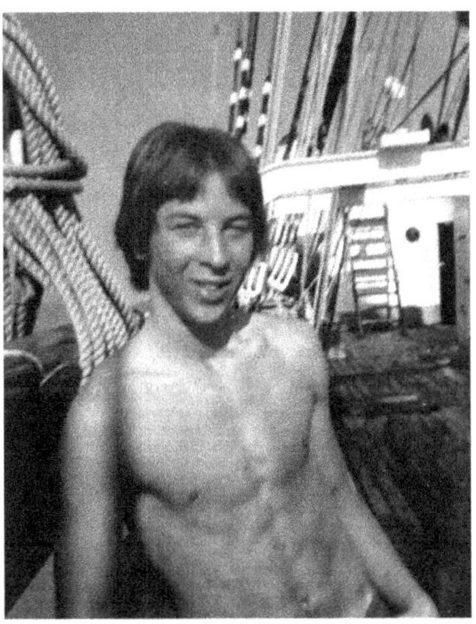

After the cut

Hollywood actor David Wayne with students

Jane and me polishing brass

ABS Jacobsen spread eagle atop the main mast

CHAPTER 13: WEST AFRICA

Alle mann pa deck! The call went out when we were ten miles from landfall on the afternoon of January 11. Cadets and crew worked together to take in all the sails. After anchors were dropped the ship remained stationary for the night. Watches continued. Aside from that, there wasn't much to do except relax and enjoy the moment.

Tom had become the chronic complainer on board. By now we were accustomed to his dry protests concerning most everything. Waiting another ten hours before docking climbed quickly to the top of his list of grumblings. Despite his continual negative slants on food, musters, watches, weather, rules, overzealous school administrators, officers, crewmen, and the fact that he had to wake up every day, Tom was a likable guy. Truthfully, he vocalized things that others only thought about but would never say. Like a trial lawyer, he creatively represented the sentiments of many of us. But he did it matter-of-factly, unfiltered, and without discretion or regard for protecting anyone's dignity. His thick long red hair, often tied back in a ponytail, accentuated his short, elf-like physique.

He was part of the small group of guys that self-formed to randomly monitor and police the behaviors of folks onboard. He, Pisacano, Perry, and Alec declared wrongs within the community, then corrected them with some sort of affirmative action, calling themselves The Brotherhood. Their proclamations were mostly humorous, depending on who was being accused and why. Once, they declared an insufficient amount of potatoes available for the cadets at dinner time. Rather than bringing a person to justice, they raided the galley supply closet and made late night French fries in the dayroom.

Another time they tied up Barry North, claiming he violated wholesome community living standards by being irritating. They accused him of being too scientific and of explaining things in ridiculous detail that interested no one. Tom was the group's spokesperson, sometimes taking on the role of both prosecutor and judge. In Barry's case, he wasted no time in declaring a guilty verdict on all charges.

Richie was brought before The Brotherhood on another occasion, gagged with hands tied behind his back. He was outspoken beyond normal tolerable levels. Simply put, Richie talked too much. Another cadet was brought to trial and charged with masturbating in a fore bathroom stall. Although he was found guilty (he pleaded guilty), his sentencing was permanently suspended due to a technicality because the only eyewitness happened to be on antibiotics at the time.

Community life onboard continued as we all waited with great anticipation for our first shore leave on the dark continent. Field trips were already being discussed among the students —mostly just chatter in hopes of being part of the first group to go. I gazed from the deck, looking eastward at the distant lights of Bathurst, trying to curtail my own excitement. I was impassioned by thoughts of setting foot on African soil, another one of my lifelong dreams.

Loren and the film crew wrapped up their interviews onboard and did final camera shots. David Wayne finished his romanticized narration as well, standing at the lookout perch gazing aloft and speaking with trained finesse. He had a great voice. After docking, several of the Hollywood crew joined the first field trip heading upriver on the *Lady Wright* riverboat for several days. From what I could tell, they had all completed their filming tasks on a good note. Amid mixed feelings concerning their presence, we looked forward to someday seeing the finished documentary. I personally felt proud to be a part of it.

Mr. Stig Floden, our third chief mate, came onboard in Gambia. He had been the captain of the ill-fated *Antarna*, another one of the Gallaghers' Oceanics boats which just the previous year was forced to surrender to Panamanian gunboats. Supposedly Mr. Kavanvik had prior commitments, just like our first chief, and didn't plan to continue after our sail to Africa. But I wasn't so sure about all that. The highest officer position onboard next to the captain had become like a revolving door. Maybe we all were driving the chiefs crazy. If so, I understood. Or maybe it was Jacobsen who caused them to quit. Regardless, the chief mate turnover seemed odd.

Ω

In 1973 Gambia's capital city of Bathurst was in the process of reverting to its original African name, Banjul. The city is located on an island where the Gambian River meets the Atlantic Ocean. Portuguese navigators settled there in the mid 1400s but by the early 1800s the island was leased by the British who attempted to abolish slave trading from the region. Their efforts were challenged by the Americans, Spanish, and Portuguese who insisted on continuing to grab slaves from West Africa. Tragically, an estimated three million slaves were transported from this place to other parts of the world.

Eventually a British military base was established but the colony faced ongoing difficulties because of routine flooding and malaria infestation. Most of the country is situated only slightly above sea level, contributing to its hot, tropical climate. Gambia finally gained its independence from Great Britain in 1965 and remains the smallest country in Africa, surrounded on three sides by Senegal. With the west-flowing river at its center, the country is long and narrow, just thirty-one miles across at its widest point, but it stretches for nearly three hundred miles from east to west.

Historically, its economy has relied on agriculture, predominantly ground nuts (peanuts) for export. The Gambia River, one of the most navigable in all of Africa, was actively serving as an important means of transportation and commerce in 1973, allowing ground nuts to be easily transported from the country's interior to the Atlantic coast.

Like many African nations, Gambia is tolerant of all religions, but is 90 percent Muslim and about 3 percent Christian. More than ten languages are spoken by various ethnic groups, including Wolof and Mandingo, but the official written language is English, which is taught in schools and spoken by most Gambians.

I knew little about the country before going ashore with Amor. Although we had become buddies onboard, she and I seldom hung out elsewhere. Ethnically Filipino, Amor was small, quiet, wide-eyed, and one of the younger cadets. As we walked together from the dock toward town, we met up with a guy named Henry who willingly offered to show us around.

Local folks were inquisitive and eager to meet anyone coming off the ship. We were forewarned of the lurking evils in Bathurst. Rip-offs, drug dealers, pimps, hookers, and worse were known to infest this third world seaport. My innocence and trusting personality had sometimes gotten me into trouble in the past so I was on the lookout for shady characters. I felt safe in the company of Henry who appeared knowledgeable, genuine, and helpful. He answered all our questions, offered information on museums and attractions, and eventually led us to a local bar where we each had a drink. The mood was relaxed but Henry kept eyeing Amor and me, seemingly trying to figure out our relationship. I thought nothing of it as he didn't ask any personal questions.

After walking back to the ship at 22:00, he suggested meeting up again the following day. I shrugged only because I didn't know my plans. But upon signing in at the gangway, I was immediately informed by Todd and Tara that Henry was one of those questionable characters. Dock authorities warned Stephanie that he was a local drug dealer. She in turn had strongly advised students not to associate with him. Unfortunately, I hadn't known about that conversation.

"Wow," I exclaimed to Todd. "How was I to know that? He seemed so nice." It was a wake-up call for me. I determined to somehow try to be wiser when meeting folks, to learn not to trust. But how could I ever tackle that one? It was incredibly out of my character not to trust, and totally against my cultural grain.

The next day was Saturday, and the entire city came to life. Folks were peddling fresh fruits, vegetables, trinkets, and colored fabric. The marketplace buzzed with activity—old men playing checkers surrounded by onlookers, mothers chit-chatting amongst themselves and carrying babies swaddled to their backs, young boys pushing long sticks with small wheels attached, and teens kicking partially inflated soccer balls on gravel lots. I ventured to the outskirts of town, beyond the president's house to a beach where goats and sheep roamed freely, feeding on stubble by the side of the road. The town was anticipating the big Muslim celebration Eid Al-Adha in two days. I was told that many of the grazing goats and sheep would be sacrificed and eaten during the feast. But on this day, they hadn't a care in the world, enjoying their time of baa-ing, feeding and frolicking.

After a long and fascinating morning walk, I returned to the ship, only to be summoned by Henry from the dock through the gangway watchman. I waved from the deck and explained that I couldn't come ashore because of my responsibilities. Conveniently, that was the truth. I was scheduled for mess duty.

Several groups had already departed for field trips, so only a skeleton crew remained onboard to handle watches and necessary ship's work. The Norwegian crew had time off as well to do their thing in bars and brothels. Life onboard was relaxed. Even mess was easy with only a few folks eating. My group was designated last for our field trip excursion and I was in no hurry to leave ship while enjoying the calmest, most pleasant time I'd had aboard.

One evening Stephanie asked me to run several errands in town. The first task was to find a particular type of movie film. The only place she thought it might be available was on a German cruise ship across the bay at the far pier. The dock pilot obliged by giving me a ride several kilometers around the bay in his Mercedes Benz. Sure enough, the Germans had exactly what Stephanie was looking for. I loved pleasing her.

She then asked me to deliver a dinner invitation to a girl named Sofia, after handing me a note on a small piece of paper with the address: 55 Lemon Street. I found the address easily enough. Sofia was a local girl in her early 20s who had helped Stephanie and Tara arrange several field trips. She greeted me cautiously when opening the door, but her face expressed a beaming smile as she read the note, then assured me that she'd be at the Hotel Club 33 at 6:30 p.m. as requested.

After an unusually long hot shower—another benefit of having few people onboard—I dressed in my nicest clothes and walked with Eiji to join Stephanie, Tara, and Sofia for dinner at the hotel. The food was great: seaman's beef, noodle soup, rhubarb, plenty of French bread and butter, and several bottles of wine. Our evening of storytelling and dialogue was a delight, much like an evening with the Smucker clan back in the States. It felt so incredibly normal that I forgot I was a cadet aboard the *Statsraad Lehmkuhl*. At one point, Stephanie spoke enthusiastically about the field trip possibilities in Gambia. As director of Oceanics, she was under a great deal of pressure. So, when things worked out well, she had plenty of reason to celebrate. That night at the Hotel club, I was exposed to only a glimpse of her ongoing work with the program.

"Interestingly," Stephanie admitted, "there is as much fly-by-the-seat-of-our-pants decision making as there is strategic planning." She wasn't kidding. "It's not that we want it that way, but circumstances force it. Funding issues, immigrations, visas, weather, balancing relationships onboard and off, and a host of other unforeseen challenges are constant."

Few sane folks would have attempted a program of this magnitude. And certainly, Chick and Stephanie could not

Stephanie Gallagher

have pulled it off without their incredibly adventurous spirits, persistence, determination, confidence, and their unorthodox ability to juggle finances, sometimes at a cost of ethical compromise that raised even their own eyebrows. Maybe they were a little crazy.

After leaving the hotel, Eiji and I met up with Bill Bacon near the docks. He was always looking for adventure, an opportunist by nature, and forever upbeat. He suggested that we should hang out together in town since the night was still young. Within minutes we were approached by Henry. Oh no! By now we all knew full well who Henry was. But there were three of us. What harm would it be to engage him? Besides, Bill was fascinated with the guy.

Henry shared the latest international news. Agents of the Israeli Intelligence Agency in Italy had just foiled an attempt by the PLO to shoot down a jet carrying Israeli Prime Minister Golda Meir. She was in Rome to meet with the Pope. Henry went on to editorialize his sentiments concerning Golda Meir's continued confiscation of farmland and property from Palestinian villages. "Her plane should have been shot down," he scoffed.

Henry continued to shake his head while recounting the Prime Minister's answer to a reporter concerning Palestinian cries for justice. She had commented soon after taking office, "What is a Palestinian? Such a thing does not exist." Henry was obviously annoyed by her disregard for the Palestinian people, by her arrogance, and by the suppressive Israeli occupation of Palestine. But he changed the subject quickly, inviting us to have a drink with him. So, we joined him for Portuguese rum at an old bar near the water's edge.

As we entered the bar, several British sailors motioned for us to join them at their table in the far corner of the large room. We declined their invitation and sat at the dimly lit counter on flat-seated stools. Behind the bar was a large wood-paneled wall adorned with portraits of stately black men wearing African Kufi hats, and one of Queen Elizabeth II who reigned as Gambia's queen from 1965 to 1970 after the country gained its independence but remained under monarchical rule.

After a brief history lesson, Henry told us about a local homemade alcoholic drink called palm wine. His detailed description of the stuff was intriguing enough for us to follow him to a place where we could get it. As we left the bar, Eiji and I wondered whether this was a good idea. I thought not. But Bill was already four steps ahead of us. "C'mon guys," he yelled back.

Henry led us through blocks of dark streets lined with small wooden homes and shacks. The night air was scented with a combination of sewer, sweat, charcoal, and goat. Several skinny dogs followed us for countless blocks, whining for toss-off treats, but they eventually became distracted by a string of garbage by the side of the road that appeared more promising than us. I was glad to be in the company of Bill and Eiji. This wasn't a night trek I would've taken alone.

We finally stopped in front of a small, unpainted, two-roomed house. Henry gave two loud knocks on the door, then walked in without waiting for a response. We followed him inside as instructed, then stood quietly along the front wall by the door while he spoke in a hushed voice to a woman sitting next to three small children on a bed in the back room. We heard only muffled tones, then saw the woman's silhouette rise and leave through the rear exit of the house. Minutes later she returned carrying several glass bottles filled with brownish, mud-colored liquid. Her dark, obedient eyes focused on the large bottle as she placed four ceramic cups on the table in front of us. Then she emptied the large bottle into three. The fourth cup remained empty.

Several old framed black and white photographs hung unevenly on the walls behind where we stood. The rectangular table in the center of the room was surrounded by four wooden chairs, one on each side. Henry motioned us to please sit down, then joined us while he opened a second bottle and filled the empty cup. A single low-wattage bulb hung from a short cord above the table, casting eerie shadows on the walls. None of us touched our drinks until Henry raised his cup with a smile and made a toast to "the best wine in Bathurst," and "to Golda Meir's survival—this time." The three of us nodded cautiously, then glancing at each other, lifted our cups as well. But we waited to drink until Henry took a first sip.

Oh my God! The stuff was potent! It burned my dry Mennonite throat all the way down through the lining of my esophagus. Bill coughed hard as his eyes lit up. Henry laughed. The shock of the initial burn was the worst. After that it was fine, one small sip at a time. None of us remembered much about our time with Henry during the next forty-five minutes. But three bottles sat empty on the table when we got up to leave. And no one was certain how much we paid. That wasn't important. I had only a few dalasi in my pocket at the start, and surprisingly, they were still there when I returned to the ship. Eiji declared the experience was worth more than the wine itself. I assume he paid. After saying goodnight, we shuffled back across town to the docks in uncharacteristic fashion. Once aboard, the three of us talked for another hour, too palm-wined and too much enjoying the novelty of this experience to sleep.

Ω

Four curious preteen boys frequented the docks regularly from the first day we arrived in Bathurst. Their hope was to meet up with anyone from the ship as we went ashore. The boys were full of questions but were always respectful and well-behaved. I made a point of engaging them and sometimes walked with them into town.

One day I invited them for a swim at the beach. The most outspoken of the four, Jericho, wanted to know if I was Muslim or Christian. I sensed that it was an important question for him and his friends. Two of them pointed to the quiet boy in the group, Daniel, and exclaimed that he was Christian. The other three were Muslim. I stopped and looked at the four boys as they waited for me to reveal my religious identity. After a short pause I said, "I am Christian."

Everyone remained silent for a few moments. Then one boy piped up and exclaimed, "Now it's three against two," pointing at me and Daniel.

I then asked, "You are all friends, right?" The boys nodded. I quickly added, "So, I'm the only one here with white skin. Am I also your friend?" Again, they smiled and nodded. I explained that being black or white, Christian, or Muslim really doesn't matter concerning our friendship. With that I threw my arms around two of the Muslim boys, Aziz and Demba. It was an enlightening moment for all of us, especially for Daniel, the quiet one. He beamed broadly, exposing his big white teeth, then walked next to me all the way back to town.

I wasn't surprised when Jericho invited me and a few others from the ship to join his family for the lamb slaughtering ceremony on the Muslim holiday known as the festival of sacrifice. The holiday honored the story of Abraham's willingness to sacrifice his son, Isaac. God, of course, provided a lamb instead, as recorded in the Bible. But on this day, I celebrated the same story with my Muslim friends through the Koran account.

Thousands of Muslims, dressed in their finest clothes, gathered for the traditional time of prayer and meditation in the large open field by the marketplace. I joined Jane, Kjemtrup, and Ellie there for the ceremony. We stood quietly off to the side, twenty feet back from the crowd. Morning sunlight highlighted the brilliant-colored fabric worn by the masses standing in reverence to God. Children were quiet. Even babies in cloth harnesses on their mother's backs seemed to understand the sacredness.

It was great to be with Kjemtrup again, away from the ship. His role onboard had been all business in recent weeks, and I hadn't seen his friendly "never mind" side for quite a while. But on this day, he was his old self, showing interest in learning about the Gambian culture. He also told us that relationships among the crew were not good. Mate Schnitler seemed depressed about things onboard with the entire community.

After the ceremony, the crowds dispersed as families returned to their homes. Jane, Peter, Ellie, and I met up with Jericho as planned, then followed him home. Steve, Debbie, and Barry also joined our group. As we walked, Jericho explained that every married man must sacrifice a goat or lamb for each of his wives and their children. "Men with more than one wife need to provide a separate house for each family. It's a sign of wealth," Jericho said. Then smiling broadly, pointing an index finger straight up, he added, "My father has only one wife. She is my mother."

He led us into his family compound from the back entrance and proceeded to introduce his younger brothers, sisters, aunt, and parents. Jericho's family was obviously poor. But their compound was clean and tidy. None of them talked much, probably because of sheer shyness amid a group of white folks. Or maybe for reasons of reverence concerning the ceremony itself.

Jericho's father dug a hole in the ground about six inches deep and eight inches in diameter. He then laid the goat on the ground, placing its neck across the hole. While the women and children secured the animal, he cut its throat. The knife was extremely dull, so the slitting process wasn't as fast and clean as it should have been. Debbie gasped. But the young male goat offered little resistance. As if it understood its purpose. As the life blood squirted and drained into the hole, Jericho's family held the goat firmly for several minutes until the twitching stopped. It was then prepared for slow roasting over a simmering fire in the back corner of the compound. Our invitation didn't include the ceremonial feast served after sundown.

Before leaving we offered Jericho a tour of the ship. His mother was already skinning the goat but nodded permission for him to walk along back to the ship. Smiling profusely, he proudly walked with me up the gangway and signed in at the registry. The eleven-year-old was full of excitement as he gazed up into the rigging, asking a thousand questions. He barely waited for an answer to one question before blurting out the next one. Jericho wanted to climb, of course, but that wasn't allowed.

By late afternoon the *Statsraad Lehmkuhl* moved from its place at the dock to a position a quarter mile out into the harbor. There we dropped anchor. Poulsen manned the launch transporting cadets and crew back and forth between the ship and dock. Visitors could no longer come aboard. I enjoyed the peaceful, secure feeling of being surrounded by water again, away from the city and its nondescript smells, away from Henry and his types. Group C worked onboard for the remainder of the afternoon, painting the ship. Then I assisted Peter on the launch for several hours. It was a fun way to while away the evening in shorts and a t-shirt. And it was a joy working alongside Poulsen transporting students and sailors, listening to the laughter, stories, and curses from their experiences in Bathurst.

Once, as the launch was leaving the dock, several girls from the ship showed up a minute too late to catch the transport. Poulsen did not go back despite their cries of protest. Janet Johnson, who was left standing on the pier, was thoroughly upset with Peter and gave him an earful of verbal unrepeatables.

That night I completed my first full journal of Oceanic adventures—nearly two hundred handwritten pages in an 89-cent spiral notebook sponsored by

Friends of the Earth. There was a photo of an ocean scene on the front cover and a message from David Brower on the back, words of profound wisdom:

"We seek a renewed stirring of love for the earth, we urge that what man is capable of doing to the earth is not always what he ought to do, and we plead that all people here, now, determine that a wide, spacious untrammeled freedom shall remain as living testimony that this generation, our own, had love for the next."

Ω

The crew and cadets on duty continued painting the ship as it was anchored offshore. We started with the tops of the masts and the highest yardarms. The West African weather was absolutely perfect for the task. Half the students were off on field trips during our first week, so the mood onboard was relaxed. We hauled the paint equipment into the rigging in large buckets using ropes and pulleys. Each cadet was then given a pail of white oil base paint with an attached pothook, a china bristle brush, and a rag. Even Jacobsen, who oversaw the painting crew, was calm spirited. However, by the end of our first workday, after consuming several stiff drinks, he climbed to the very top of the fore mast then went spread-eagle on the mast-head, on his stomach, as we watched in jaw-dropping disbelief!

Malcom, one of the most easy-going cadets onboard, was a southern boy who just quietly fit into his surroundings. He and I worked together painting in the rig the first several days. One of our tasks was to paint the merse yard in its entirety, eighty feet up. We stood on the thin cable underneath the arm, held onto the yard itself with one hand, and painted with the other. The paint pail hung from anything close, like a cross-cable, pulley, or rope. It was awkward at best. I started at the end of the yard on starboard side and worked my way toward the mast. Malcom did the same from port side. It was impossible not to get paint on our hands, legs, arms, and hair. Although Kjemtrup wasn't there to say it, we determined that to be a "never mind."

Administrators Mike and Steve joined our crew as well, adding to the fun. We told stories, engaged in philosophical discussions, and laughed plenty. Jacobsen was jolly every day and seemed pleased with our progress, except for an incident on the third day.

After coffee break, Malcom dropped a pail of paint from the stumpe yard, fifty feet up. As it slipped from his hand, he let out a southern boy yell that pierced the late morning calm. Richie and Jacobsen were below and looked up in time to see

the pail come crashing to the deck. White paint splattered on everyone and everything in every direction within twenty-five feet. It was one big maritime mess!
Fortunately, I was high above the ruckus. But my ears weren't protected from the
five solid minutes of animated Norwegian cursing like I'd not heard before.

That same evening as Bill Bacon, Eiji, and I were having dinner, Bill reenacted
Jacobsen's verbal barrage. It was a hilarious, nearly perfect imitation of the foul-
mouthed sailor, complete with syllable emphasis and pronunciation. I laughed
till tears ran down my sun-weathered face and dripped from my chin!

Jacobsen got over the mishap by the next day and our painting tasks continued in normal fashion. We all developed a unique camaraderie during our several
days aloft, without once complaining. And we all agreed that painting a sail ship
in Africa would most certainly improve our future resumés.

Ω

When the second week field trips were determined, I got my wish to join Eiji's
group along with Jill, Katie, Bill Bacon, Malcom, Tom, Gary, Mark, Blake, and Willy.
Eleven people total, and a diverse group at that.

Mr. Brewer was a British conservationist and manager of the Abuko Nature
Reserve, half an hour out of town, who had lived in Gambia for the past fifteen
years with his family. He came aboard one evening with his pet chimp, Pooh,
and formally briefed us on the culture, wildlife, things to expect, and necessary
precautions while traveling to the interior. He warned of venomous snakes.
That sent chills up a few spines. The venom of one snake bite slowly destroys a
person's body tissues, causing him to bleed from his eyes, nose, and mouth until
dead. He went on to say that Gambia has been called the white man's grave for
good reason. For many years white folks came to West Africa seeking adventure,
then died. "Even today, malaria continues to be a major killer in the country," he
added. Mr. Brewer was a nice guy, but I questioned whether he really needed to
say all those things.

The next day, our group headed to his nature reserve to clear brush. We were
given machetes and assigned to work alongside several nationals who showed
us the technique of swinging and chopping. The morning hours were a breeze,
but by afternoon the sun was extremely hot, and the work became physically and
emotionally exhausting, even for those of us who had determined to stay positive.

It was no surprise that Tom was first to complain. His sarcasm and complaints
continued throughout the afternoon, bringing some necessary humor to the situation. Gary was next to go negative. Although his complaining was deliberate and

serious, it added hilarity to Tom's comments. Bill and I did our best to keep the mood light. It was January 19, Bill's eighteenth birthday, and he was determined to make it a good day.

We were promised lunch would be delivered by 12:00. Assuming the importance of lookout watch aboard ship, we decided to apply the same value to lunch in the jungle and created a watch shift to make sure the food deliverer could find us. Shifts lasted half an hour each, starting at 11:00. The watchman sat by the side of the road in full view of any vehicle coming from either direction. Sadly, there was no traffic, and our food didn't arrive until 14:30. When it finally came, we were sorely disappointed. The stuff wasn't worth the cost of the taxi nor Tara's time to bring it. Each sandwich consisted of two slices of inch-thick stale bread and one slice of cheese or salami, but not both. No butter, no mayo, and no mustard, drier than the hot African air itself. It was so ridiculous that all we could do was laugh, cuss, and chew. Even Tom and Gary were silenced beyond belief.

By 16:00 we were famished, dehydrated, and unproductive. Just one of the local guys remained. Who knows what he must have thought, but he kindly suggested we take a short tour of the reserve. He guided us along narrow winding paths through the beautiful thick lush jungle. A colony of chimps were barking, grunting, hooting, and swinging on vines. Pooh, Mr. Brewer's pet chimp, was also there playfully showing off as we passed by.

If nothing else, our day at the reserve helped develop a special bond within our group. Maybe that was falsely optimistic, but at the end of the day a very tired bunch piled into Mr. Brewer's Land Rover and headed back into town. He gave us a sack of grapefruits to take aboard, but we devoured most of them enroute. We had earned the right to eat every morsel of food within our reach.

Ω

For centuries the Gambia River has played a key role in the country's economy concerning trade and transportation to and from the interior. Dirt roads were often not passable, and certainly not as reliable for transporting goods as the river. The *Lady Wright* riverboat, built in 1951, provided regular local transports in both directions between Bathurst and the region of Basse, 300 kilometers inland. Small villages, farms and huts lined the river. At each designated stop, large gatherings of community folks came to sell their wares, play music, and be a part of celebrating the riverboat's arrival, which served as their main social event of the day.

There were three private rooms available for rent aboard the *Lady Wright* for those who wanted privacy and could afford the convenience. Although simple and antiquated, the wood-paneled rooms were set up with single beds, two small tables, and a bath large enough only for a sink and commode. Steve and Debbie Hilbert decided to join the student group heading to Basse after hearing about the room options aboard. Debbie insisted on having her own, but there was just one available when she reserved. Fortunately, it was the largest room with three single beds. But to her disappointment, it was shared with our whole group and a fifty-five-year-old Scandinavian guy, completely dashing her hopes and expectations of a leisurely excursion upriver.

Our group boarded the *Lady Wright* at 17:00 at the river port in Bathurst after prepping and exchanging currency. I helped Poulsen haul several loads of garbage from the ship to the dock via the launch earlier in the day. It was Saturday, January 20, 1973. Back in the States, Richard Nixon was being inaugurated for his second term as president. But aboard the *Statsraad Lehmkuhl*, no one cared a rat's ass about that. Certainly not me. In my opinion, Nixon's inauguration wasn't something to celebrate.

Hundreds of folks boarded the boat with us, many dressed in colorful clothing. The collection of smells represented the diversity of the passengers themselves, from body odors and sweat to hints of urine, animal feces, greasy food, overly ripe fruit, charcoal smoke, and tobacco. There were occasional whiffs of sweet perfume as well. Many passengers carried overnight satchels.

A variety of supplies and sacks of grain were loaded before we pulled away from the dock. Uniformed men positioned themselves on deck and on the dock for crowd control, obviously accustomed to the chaotic boarding process. They kept passengers moving impressively well. The outside railings of the boat became prime real estate as folks packed against the perimeters of the deck. Good views and good air were in high demand. Our group was warned of pickpockets and bandits, so I zipped my passport and cash inside the travel security belt strapped around my waist, out of sight under my shirt. Several kids had secret pockets sewn inside their pants, shirts, and bras. Others hid valuables in their shoes.

Debbie's room was great for backpack storage and bathroom usage. The lone Scandinavian, a funny character, grinned and nodded constantly but contributed little to our conversations. He mostly stayed on deck except to sleep. However, he adamantly claimed one of the beds while Steve and Debbie secured the other two. The rest of us, thrilled with the novelty of riding a riverboat in Africa, weren't concerned about sleeping arrangements. The boat, although not luxurious, was equipped with a small bar and dining area.

After leaving Bathurst, it didn't take long for the students' secret stashes to come out. Blake opened a bottle of whiskey. Beer bottles appeared from other kids' side pockets. Eiji grinned boyishly as he opened a bottle of French Cabernet Sauvignon. There were plenty of shared drinks for anyone who wanted. As nightfall approached, the starlit sky and cool soft breeze had a calming, blanketing effect onboard. Local folks quietly found their places of refuge. We found a secluded area on deck as well, sat cross-legged and discussed everything from religion to politics to pot. Then one by one we drifted off to sleep, cradled by the lazy motion and humming of the diesel engine.

I woke sometime during the wee hours of the night and found myself huddled under a blanket with Blake on my right and Jill on my left. The others were scattered nearby. It felt secure, like memories of my sleeping arrangements as a young child on the farm in Bird-in-Hand with my siblings.

After sunrise, I began feeling seriously ill. My body burned with fever while my head throbbed. I couldn't eat. Eiji supplied me with bottled water to prevent dehydration as I sat on deck watching the Gambian countryside pass by, listening to muffled conversations around me without comprehension.

When the riverboat stopped at village ports, I remained seated, enduring the pain that now had spread throughout my body. My condition worsened. Eiji started me on penicillin, sensing I must have an infection. Thirty minutes later, I experienced a violent reaction to the medication—acute stomach pain and cramps which spread throughout my entire abdominal area into my chest. I was certain my appendix must have burst. I labored to breathe. Mind games played havoc with my emotions. I was consumed by thoughts of death. It felt like my body was shutting down, like I was slowly suffocating. Images flashed through my mind. Eiji stayed silently by my side. Time as I knew it stood still, but somehow the day passed.

After dark, I pulled myself up and stood by the railing under the moonlit sky as Mr. Brewer's words echoed loudly in my ears like a repetitive recording with no end, "GAMBIA IS THE WHITE MAN'S GRAVE!" Dim lights partially illuminated a scene of grass huts nestled among tall coconut trees just beyond the riverbanks. A lone dugout canoe with two skinny silhouetted figures quietly paddled alongside the *Lady Wright*, like demons waiting for my soul. Maybe I was hallucinating... I collapsed into unconsciousness.

When I woke, I was in serious pain and struggling to breathe. Within minutes I passed out again as Eiji and Blake looked on. They poured water on my face and shouted at me. No response. Eiji told me later that he knew my fate belonged to powers beyond him. He didn't remember how long it was before I opened my eyes, but a calm spirit emerged from my waking. The strain was gone, the severity of my pain had disappeared, and my breathing was no longer labored. Something unexplainable had happened. Like an angel quietly intervened, whispering to the demons, "The boy's time is not up."

There was no logic for what happened that night. Not for the cause, nor the recovery. It felt strange. I now understood, at least in part, what my father must have experienced in his final hours—the fear, the determination to live, and the daunting reality that life was slipping away. He died of tetanus. Lockjaw. And in the end, he suffocated.

This traumatic experience aboard the *Lady Wright* was a reminder that I am living by the grace of God. Life is a gift not meant to be wasted. As for the existence of guardian angels? Hmmm, maybe so. This was my second such experience in less than a month.

Ω

A beautiful morning greeted us the next day. There was no one happier to see the sun than me. I quietly stood on deck by the railing watching monkeys swinging in the trees. Colorful birds tweeted from their lofty perches, two eagles soared overhead, anthills onshore stood taller than humans. Eiji joined me by the railing as we stood reverently for several minutes, enjoying our serenity.

He finally broke the silence, "I thought we lost you last night." I nodded, then responded without looking at my friend, "Me too."

Jill shared her breakfast with me—a grapefruit, several pieces of cheese, and wafers. She then offered me spicy rice and fish for lunch as I eased back into the realities aboard the riverboat. It felt amazing to be alive. I was blessed with a renewed understanding of the importance of my friends.

At twenty hundred hours on the evening of January 22, the *Lady Wright* finally docked in Basse. It looked like the entire town was there to celebrate our arrival. Several men had just killed a twelve-foot crocodile that lay motionless, stretched out on the riverbank. It was a beautiful looking beast as long as it stayed dead, but it caused plenty of excitement. The mood remained festive with live music, drums, and dancing as we disembarked.

We found the Catholic boarding school, our destination for the night, about a mile out of town. Unfortunately, the school administrators hadn't received notification concerning our group's arrival. Amidst last-minute scrambling, the school director welcomed us warmly, calling quickly on several teachers to assist with arrangements. I was accustomed to this sort of spontaneous hospitality in Lancaster County, but several kids in our group found it awkward and decided to sleep outside on the compound grounds, despite being offered accommodations inside.

I was introduced to a teacher named Daniel who insisted that I take his room for the night. We talked past midnight discussing Gambia's social and economic future. He was optimistic, impressively energetic, and well-spoken with a positive personality. And his bed was great, with mosquito netting and all.

The next day we spent time at the school. Students dressed in navy blue uniforms stood in straight lines while reciting morning prayers as the school day began. Two Peace Corps volunteers from the States were assigned to work alongside the administration as nutrition and health advisors. They gave us a formal tour of the school and shared news from home. Former president Lyndon B. Johnson had died the previous night.

Several in our group decided to split off on their own. Enough of the boring stuff. Oceanics guidelines supported education through experience, suggesting that learning could be as varied as the kids themselves. There was no resistance from the rest of us as five fellow students headed to the beach for the next few days. Who could honestly say whether or not beach bumming in Africa fit the Gallaghers' criteria for education?

After Steve and Debbie also parted ways, the remaining six of us hoped to visit Niokolo-Koba Game Reserve in Senegal. Bill Bacon and Eiji returned to Basse to bargain for a transport. Mark and I walked curiously through a nearby village where houses were constructed of grass and mud with thatched roofs. Topless women attended to children while laundering clothes in the stream. Men sat lazily under shade trees, watching their women. It was the hottest time of day, and the air was nostril-burning dry. A light breeze kicked up dust from the sandy pathways as Mark and I meandered about. Folks were cautiously friendly. Several children greeted us, shook our hands, then ran away. It was a setting from the pages of *National Geographic.*

As planned, we met up with Eiji, Bill, Katie, and Jill, and all piled into the transport headed southeast to the Senegalese border. It was bumpy, dusty, and terribly uncomfortable. In Senegal, we had difficulty finding affordable transportation to the game reserve. Negotiations broke down after twenty minutes of hard bargaining.

The six of us collectively had only enough cash to go from the border to the reserve and back, leaving no funds to get back to Bathurst, 300 kilometers away. Bill, always the risk taker, suggested we go to the game reserve anyway. "We'll find a way," he said with a confident smile.

I loved his spirit, but in this case, I voted with the majority to go back. Bill had just one vote. Disappointed, we recrossed the Senegalese-Gambian border and headed to Georgetown riding on the back of an open transport. The driver was a maniac, jostling his twenty-five passengers in every direction, speeding over bumps and around curves. It was a dusty, butt-broaching ride. Not fun at all.

Georgetown is located on McCarthy Island where a Wesleyan mission first introduced groundnuts to Gambia in 1823. But we didn't care much about peanut history or the freaking mission that day. We were exhausted, dirt-covered, and humbly happy to arrive alive. Without smiles.

We found dormitory accommodations at another Catholic school, again with no forewarning of our visit. They fed us well, then I endured a very cold shower as layers of road dirt and sludge washed into the floor drain. This bed had no netting and mosquitoes buzzed by my ears all night—African mosquitoes, the same ones that probably harass the elephants. The worst kind.

The next day was spent in part with students from the school. But I also met and hung out with a 23-year-old American girl traveling alone through West Africa. We became instant friends. Barbara shared several absorbing stories from her travels and was obviously blessed with a culture-savvy spirit of adventure. That night we sat together interacting with a group of local students, answering a million questions about life in the States. Her smooth reddish hair was pulled back loosely into a short ponytail revealing her pretty, sun-weathered face. I couldn't help noticing her soft eyes glowing in the candlelight when she smiled at me. Barbara was attractive—even her faded jeans and beige flowered blouse were pleasing. I was only mildly distracted by amorous thoughts, however, as the kids' questions kept coming.

We did our best to satisfy their inquisitiveness while comparing cultures. Barbara articulated her answers well as the hopes and dreams expressed by the Gambian students were as genuine, optimistic, and refreshing as any I'd ever heard. They honestly believed the efforts of their generation could solve many of the world's social challenges, end wars, abolish racism, and overcome economic injustice. They identified international social needs correctly. And they determined this was their world to change, starting first with their own country. It was an unexpectedly stimulating conversation in a most unusual part of the world. And it felt oddly romantic teaming up with Barbara.

Ω

The next day the remaining Oceanics students paid several Dalasi to take a ferry from Georgetown to the mainland. From there Mark, Bill, Todd, and I caught a ride on a small transport headed toward Bathurst. After our efforts to visit the game reserve failed, we were left with no backup plan, and suddenly found ourselves flying by the seat of our pants. I suppose it was right out of Stephanie's master script.

We endured 300 grueling kilometers huddled with thirteen passengers bouncing and tossing our way to the capital in the back of a Datsun pickup. None of us had enough rear-end padding to absorb the bumps well. Mid-route the driver was cited by local police for having too many passengers. The guy paid his fine, a payoff no doubt, then continued with all thirteen of us piled in the bed of his truck. I suppose our educational experience that day came by way of endurance development and character building.

After arriving in Bathurst, the four of us bought food to prepare for dinner then headed straight to the beach where we met up with Eiji, Joe, Katie, and Jill. We found a quiet place on the sand to set up camp for the night and collected enough driftwood and sticks to build a fire.

I sat by the water while small waves slapped the shoreline, and as the soft sea breeze caressed my hot, dry skin. The sky above hosted a thin quarter moon and a million stars. Bill made enough spaghetti and bean soup for everyone over the fire, and we shared several bottles of red wine, responsibly. It was a time of group reflection, spiritual awareness, appreciation for life, and appreciation for creation itself. Also, for the relationships bonded by this trip. Good friends and warm sleeping bags on a West African beach. It was a relaxed, most fitting finale to our time in Gambia.

The morning sun rose quickly over Bathurst. I enjoyed the sounds of the sea and of honking gulls from inside my sleeping bag during my final waking minutes. It was a personal time of thanksgiving. I felt more complete than I had just one short week ago. Something deep inside me had changed. I spent the day at the beach with my friends, but savored alone time as well, walking, running, swimming, collecting shells, basking in the sun, and meditating. It was a perfect day.

Anchored in Bathurst, Gambia

Work Crew – (L to R) Tom, Nancy Graham, Susan, Jack, Mary

Captain Fossa and his whole motley crew aboard ship

1st Mate Schnitler and 2nd Mate Kjemtrup

CHAPTER 14: THE CROSSING

Back in town we enjoyed one last meat pie and bowl of fresh fruit at the Gambia Restaurant, then boarded ship as evening approached. Life as a cadet was about to resume—discipline, musters, ship's work, watches, cleaning stations, whistles, classes, and community life onboard. I was ready to sail.

On Saturday, January 27 at 13:00, we pulled anchor as the *Statsraad Lehmkuhl* turned west and slowly navigated out of the West African harbor. Several sails were quickly set to catch the soft afternoon breeze as the ship's slow, easy, rolling motion brought joy that only a sailor could understand. I stood on deck watching the dark continent slowly fade from sight, with a smile, as I felt the comfort of my surroundings, my home. Nothing but sky, sea, and some newly created fond memories. The sun appeared as if through a smoke screen as light haze enveloped the skies, casting unusual reflections on the water.

The mood onboard was good. Crew and cadets seemed pleased to be sailing again. As the transatlantic trip began, significant changes were made to the watch schedules. Each group was now scheduled for four hours twice a day, rather than serving six- or eight-hour shifts as before. There were few complaints concerning the new schedule, not even from Tom. But it's been said often that a new broom sweeps well.

Our excitement on the first day at sea included a galley fire after dinner. One of the ovens over-heated and several loaves of bread caught fire. No one was close by as the fire spread to cardboard boxes in the galley. Within minutes the commotion was over as the fire was doused. Thank God for hydrants on deck and fast responses by two able-bodied seamen. It seemed unimaginable to me that fire could destroy a ship at sea surrounded by water, but I was told it could and that it had in the past.

Classes officially restarted on day two, but the most notable event was Rick Goodfriend's haircut. Previously, he was one of the die-hard holdouts against cutting his hair, so his decision came as a surprise. Jane cut off a full twelve inches of his brown locks with Bosun's scissors, leaving less than half an inch of stubble on his scalp. His beard remained. Celebrative crewmen cheered and hollered as

Sargent bellowed from the halfdeck, "This is the best thing that happened today!" (in Norwegian but translated with gusto by Jacobsen).

Tom and I climbed high to help set the top sails, just as the sun was rising. What an extraordinary contrast from doing the same task in the North Sea, now as the warm breeze and first rays of sunlight caressed our faces. I enjoyed Tom, more so when it was just him and me without a swarm of shipmates around. He cussed less. So, my day was off to a good start and remained so until lunch was served— bones, fat, and gristle. The smell alone killed my appetite. I'd have endured Tom's cussing for better food in a heartbeat.

Group C took in the high sails at dusk, despite good weather. Captain didn't want to risk the possibility of a night squall or a sudden storm after dark. Jacobsen told me that setting sails at sunrise and taking them in at sunset would be our new daily routine while crossing the Atlantic. East to west trade winds became our ticket for good sailing from Africa to South America. However, our speed was a slow three knots for the first several days. It felt like a storybook experience in slow motion as the ship rocked gently, creaking from top to bottom in rhythmic pentameter. I was reminded of the days Mom read to me as a child sitting on the old green glider on Grossmommie Smucker's front porch. The sounds were the same. And the security.

On the third day, Schnitler announced the ship's official time would be turned back two hours—ten minutes each hour over a twelve-hour period—to accommodate watch schedules. The time adjustments started at midnight.

My morning routine included climbing high to set the bram and royl sails. It was an easy, satisfying task to untie sizings and unfurl canvas. I sometimes stayed aloft after my work was completed, gazing out at the vast 360-degree horizon. Nothing in the world compared, and no words in any language could adequately describe the experience. It felt like heaven at sea.

During the crossing, I read several books: *Who? Me?* by Yoram Matmor, *The Temple of the Golden Pavilion* by Yukio Mishima, *Islands in the Stream* by Hemingway, and *The Sailor Who Fell from Grace with the Sea*. One day while reading in my room I heard unusual sounds coming from the union mess. I sat up and listened curiously.

Yappi, the student from Ivory Coast, Jaime the Mexican, and Arturo the Puerto Rican prof, had formed an impromptu a cappella trio. I was amazed how terrible their blended voices sounded but impressed by the enthusiasm and expressions of the three, especially Yappi. I couldn't understand the jumbled French, Spanish, and English lyrics, and I doubt anyone could've possibly recognized even a single chord. Arturo, the only musically talented one of the bunch, was completely disqualified by the other two. More kids gathered, also curious about the alien sounds coming from the mess hall. Soon audience participation of foot tapping, nodding, and hand clapping turned this strange performance into a one-of-a-kind, unheralded sea choir. Although not pretty, it added hilarity and joy to another day at sea.

With each passing day, the number of "long hairs" were dwindling. Dave Freedman and Clark were next. Holdouts watched from the back shadows, shaking their heads disapprovingly as shipmates continued reshaping their heads. Crewmen cheered and blessed each cut of the scissors. One evening while Jones was getting his hair cut, a school of flying fish flew across the deck overhead. Several hit the side wall, startling all of us standing nearby. It was surreal. I had never even heard of flying fish. Quickly, I positioned myself by the railing, peering into the open sea, hoping for more. Sure enough, within minutes another school of the sleek wing-finned fish suddenly rose up from the ocean, seemingly on cue. Scores of them skimmed across the sea like birds, then climbed high enough to clear the deck, staying airborne for thirty seconds. Malcom timed them. It was an amazing spectacle. One fish flew through an open porthole near midship and landed on someone's bunk.

After the excitement, I had a one-on-one session with Mike to discuss my credo. He asked me to read it to him aloud. Not feeling up to it, I reversed his request, politely asking him to read it to me. Mike responded with a stare of surprise, then proceeded to read the entire credo, slowly with good expression. It felt strange but I was better able to critique my work as a listener. His voice was deep and strong with clear pronunciation, the kind of voice I wished I had. When he finished, Mike commented on several points of content, corrected some punctuation errors, then encouraged me to keep developing vocabulary and writing skills, adding, "Marlie, this is good. It reflects who you are." I thanked him.

Ω

The trip from Bathurst to Belém was estimated to take approximately two weeks. After the slow start, the winds finally picked up as the ship began cruising moderately at seven knots.

One day Linda forgot to sign off at the end of her banjer watch shift. Kjemtrup promptly decided to give her an additional lookout watch shift as punishment. She was assigned to my watch, meaning I now had to scrape rust for an hour. I balked at the unfairness, explaining to Kjemtrup that it felt like I was the one being punished. His response shouldn't have surprised me: "That's a never mind!"

Day six started with the *Statsraad Lehmkuhl*'s nautical position at 9' N latitude, 28' W longitude. It was February 1, 1973, but none of us cared about the date. Nor did we enjoy lunch much as few of us were fans of liver. Todd and I declared it to be the steward's second worst concoction. But I managed to chow down two large slabs of the stuff with plenty of gravy and ketchup. My body needed iron. I commented to Todd, however, that it was more fun washing dishes that day than eating. I suppose the liver gave us something to talk about. Boredom was starting to set in onboard for the first time since leaving Norway. The trade winds were spoiling us.

One early morning, Ellie and I climbed to the bram yard on the main mast to untie sizings. Unfortunately, one of us missed a sizing in the middle of the sail. Poulsen yelled some choice Danish words across the deck as we descended, cuss words, I'm sure. Obviously, someone had to go back up. And according to Ellie, that someone wasn't going to be her, as she claimed complete innocence for the mess-up.

Climbing high twice during any shift was a workout. I could've complained, knowing full well it wasn't me who missed the sizing. But honestly, I should've double-checked our work before descending. Pointing a finger at her, with three pointing back at me, would've been wrong. That's what I was taught at home. So, I relied on my adrenaline for strength and climbed. When I reached the bram yard I looked forward and saw Jill doing the same thing on the fore mast! Seriously? She appeared to be very unhappy, so I didn't mention anything about our morning fate to her at breakfast.

After fixing the problem, I stayed in the rigging for fifteen minutes, enjoying the view and riding the sway from the far side of the yard. The sails were full as the ship listed slightly toward port, cutting through modest swells at a good clip. That was the silver lining. The only sound I heard was the soughing wind blowing steadily from the east. I was alone, relishing my brief magical solitude amidst the sails. It was better than a fairy tale.

One of the great things about our sail from Africa to South America was our free time. I had time to think, reflect, and connect purposely with creation, and to sometimes feel twinges of homesickness, missing my friends back home. I had cautiously kept my relationships onboard at arm's length, afraid to become too involved with anyone. Sometimes I felt inferior to many of my shipmates.

Food quality was noticeably better after leaving Africa, except for the occasional bones, fat, and gristle. Meat selection was improved, potatoes were fresher, and tropical fruit was a nice supplement to many meals. The Brotherhood had little to say concerning the food. One day the cooks made beef steaks and a ton of French fries. Kids at my table were in rare form, trying to out-do each other by scarfing down volumes of food. Eight of us devoured more than was reasonable, eradicating all possibility of anemia.

Later that night, Pisacano and Freedman were sitting under the halfdeck overhang playing guitar and singing. A beautiful starlit sky displayed its grandeur overhead. Unfortunately, Pisacano lost track of time, unaware that he was supposed to be at muster with his group. Jacobsen did roll call that night and became infuriated by the fact that a cadet missed muster under his watch. He ran from his position on deck with intent, grabbed Pisacano by the neck and aggressively threw him into line, tossing his guitar aside. It was a violent act. Professor Soja, who was standing nearby, approached Jacobsen and told him to "lay off," which triggered an impassioned response.

Fiery-eyed and bristle-necked, Jacobsen shot back, "Shut up or I'll do the same to you!" This was the first time I was aware of a crewman laying hands on any of the cadets in anger. It was cause for concern, arousing feelings of deep vexation. The incident sent me into an emotional spiral. It wasn't just about Jacobsen and Pisacano. I began questioning my own self-worth and my ability to function productively as a cadet, as a student, and as a human being.

Minutes passed. I felt empty inside, surrounded by invisible walls. My optimistic hopes of somehow making the world a better place were gone. Even my desire to do so vanished. And worse still, I felt incredibly lonely and broken. This stupid little two-minute episode on deck triggered feelings I didn't know existed—feelings that I had subconsciously suppressed. Suddenly, I found myself in the middle of a serious internal emotional struggle.

Numbed and chilled, I stood alone on the fore deck for a long time staring at the sea, fighting my emotions, resisting thoughts of negativity, determined not to allow this surge of inner weakness to define me. I had too much to live for and even more to hope for.

I looked heavenward and whispered aloud, "I must claw my way out of this funk!"

The sea, with its many mysteries and moods, somehow calmed my spirit and redirected my thoughts. Like tacking into the wind, my mind demanded a course

change. I stood by the starboard rail for a very long time, not speaking or interacting with anyone, allowing my soul to reboot.

Ω

One day Kjemtrup said we were approximately midway between Africa and
South America. Except for that tidbit, there was no news from anywhere. The world
could have been blown to smithereens and no one aboard the *Statsraad Lehmkuhl*
would've even known. It was mind-boggling to be living in such oblivion. Mark,
Tom, and I were hanging out in the music room that night talking about Swamp
Apes in Florida, the Abominable Snowman, and death. With little connection
to the outside world, no news, no television or radio, I suppose we had nothing
better to discuss or to prompt our imaginations.

During night shifts, there was little for us to do when not manning one of
the four watches. I usually sat with the rest of my group under the roof outside
the guest saloon, staring into the night, trying desperately to stay awake. We
weren't allowed to sleep, and without lighting we couldn't even read. So, Kjemtrup
decided to do us a favor one night. He wrapped an old sail around the porch
where we sat and turned on a bright light so we could read, study, play games, or
do whatever we wanted to pass the time. Anything except sleep. But alas, Linda,
Willy, and Pisacano fell asleep. So, Peter tore down the sail in disgust, turned off
the light, and gave the three sleeping cadets each an added watch shift after our
group went off duty.

As we inched closer to the equator, Tom tried convincing a few students
that everything works in reverse in the southern hemisphere. Like the water in a
flushing toilet swirls the opposite direction, and ceiling fans, lawn mower blades,
and merry-go-rounds spin the opposite way. I'm sure Lotion, if he heard Tom's
nonsense, would have been the only one who believed it.

We continued scraping rust and painting the ship daily. The task was as easy
at sea as it was in port. Waters were calm, the breeze constant, and skies were
mostly clear. At night the constellations were spectacular, with more stars visible
than I had ever seen. The Southern Cross was a new one, as was Canopus, the
brightest star in the south. Familiar constellations of the northern hemisphere
appeared to be upside-down and close to the horizon as I looked north from
lookout watch. I wasn't an expert by any means, but the skies fascinated me day
after day, night after night. Uncle Dan would've declared it to be God's handiwork
on display. And who was I to disagree?

The saltwater shower was hooked up and left running for a solid forty-five minutes one day as we lathered away the sweat, grime, and unseen tropical crud from our bodies. By this time, most everyone was bronze toned except Katie, Jim, Janet, Nancy, and a few others blessed with fair complexions. The shower scene on deck transgressed from normal enthusiasm to aggressive behavior after The Brotherhood determined that everyone must get in. Not only did they round up those on deck who refused to shower voluntarily but searched the banjers for cadets in hiding as well. Few escaped. According to Perry, a thorough saltwater cleansing of the community was imminent. The shower felt good, but the sticky after-effect of saltwater on my skin didn't fulfill the freshwater purification I so badly needed.

Unfortunately, in an unrelated incident, a freshwater spigot had inadvertently been left on a few days earlier. As a result, the ship supposedly lost nine tons of water, which limited our freshwater access in the washroom areas to three times a day, one hour at a time. The kitchen crew was ordered to boil potatoes and vegetables in saltwater.

After the on-deck saltwater shower excitement subsided, Kjemtrup invited some kids to shave his head. He never allowed his crop of thick brown hair to grow longer than several inches anyway, but this involved a razor cut. The scene on deck was certainly entertaining as kids took turns with the razor. Peter patiently endured it all, grinning from ear to ear. Without hair, his strapping frame loomed even larger, and his squinty Danish eyes gave him a Martian-like appearance.

Some nights, when not on duty, I slept atop the galley roof with other cadets. It felt fresher and less stuffy there than in the banjers where heat and humidity created stale, smelly air. Plus, drifting off to sleep on the galley was soulfully soothing—lying directly under the fore mast that towered high above, creaking and swaying lazily with the motion of the ship.

By day twelve, there was a serious wave of listlessness developing among the students and faculty. I was feeling it too. My daily routine had become monotonous. We all seemed to be wallowing in stagnation, lacking motivation to do anything. Mike addressed the issue in English class, acknowledging the fact that there was no escaping the confines of the ship while in the middle of the Atlantic. But he went on to compliment the educational aspects of this character-building period within the Oceanics experience.

"All of you are forced to face your feelings, your breaking points, and your tolerance levels. Unfortunately, some of you won't appreciate any of this until long after it's over." He then added, "I challenge each of you to look inwardly and find the strength to endure the present for the sake of the future. You are some of the luckiest kids in the world."

I took his words to heart, agreeing with everything he said. At least in theory. And I thanked him after class. But doing the inward work and applying it to my situation at sea within this close community wasn't as easy as I wished. Like others, I tended to withdraw in search of solitude when not on duty. Even then, I found it difficult to write creatively or with any fluidity. I felt forced to expand my zone, to find something new each day, to embrace the unusual, and to connect with the abstract.

Every day the early evening cloud formations in the west were significant enough to spend time viewing. And to write about. One evening the cloud patterns that spanned the entire western horizon resembled cracked mud on the bottom of a dried pond after hardening, then getting flushed by enough rain to soften the edges—except it was a thousand times more beautiful than that! Colors on the horizon were brilliant orange and red. Directly overhead, the sky appeared tie-dyed in yellow and white, painted on a vivid blue background. The north was mostly clear with a few small scattered puffy clouds. A thin sliver of moon accented the eastern horizon, completing the spectacular panorama. I quietly surmised that the sky symbolized the future—the unknowns—and the sea represented the present. Now I understood the significance of the old proverb, "Red sky at night, sailor's delight. Red sky in the morning, sailors take warning." Its truth was proven a hundred percent of the time when at sea.

The breakfast pancakes were above average the next morning. I scarfed down six of them with plenty of butter and syrup. Work duty started at 09:00 for Group C. By now, everyone knew exactly what to do to make our tasks go well. Some cadets worked better together than others. Several worked harder. But overall, our group adjusted to each other's strengths and weaknesses. On this day, the mess crew of Pisacano, Bill Wright, Robert, and I functioned as well as any mess crew ever. Robert, the Norwegian, was a no-nonsense guy who knew how to get things done. He set the tone. After our work was finished, we all high-fived each other, impressed with our own efficiency, and we bragged to anyone who would listen.

Setting sails that day was a breeze. But as time passed, the skies became noticeably hazy, and the air grew heavy with intense heat and humidity. Portholes were closed because of choppy seas, and the banjers became unbearably stuffy. They stank. The sea was rougher than at any point since leaving Africa as the ship experienced agitation nearly equal to my own restlessness.

While helping to set top sails on both the fore and main mast at 05:00 hours, I noticed what appeared to be a ship far off on the northwestern horizon. Within minutes it changed course and headed directly toward us. After returning to the deck, I reported the ship sighting to Mate Schnitler, but he had already picked it up on radar. I shrugged as he thanked me anyway. Schnitler was a tough dude, and seldom went out of his way to compliment anyone. I believe he appreciated my efforts most times when he was the officer on duty, although he rarely said so.

Several officers lined the railing as the Greek freighter approached our starboard side, then slowed considerably while maneuvering closer. Obviously, the Greeks were fascinated by encountering a sail ship in the middle of the Atlantic. The sailors aboard stood by the rail on their deck and saluted as they passed by heading the opposite direction, followed by three long blasts of the freighter's horn. Aboard the *Statsraad Lehmkuhl*, we all did the same, and someone blew our horn. This was protocol, I was told, a mutual act of respect when meeting another ship on the high seas. We passed close enough to easily see the faces and expressions of sailors on the Greek freighter.

Group C had classes in the afternoon. In English, our discussion centered around apathy. Philosophy class was consumed by the question, What is truth? A subject deeper than the ocean itself. We concluded that there was no way to measure the depth of either. Frank loved ending his sessions with questions. Bill Bacon and I embraced his class-ending antics, but Bill believed he could find the answers. Everything was tangible. In contrast, I was willing to continue seeking for a very long time without answers. I didn't need them to survive. As a matter of fact, I still had questions from childhood swirling in my head. And probably always would.

On the lighter side, we watched a movie that evening, *Mrs. Brown You Have a Lovely Daughter*, starring Herman's Hermits. It was a poor quality film, probably the worst I'd seen onboard. Pure entertainment that required no further thought or dialogue—perfect for a guy like Jacobsen. Someone suggested that he and the film shared equal intellectual depth. I couldn't have agreed more.

Ω

The sun at twelve noon was directly overhead on day fourteen, literally straight up in the sky. An hour later all normal activities aboard came to halt—no ship's work, no watches, no sleep time, no classes, no sea schedule. Something strange was brewing.

There has been a long-standing nautical tradition of ceremonially initiating sailors who cross the equator for the first time. It's an event that theoretically ushers in a sense of one's belonging to the sea. High energy and grandeur are known to characterize the ceremony. Sailors who have previously crossed the equator are known as Shellbacks, or sons of Neptune. Those who have not are called Pollywogs. King Neptune, of course, is known as ruler of the seas. So, the entire shindig is meant to appease and earn favor with the King in hopes of protecting sailors from the perils of the sea. In short, it brings good luck. I cautiously questioned how the ceremony would involve me. How much good luck did I need? But I prepared myself for whatever might happen, knowing it had nothing to do with luck. And I didn't trust the Norwegian crew.

In the case of the *Statsraad Lehmkuhl* in 1973, sail master Bernes role-played King Neptune, complete with scepter, gown, and crown. The Sargent was dressed as his ugly hairy wife, Queen Amphitrite, who assisted him. Jacobsen was the doctor, while Schnitler, Kjemtrup, and Poulsen dressed as Pirates. Their job was to stretch out and hold down the initiates, allowing Doc Jacobsen and Judge Bosun to perform their ceremonial rituals on each cadet.

The launch boat was placed in the center of the main deck and filled with sea water next to two benches side by side forming an operating table. Remaining crewmen formed a large circle surrounding the area. We were told the ceremony was mandatory for all Pollywogs. Either we cooperate and do it voluntarily, or it would be done by force. No exceptions. No opting out for medical, emotional, intellectual, gender, or any other reasons. We were instructed to wear shorts or swimsuits. Although most everyone was on deck at the start, an official Norwegian search squad was formed to find any elusive resisters in hiding. The initiators list was complete with the names and numbers of each cadet, faculty member, and rookie sailor aboard.

Several cadets volunteered to go first, just to get it over with, while those of us with apprehensions looked on from the sidelines. I stood back by the railing on port side, quiet and solemn as a belay pin, hoping to blend in with the crowd of cadets who had the same fears as me. Trying not to be noticed. Not that I was scared—no one was going to throw me overboard. But the idea of being vulnerable to King Neptune's Court was discomforting—a bust on anyone's self-esteem. It felt humiliating.

Jane, Todd, and a few other brave souls got the ceremony started. Each victim was laid face up, sprawled out on the operating table. Their arms and legs were held tightly by the three Pirates. Then Jacobsen went to work with a devilish grin, first squirting ice-cold water from a large syringe up each Pollywog's crotch. For some, he pushed a large chunk of ice inside their pants and rubbed it around from the outside, then took a rubber mallet from his tool pouch and pounded sparingly on their stomach, chest, and thighs. With scissors, he randomly removed a lock of hair from each victim's head and handed it to the Sarge.

Bosun had mixed up a strange sticky concoction of goop. Ingredients included peanut butter, mustard, margarine, cooking oil, and mystery stuff, notably hard to remove. The goop was first smeared over the pollywog's face and hair. Anyone sporting a beard received a double dose. There was an added procedure for female cadets. Doc wore a homemade stethoscope around his neck made of a toilet plunger and rope which he used for breast-beat analysis. In the case of well-endowed girls, he plunged their breasts. Most everyone onboard knew Jacobsen to be a pervert. Several shots of whiskey before the ceremony only encouraged his bad-boy behavior. There was little anyone could do to tame his exploits as this equator crossing initiation came directly from the Nautical Bible. He had the full support of Captain Fossa, Chief Mate, and all the officers, so we were totally at his mercy. Besides, it was 1973 and we were somewhere in the middle of the Atlantic Ocean. Who were we going to call? (Ghostbusters was not yet an option.)

Smiling like the devil himself, Jacobsen pulled Mary's top completely down, exposing her breasts, then proceeded to plunge them both. He was in no hurry, pretending to listen for something inside. Several times he pressed the plunger into her crotch as well, between spread legs. She wasn't the only female to receive such treatment. Although Jacobsen claimed to be role playing, everyone onboard knew better, including the captain. Jacobsen enjoyed every initiation moment with every female cadet. Dear old Great Uncle Dan should've seen this!

After forcing a spoonful of prescribed medicine (vinegar, hot peppers, and tabasco sauce) into the initiate's mouth, Jacobsen gave a nod, signaling the pirates to throw the Pollywog into the lifeboat for a saltwater rinse. Each cadet was congratulated by fellow sailors with high fives, celebrative laughter, and lots of hooting and hollering as they climbed out of the launch, now transformed into a Shellback.

Suddenly, I felt the urge to get it done. I knew nothing about Pollywogs before this day, but now I was already sick and tired of being one. Stepping forward toward the operating table, I was roughly greeted by the Pirates who grabbed my arms and legs and laid me out. I felt the cold water in my crotch, the goop across my face and chest, the medicine on my lips, and I heard the snip of hair being cut above my left ear. Although we were no longer necessarily known by our cadet numbers, I felt very much like #45 that day, rather than a person with a name. But my initiation was fast. By comparison, I believe I got off easy. Maybe my ongoing cooperation with the officers and crew, and the fact that I was never loud or boisterous onboard paid off. Or maybe I was just lucky.

The ceremony continued on deck for several hours. A few cadets were missing from King Neptune's list: Willy, Nancy Graham, Kevin, Ellie, Emil, and Yappi. But with only a limited number of places to hide aboard ship, time was not on their side.

Perry took it upon himself to make his own goop in preparation for the missing seven. A large container of pancake syrup, mustard, ketchup, eggs, flour, milk, and canned sardines were stirred into several gallon containers. One by one, the missing Pollywogs were brought to justice, held down, and doused with Perry's sticky stuff. Two pillows were then torn apart, and the feathers dumped onto the victims.

That action triggered angry shouts of disapproval from several cadets who thought the punishment went too far. I remained silent with no feelings whatsoever. Like it or not, I understood the consequences of nonconformity from my childhood experiences. Ellie, the hardest Pollywog to find, was the last cadet to be initiated. After being 'tarred and feathered', her mouth was stuffed full of sardines. Then, with hands tied behind her back, she was blasted with the saltwater pressure hose. Her appearance during initiation wasn't pretty by any stretch of anyone's imagination as she suffered through the ramifications of not submitting to King Neptune's court voluntarily. I believe Ellie was intimidated for all the same reasons as me, only multiplied by ten. But I never discussed it with her, assuming that particular memory was better left alone.

After the ceremony was completed, King Neptune himself presented each of us with an equator-crossing certificate, complete with the *Statsraad Lehmkuhl's* official stamp. He then welcomed us to the documented Shellback community. Supposedly, there were no longer any Pollywogs onboard. As a friendly gesture, the crew gave each of us a beer. Jane then proceeded to have her head shaved, allowing Kjemtrup the honors. I suppose crossing the equator by ship really was a big deal.

Tom questioned whether everyone was inwardly transformed. He continued using the term Pollywog to address several shipmates. It was a fitting one-word description, and a great word to repeat over and again, "Pollywog, Pollywog, Pollywog!" I thanked God I no longer was one.

Ω

We quietly crossed the equator on Saturday, February 10, day 15, at 0' latitude 45' longitude off the east coast of Brazil. Expectantly, Lotion stood on deck looking for a rope or cable. His disappointment was less imaginary than the line itself—there was no cutting or splicing.

Only the necessary work of setting sails was done in the morning. Otherwise, we enjoyed a day of leisure. My time was spent talking and reflecting with students and faculty. Eiji shared his experience of trying to avoid the US Military draft. Jim Soja told his story as well. After becoming an officer in R.O.T.C. during college, he realized that he couldn't conscientiously participate in the Armed Forces. But it required extensive articulation to argue his case before the interrogating committee, while not being a member of the Amish, Mennonite, or Quaker churches. His position was clear, however, and he didn't waver from his convictions which led to his eventual dismissal without further consequence.

Rain started early and continued throughout the day, heavy at times. During the hardest downpours the wooden deck became slippery, prompting reckless running and sliding by us stir-crazy cadets. Sam fell hard and broke his collarbone. During the frolicking frenzy, Soja and Dave Freedman stripped Pisacano naked on deck. Interestingly, no one seemed to care, including Pisacano. I suppose by now there was little shame left to be exposed onboard. But the incident raised a few eyebrows and caused some whispering among female cadets concerning his endowment.

Ω

Welcome to the tropics. By now, conditions had become remarkably hot and humid. I continued sleeping on the half deck at night. During the day, I spent as much time in the rigging as possible. One hundred feet up was the only place to feel any breeze. After receiving my allergy injections from the Doc on our final day at sea, I weighed myself on the small scale in the corner of his cabin—145 pounds, the exact same weight as when I left home. But in the past months I had gained muscle and lost fat. I felt like a million bucks.

At 08:00 the lookout watchman rang the fore bells, indicating that he had spotted land. Backed by favorable trade winds, we had successfully crossed the Atlantic. At midday a Brazilian pilot came aboard from the tug, then guided us nearly sixty miles up the Para River, part of the greater Amazon River system. We anchored one mile from the port of Belém. Our toughest emotional challenge of the day was waiting to go ashore until the following morning.

I was within earshot when First Mate Schnitler said something about the freshwater showers being turned on. Quietly I grabbed my towel without uttering a word to anyone and ran for the guys' shower room. After sixteen days at sea, I could think of nothing better than a nice, hot freshwater drenching. And it was great! But as I was finishing, I looked up to see Jane enter the room. Obviously, she had no inhibitions about disrobing in what had suddenly become a coed shower.

"The girls' shower room has a line," she smiled matter-of-factly.

I tried to hide my astonishment while we exchanged pleasantries. It was difficult to know where to look as we talked. Or truthfully, where not to look. Jane's casual spirit helped ease my excited discomfort, as she lathered her body. I managed a few side glances while drying off. Bare breasts weren't foreign to me, but hers were.

I rationalized the situation in the moment. We were both students and sailors onboard for the same reasons, and both shared a passion for life. There was nothing romantic between us—we were shipmates. We worked the rigging together, polished brass, scrubbed decks, served meals. This was no big deal, right? Showering was just one more thing we now did together. Like lining up for muster. But somehow my forced rationale wasn't convincing. This did matter. And as much as I questioned my conservative teaching, so did modesty. But this was also rousing. I smiled, did a quick glance-back then wrapped myself in a towel and left the shower stall, uncertain of proper protocol. This was different than untying sizings together on the royl yard.

Equator crossing ceremony on the deck

Captain reading the Pollywog call list

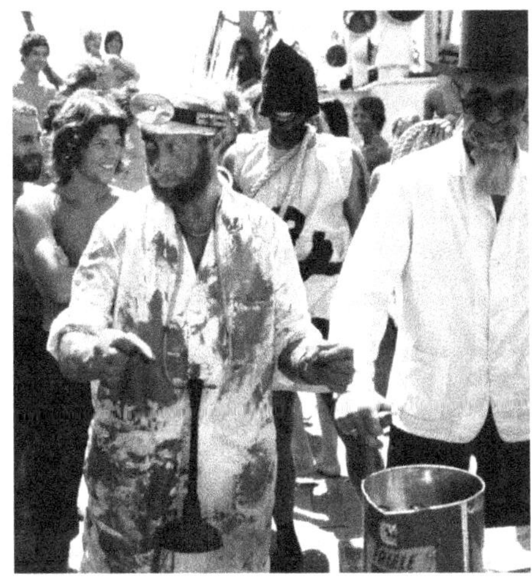

Doc Jacobsen performing initiation tasks

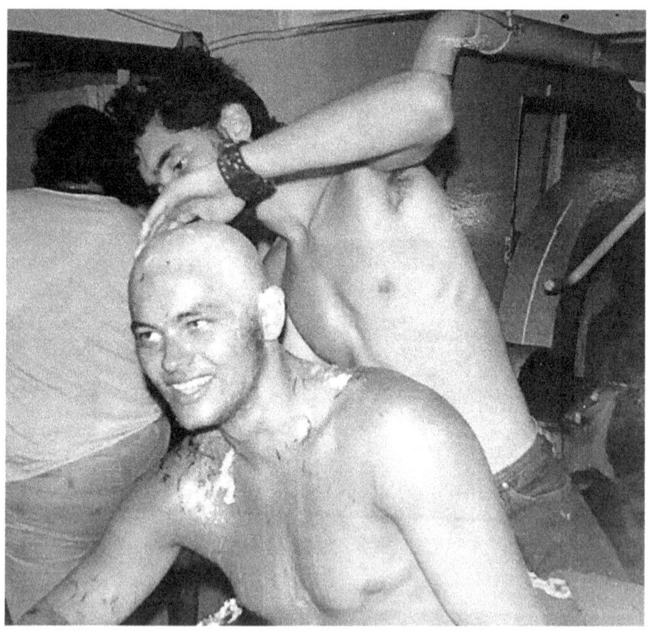

Transformation from Pollywog to Shellback

Bill Bacon shaving Kjemtrup's head

CHAPTER 15: BEM-VINDO AO BRAZIL

After breakfast, we all gathered on deck for mooring stations. It was great to finally arrive at the docks in Belém at 09:00 hours. I checked my remaining bank account with Steve and Debbie before going ashore and was pleasantly surprised I still had ninety-two dollars and change. I determined it should be enough for the next several months if I was careful about my spending.

Stephanie greeted us onshore, adding to our exuberance with a large box of mail from home. I received eighteen letters from family and friends—certainly a highlight of my morning. But best of all was walking on dry land again! Explaining that feeling to anyone who has never spent sixteen consecutive days at sea is impossible.

After lunch we were given a brief orientation of the city, Brazilian culture, and an intro to the Portuguese language. The dock was lined with photographers, reporters, business professionals, bums, and prostitutes as Pisacano and I curiously made our way down the gangway, then out along the large concrete dock to the street. It was an overwhelming welcome for sea-weary sailors—an invitation to see, smell, feel, and experience so much good and evil.

Belém is the Portuguese word for Bethlehem. Geographically, the city is situated at the mouth of the Amazon River, classifying it as a busy port for trade and commerce. Founded in 1616 by the Kingdom of Portugal, Belém became the first European colony in the Amazon region. Sugar trade started quickly but the city's economic importance rose and fell with eventual cattle ranching and agricultural products: rice, cotton, and coffee. As settlements developed in southern Brazil, Belém's economy declined, only to be revived by the rubber industry in the mid 1800s, along with aluminum, iron ore, and Brazilian nuts. The port continues to be the main commercial shipping center of northern Brazil.

In 1973, tourism was also an important part of the economy, as cruise ships and merchant ships visited the city. When we arrived, Belém was bustling with opportunities, including a plethora of nightlife activities for pleasure-seeking sailors.

Pisacano and I wandered through town. It was a great exchange for the
boredom we had experienced onboard during our recent ocean crossing. I was
completely absorbed by my surroundings. We bought beers at an outside bar
and shared stuff about our lives, dreams, and expectations. I enjoyed becoming
better acquainted with him away from the ship. Like Tom, he also didn't cuss
much when it was just him and me. Aside from his antics with The Brotherhood
and his earthy humor, Pisacano was intelligent, understood practical realities,
showed common sense, and was fun to engage in serious conversation.

Two young girls caught our attention from the sidewalk, obviously wanting
to hook up. We tried to pay them no mind initially. But it was impossible not
to notice their beckoning smiles—smiles that could melt the heart of a priest.
Brazilian street girls seemed to know intuitively how to lure a guy into their world.
I suppose that was their job. And we were love-starved teenage boys, not priests.
My internal battle between cultural teaching and the allure of persuasion was
both confusing and thrilling. But Pisacano and I decided to head back toward the
ship. After we parted ways, I did a full circle with the intent of hanging out in town
a while longer just to feed my curiosity and learn more from the street culture.

Bebe was one of the girls Pisacano and I had previously encountered on the
sidewalk. She spotted me before I saw her, then greeted me like an old acquain-
tance. I was taken aback by her forward approach, but she presented herself in
a spirited manner, not like the artificially toned ladies by the docks. Although
her English wasn't perfect, it was a far cry better than my Portuguese. And she
was dashingly cute, dressed in a snug fitting black mini skirt and sleeveless blue
button-down blouse, opened at the top. A white pearl necklace hung from her
neck, contrasting her exposed bronze skin and the straight black hair gathered
loosely on her shoulders. Bebe was any teenage boy's dream girl—Mennonite boys
not exempt.

Our conversation wasn't long or deep, but it was fun. She enjoyed pronounc-
ing my name, revealing dimples on her cheeks every time she said "Morli." Her
spirit stirred excitement within as she locked her arm in mine then pointed to a
side street. My heart pounded with nervous desire, now fully engaged without an
ounce of resistance. Nothing seemed important to me beyond Bebe. I followed
her into a building and up a staircase to a dimly lit second floor room.

Her twenty-two-year-old eyes were true and sweet, sparkling with aspiration,
bearing my own reflection, if only for a time. And her touch was unrestrained.
I wanted to take her home and love her forever, to fix her life and justify mine, to

eradicate my guilt for participating in such exotic love. To turn my short-lived fantasy into lifelong reality.

But Bebe understood her role and her place, cognizant of the pleasures she provided, and why. Tenderly, she removed a thin braided leather bracelet from her wrist and tied it around mine in the quiet moments that followed. "Bem-vindo ao Brazil, Morli," she whispered. It felt like the sweetest thing in the world. I didn't want to leave.

But in the end, it was I who felt lost. This was Belém, not Bird-in-Hand. I was in her town on her ten-dollar terms. After returning to the ship, I stayed aboard for the remainder of the evening, reflecting, immersed in my solitude, safely distanced from the crowds, the confusion, and further evils of the night. I felt very, very lonely and empty, vowing never to tell a single soul about my encounter. And I didn't.

Few cadets stayed aboard that first night as curfew wasn't strictly enforced. The Norwegian crew was as stir-crazed as the cadets. Jacobsen and Morgan Kane got drunk. Bars and brothels were well-patronized by the sailors living up to their global reputation. I had always thought myself better than that. But this night was different as Great Uncle Dan's words echoed in my head: "WE BECOME LIKE OUR SURROUNDINGS!"

Ω

Poulsen also stayed onboard. According to rumors, he had a special interest in Janet, the tall blonde quiet cadet from Minnesota. The same one he'd left shouting at him from the dock in Bathurst. Janet appeared emotionally stable and more private than most of the students. I believe Peter liked her from the first day she arrived. But somewhere mid-Atlantic, or maybe before, their mutual affection blossomed.

His demeanor onboard changed noticeably as their relationship developed. He was kinder, less intense, more patient, smiled more, and engaged us in conversations beyond work. If ever there was a transformed sailor, surely it was he. His personal work ethic didn't change, he was still a bull on deck and in the rig. But he modified his expectations of us after better understanding the cadets' perspective. I suppose Janet's influence could accurately be credited for that. My relationship with him was always good, but now it was even better. On our second day in port, February 14—Valentine's Day in the States—Peter shaved his head.

Ship's work continued while docked in Belém, just like in Africa. Field trips were staggered. Group C had the privilege of washing the masts while in port. Todd and

I hoisted all the way to the top, then using Bosun's chairs and pulleys, we hung from the rigging and descended, cleaning as we went. I never tired of views from the rigging, nor the euphoria I experienced during those moments. Additionally, I enjoyed the humor Todd and I shared while doing menial tasks. He got the biggest kick out of retelling stories he heard from other cadets. By the third or fourth time he told them, the tales became hilariously embellished.

Ω

Being docked in a city with all the temptations of the world at our fingertips proved to be more than some of us could handle. The administration was losing control over the students after just two days. Rules were broken, respect for authority diminished, and self-gratification became the motivation for most everything. Cluttered banjers, unmade beds, missed watches, curfew violations, and excessive drinking were daily events.

The paid crewmen didn't necessarily set good examples in port, but onboard they performed their tasks well and kept their areas of the ship tidy. Unlike many of the cadets.

Finally, Mike had seen enough, totally fed up with drunk students, irresponsibility, and reckless behavior. Without warning, he suddenly turned from administrative director of education to school dictator wielding an authoritative hammer. According to Tom and others, he had become unhinged.

Mike called a brief meeting during which he outlined an official end to all the nonsense. In a raised voice he exclaimed, "From now on, I will call the shots. I won't discuss anything concerning any rules with any of you. When I say something, you WILL do it. I will NOT entertain questions. Anyone who violates rules or policies will receive points. Three points will result in a red-ring, and a red-ring means no shore leave." His tone wasn't one to be second-guessed as he continued, "If you're late for muster, if you swear at an officer, if you don't make your bunk, if your locker isn't tidy, if you don't clean your cabin or dust off the top of your locker, you'll receive points." He was on a dictatorial roll, "Before shore leave, there will be an inspection of the banjers and individual cabins. If standards aren't up to snuff, no one will go ashore until they are. I don't care if you all stay on board for the next two days!"

I shuddered, not so much at his words but at his tone. There was grumbling afterwards, of course, even among the faculty. Arturo suggested, "If this year produces only Norwegian cadets, then the Oceanics program has failed miserably." He was referring to educational opportunities and shore leave being stymied by ship's work and discipline. I understood the need to curb the anarchical direction infecting the ranks of the student body, but Mike's actions felt excessive. However, if we couldn't correct it ourselves, then I suppose it had to come to this. But not before we were given a fair chance.

One evening about twenty students piled into several taxis and went across town to a professional soccer game. Actually, two games. The first was minor league play with developing players, but the second game demonstrated the skills and brilliance of professional Brazilian soccer. The crowd was incredibly enthusiastic and nearly as entertaining as the game itself, screaming and dancing euphorically. A group of about twenty-five banner-wielding nationals danced back and forth along the near sideline chanting, choreographing their aerobic dance steps and acrobatics. It was extraordinary. Even a heavy, fifteen-minute rain shower didn't hinder the crowd frenzy. Several of my shipmates did their best to keep up with the locals by drowning themselves in vodka and Pepsi.

When the game ended, the festivities spilled into the streets. Alec, who was absolutely plastered, separated from his group. I found him staggering aimlessly, oblivious to the fact that he was lost. Sensing his inability to walk further, I hailed a taxi and accompanied him to the docks. There, several of us tried convincing him of the importance of boarding the ship quietly. But Alec wasn't cooperative.

He responded to our advice loud and slurred, "I love atten-TION where-EVER I can get it... ya hear me? People gotta acCEPT me for who I am... a fuckin' haa-appy hippie!" Then he laughed. In fact, Alec laughed so hard he fell, sprawled on the concrete dock a hundred feet from the ship. The night was muggy warm as the three-quarter moon hovered just above the horizon. Alec decided to sleep right there on the damp grungy dock. It wasn't an easy task convincing him otherwise, and even tougher getting him onboard. Alec was a big guy. Eventually, George, the gangway watchman, and I managed to push, pull, drag, and roll Alec safely back to his cabin, without the scrutiny of attending officers or administrators.

Not everyone was as lucky. Bill Bacon and Rick Goodfriend decided to drink quietly on board that night. Bill had a hidden bottle of whiskey. They thought they could keep it secret, but after feeling a preponderant buzz, they raised a ruckus at gangway, engaging folks as they returned to the ship. In their stupor, the boys attempted to high-five Chief Mate when he came aboard—definitely a behavioral miscalculation. Chief wasn't amused, and the guys paid their dues.

Mark came back alone that night unapologetically at 03:00 with no explanation, but wearing a boyish grin as wide as the mouth of the Amazon River. He always carried himself with quiet confidence, not needing approval from others. He was a tall, handsome guy. And he didn't need encouragement to accomplish the things he set out to do. Mark was fun to hang with, and seldom complained about anything. My times with him were always more heady than wordy—more thoughts than spoken words. He wasn't caught up in the details of other folks' business, nor was he excited about sharing his own. But that night he was smiling profusely.

It was no surprise that nine red-rings were issued the next day including to Mark, Bill Bacon, Goodfriend, Pisacano, Bill Wright, Kavasic, Tom, Perry, and Del Hagen, for either coming in late or for excessive drinking. It was the perfect number as the captain had determined that at least nine cadets needed to always be onboard while in port, along with the on-duty crewmen. So, the nine red-ringers served a productive purpose for the rest of us. I thanked Bill Bacon with a selfish grin as I headed onshore. He just shook his head and smiled back, always a good sport. Group C would have been scheduled to stay on ship for six hours that day.

Ω

Field trips were posted after our second day in port. Twenty-five students signed up for the first one available. I declined because of the numbers alone. That was just too many kids. Eiji mentioned the possibility of going to a Japanese community 230 kilometers down river from Belém at a place called Tomé-Açu. If that trip worked out, obviously Eiji would lead it, being the only one onboard who spoke Japanese. I was excited about the idea of another riverboat trip. As it turned out, I was chosen to join Arturo, Frutchi, Malcom, George, Mitch, Rufus, Willy, Emil, Tim, Tara, Nancy Graham, and Eiji—thirteen total.

After cleaning stations and breakfast, George, Malcom, and I went into town to buy snacks for the trip: five liters of Pepsi, cookies, fruit, miscellaneous packaged items, and cheese. We also grabbed cans of sardines from the galley. Stephanie helped us with last minute details, including supplying each of us with a hammock. We piled into several taxis that transported us to a river dock on the west side. After a hectic start, our entire group boarded a small riverboat at 12:00, heading into the interior.

By comparison, this boat was smaller and nicer than the *Lady Wright* in Gambia. And the landscape was greener and lusher than any place I'd ever seen before. Locals maneuvered dugout canoes near the shore not far from thatched-roof huts scattered along the river's edge. I was excited for this new adventure. As an early teen, I had read about the Amazon River basin in *National Geographic*. At the time, I could only read and dream about the place. But on this day, the Amazon River became as real as the sun in the sky.

Local staff sold food from a small kitchen onboard. Our group shared several large platters of rice with snippets of meat. We added sardines from our stash. The fresh fruit juice looked great, but we were told not to drink it for fear of impurities in the water.

Many Japanese folks were onboard as well, assumed to be going to Tomé-Açu. They were friendly and responsive when Eiji addressed them in their native tongue. However, they knew no English at all, and ironically, some of the teenagers spoke Portuguese as their first language.

Through conversations on deck, Eiji gathered information concerning their community. A beautiful fair-skinned, black-haired girl caught my eye as we exchanged glances. I was enticed by her friendly smile and joined her by the rail near the bow. Although awkward at first, we communicated with hand signs, gestures, expressions, and a few words. Conveniently, Eiji joined us for several minutes to translate, providing us with basic introductions.

Her name was Etsuko, meaning joyful child, which seemed fitting for her personality. She was seventeen years old. We spoke in turn, she in Japanese/Portuguese, and me in English. I suppose neither of us comprehended much of what the other was saying initially, but it wasn't due to lack of effort. We kept trying.

She showed me several books from her pack with photos of jungle clearing projects in the Amazon basin in the 1900s. As the saying goes, "A picture is worth a thousand words." Etsuko's parents and grandparents were some of the first ethnic Japanese to immigrate and settle in Tomé-Açu in 1929. Two years later, her grandfather—a man she was quite proud of, but never met—died of malaria. Forty-two families, 189 people total, arrived in Brazil's Para district in 1929. Their reason for choosing this place was to develop farmland. But the group's efforts were met with challenges beyond preparedness for this harsh tropical climate. Disease, mostly malignant malaria, riddled the community in those early years. Numerous deaths resulted. Folks involved in the development project renamed the Amazon River region "Saga Vermelha," meaning "Green Hell."

I read details concerning the history of Tomé-Açu after my time with Etsuko, but my fascination with the place was inspired by her, a living descendant of the folks whose determination and diligence developed the community into what it had become today.

She and her aunt were returning home from visiting family in Belém. They knew the routine aboard the riverboat after dark. Nightfall comes quickly in the tropics. So, after the sun set, Etsuko was summoned by her over-protective aunt. Sadly, for me, it was time to part ways. Smiling, she squeezed my arm and gave me a quick hug, then stepped back, clasped her hands together and bowed respectfully before turning and walking to the far side of the boat. I watched as she vanished from sight, thinking to myself how perfect she was.

Many folks had previously hung hammocks from hooks placed on deck posts for that purpose. Most of our group did the same. Several were hung directly above others, like hammocked bunkbeds. However, by the time I tried to find a place, all the hooks were taken. It became nearly impossible to move freely around the deck because of the proximity of hammocks with little space between. The only privacy available was the thin material of the hammock itself. A person could wrap it completely around themselves and sink deep down inside.

I smiled as I looked across the sea of hammocks creating a most unusual slumber party aboard. Most folks were quiet, but not the Oceanic kids. The only logical place to gather vertically was along the outside railing. So, that's what we did, although the views were gone. Nothing could be seen outside the boat beyond the blackness of the night. Aside from lights fore and aft, it was also dark on deck as the diesel engine hummed its laborious continuous song throughout the evening and into the wee hours. I eventually curled up inside my hammock rolled out on the hard wooden floor below Tim and Rufus. Past life experiences had conditioned me for this. I could sleep soundly most anywhere.

At 06:00 we disembarked in the town of Tomé-Açu. Several VW minibuses transported us to a community center twelve kilometers away. This Japanese agricultural community was comprised of several small villages scattered across the region. During the previous forty-three years, thousands of acres of jungle had been cleared and developed into productive farmland in a concerted effort to grow various vegetables. Peppers eventually became the predominant cash crop as Tomé-Açu became home to one of the largest pepper-harvesting plants in all of Brazil.

I enjoyed watching Eiji engage with his culture. It was a side of him none of us had seen before. Locals were friendly and welcoming, and seemed impressed that Eiji brought a group of kids to their island. We were on our best behavior when in the company of the community folks. An older couple invited us to their house on the edge of town for coffee and cakes. Interestingly, they were two of the original 189 who had settled in Tomé-Açu nearly forty-four years earlier.

Fuyuki, the old guy, had studied plants his entire life and acquired a doctorate in botany. He operated an experimental farm, analyzing plants to find which ones best thrived in this tropical climate. As one of the pioneers, he was instrumental in developing the first pepper farms in the region and was also impressively knowledgeable in soil treatments. His wife was a dear lady who thoroughly enjoyed serving our group with a continuous smile. Fuyuki informed us that it was she who maintained and cared for the beautiful, magnificently colored flowers outside their house.

We were then treated to a complete Japanese meal in a local dining hall. It was my first time ever eating with chopsticks. Although food kept falling off my sticks, I managed to get every morsel from the plate to my mouth. Malcom and I joked that our first bites were probably digested before the last ones were swallowed. But regardless, the meal was great: tons of rice, noodles, breaded beef, tomato and onion salad, hibachi soup, raw fish—my first time for that as well. And Pepsi. The raw fish was a serious topic of discussion among us first-timers.

Ω

In the early afternoon we all piled into the back of two pickup trucks with our luggage and rode two hours on dirt roads deep into the bush. It wasn't a ride of comfort. The dense jungle surrounding us was both fascinating and scary. At one point we saw a huge tarantula on the road. Our driver stopped to allow us a closer look. Everyone jumped out except Tara who remained frightfully glued to the bed of the truck directly behind the cab.

Our destination was a large unpainted wooden building resembling an over-sized primitive cabin with lots of windows. It was surprisingly clean inside. Oinishi, one of the drivers, explained that the building is used to host Japanese immigrants when they first arrive. Since it was unoccupied at the time, it became the perfect temporary jungle-home for us.

Our butts were sore from the ride, so Malcom, George, and I went for a walk after being forewarned about the jungle critters. We encountered another tarantula with bright orange rings around each of its eight legs, slowly walking in the same direction as us. With our eyes glued to the hairy creature, we stayed in the far-right lane of the dirt road as we passed, then returned to the shelter just before dark. Sounds of the jungle filled the air as if from a huge multiple-speaker stereo. Fears were exaggerated at night, as my ears and nose replaced my sight, respectfully acknowledging the unknowns just outside the walls of our cabin.

Oinishi lived only fifteen minutes away. He later hauled the entire crew to his house for dinner on the bed of his pickup truck. Again, the meal was great, with unchilled sodas and whiskey to drink. Arturo began telling stories, setting the tone for a fun evening of entertainment and humor.

Back at the cabin, George pulled out a huge bottle of rum from which he filled multiple tumblers. It was time to celebrate this Amazon getaway, far from the work, discipline, and restraints of the ship. With no mates or officers looking over our shoulders, we hadn't a care in the world. Except to stay inside. Laughter, wedgies, purple-nurples, and plenty of junior high rum-induced behavior continued into the night, which was quite out of character for this group of kids. We weren't considered part of the rowdy crowd onboard.

I eventually tired of it all and curled up in one corner of the large room in my sleeping bag. But George bribed me with another Rum & Coke, insisting I should get up. He was a good guy who sincerely cared for the welfare of his friends. I respected him a lot. Considering that, I got up, nursed the drink, and rejoined the fun. Friends were important to me and I didn't care to be perceived as a party-pooper. But when George handed me a second glass of rum, I casually stood by the window and poured it out through the screen, inconspicuously. Sometime after midnight everyone crashed. The cabin was a remarkable mess with stuff strewn everywhere amongst kids sleeping on the floor, giving the appearance of a jungle inside as well.

No one was eager to get up the next morning but our schedule went as planned. After breakfast with Oinishi's family, he transported us even deeper into the rain forest until the road became muddy and impassable. From there we walked another kilometer to a large clearing where several men were hacking away at the brush with machetes. Clearing jungle was no easy task. Oinishi handed out several machetes and warned us briefly of the dangers. There were venomous snakes—pit vipers that hung in low trees and shrubs, coral, and bushmasters. Also, poisonous dart frogs, bullet ants, wandering spiders, and freshwater piranhas, in addition to jaguars, anacondas, and boa constrictors. This quick orientation was enough to ensure keen concern with every step we took, eyes darting, watching for any potential danger within sight. But it also paralyzed several kids in our group, even without the actual venom, nixing their desire and ability to wield machetes.

The jungle sounds were fearfully foreign, intensifying our anxieties. And of course, there was exaggerated talk among the students. Willy dryly shared his understanding of the little vipers that hang from trees, explaining that when someone walks underneath, the snake attacks from above and bites its victim on the head.

"Here's the best part," he said with a grin. "The venom works incredibly fast, so the victim has only minutes to live. He first starts bleeding from his eyes, ears, and nose, then twitches uncontrollably until the nerves slowly die, long after he stops breathing." Willy dramatized the twitching as he spoke. Tara challenged the truth of his description, but no one knew for sure. And Willy just smiled with no reason to say more. None of us could unimagine what we had just heard.

Oinishi's expectation for our jungle-clearing time was more about the experience than about productivity. We were free to explore, hack with machetes, or just hang out for the next few hours. Arturo, Malcom, George, and I found vines to swing on. We cleared brush from underneath the swinging area, then behaved like chimps showing off. We each grabbed a vine and played the jungle version of king of the mountain, bellowing loudly as we swung. George rightly became "George of the Jungle." According to Arturo, monkeys in nearby trees were astonished and entertained. I nodded, smiled, and suggested that it wasn't just about the sounds. These Brazilian monkeys had never seen a fat Puerto Rican swinging on their vines.

We hiked a bit further but didn't stray far from the narrow dirt road. Because of the dense green canopy overhead, the sun's rays seldom reached the jungle floor. But the random sunlight that filtered through added surreal beauty to this amazing piece of creation.

Oinishi and his wife cooked dinner over an open fire. It was a hot day, and the humidity was intense. Our pungent body odor was beyond tolerable levels. We all stank! Emil and I walked to a nearby small freshwater pond, stripped down and jumped in, hoping to vanquish the smell. Within minutes, three young boys came running to us, waving their hands, and screaming in Portuguese. Without verbal comprehension, we got out of the water quickly, only to realize there were electric eels in the pond.

Maybe Oinishi had forgotten to mention them when naming all the critters. Although a jolt from an electric eel might not kill a person, it could give him a shock of 500 volts—more than four times that of a regular North American home receptacle. Emil and I were innocently taken aback. But we no longer stank.

Others in the group took bucket baths. I seriously questioned whether a bucket held enough water to totally eradicate their BO.

Ω

All thirteen of us spent one night in the home of a wealthy pepper farmer in the region. Hideshi and his wife owned a very large, beautifully furnished home in town. They were an interesting, educated, and socially entertaining couple. Through Eiji's interpreting, they shared historical and present-day challenges of the region. I was personally proud of our group. Most of the kids stayed engaged in the conversations, asked intelligent questions, and behaved respectfully throughout the course of dinner. We later read, journaled, and reflected on our recent experiences as music played from the large stereo in the living room. The house provided sufficient space for all of us to sleep with comfort, especially with the provided mosquito nettings.

The next day, I persuaded Malcom to start keeping a journal. That was no easy task as he claimed solid arguments against it, including the time involved, lack of reflective focus, and laziness. But in the end, I convinced him to write, stressing the importance of doing it for the sake of his future grandkids. In fact, he was so moved that he started writing that very night in Tomé-Açu. In typical Malcom fashion however, and after several minutes of serious focus while gripping his pen, he looked up and remarked, "This is a real pain in the ass! You can't tell me otherwise. But you make a good point—maybe, just maybe, when I'm old on my rocker, I'll tell my grandkids stories from the good old days—like when I was a sailor in the jungles of Brazil. And only because I kept a freaking journal inspired by a Mennonite boy."

Then he asked, "Is that why you write so much? So you can someday tell stories to your grandkids?" I didn't answer but thought about his question. I never imagined myself being a grandpa. But if ever I was, I liked the idea of sharing some of these stories with my grandkids.

Later, after seeing the beautiful spotted saint wood at a shop in town, Malcom and I decided we might want to become whittlers. The old man who owned the shop made a variety of things from the hardwood—chopsticks, canes, rules, and creative wood carvings. Revered in the community as a professional whittler, the guy was obviously talented. Malcom figured whittling was as noble a profession as anyone could have, and a goal he could attain with lots of practice and patience, concluding he already was blessed with patience gleaned from just being around all of us.

In truth, Malcom was probably the most patient character on ship. Being from the south, he maintained an unhurried pace and was seldom anxious about anything, except maybe this latest venture in journaling. When I questioned him further concerning his fascination with whittling, he grinned and repeated his desires in a tenor southern draw, "Yup, I just wanna be a-sittin' and a-whittlin' all day long, ever-y day."

Our group came away with a significant combined number of crafts. I bought seven sets of chopsticks for gifts. I thought of Dad. He would've been fascinated with the old guy's craftsmanship.

Ω

The riverboat experience on our return trip contrasted the trip in. First of all, the boat wasn't nearly as nice, nor were its passengers. And Etsuko wasn't there. We sensed a disquieting energy from the start, like we were being watched. Dark, shady characters meandered about in the shadows. Two scrawny-looking guys sat by a wall on deck playing a game involving money, in which the winner takes all. It appeared to be a simple game—easy to play, easy to win. But it turned out to be a scam. Several of our group watched with intrigue, then were lured to join in. Unbeknownst to any of us, the two dudes were working together. In the end, innocence proved costly. Several kids lost the equivalent of 25 dollars before catching on to their scheme. It was a good lesson in Brazilian riverboat gaming and in trustworthiness.

By now our group had become the center of attention. Other characters were inspired by how easy it was to swindle money from the Americans. So, all thirteen of us became targets. Keen to the situation, Arturo and Eiji warned us, "Keep your valuables and passports protected and out of sight. Guard your packs. Leave nothing unattended."

We stayed together, feeling heavy stares from dark eyes. In daylight hours, we felt better equipped to fend off any thievery. But as nightfall approached, apprehensions increased. We scheduled hour-long "bandito watches" throughout the night, with two of us on duty at a time. Watchmen's tasks were defined: keep a close eye on the group's possessions, make yourselves visible, and send a clear message to all potential crooks, "No way Jose, not on my watch!" As with banjer watch aboard the *Statsraad Lehmkuhl*, the riverboat watchmen moved around.

In the wee hours of night, during my watch, two men crawled underneath several students' hammocks. I quickly positioned myself next to them and stayed until they left. None of us lost anything that night beyond the initial cash to the game swindlers. And, oh yes, Emil lost his dinner. Several times he hung over the rail and puked his brains out. Malcom was amused by it all and snapped photos—certainly not the most sensitive thing for a good southern boy to do. But it added humor to a night that needed more.

We disembarked in Belém at 06:00 with all our possessions, emotionally and physically exhausted. But we decided to extend our time to include breakfast in the city, postponing our reacclimation to life aboard ship. Then I got sick—acute stomach and earache, fever, and pain throughout my body. I stayed in bed for the rest of the afternoon. It must've been a reaction to something I ate or drank.

With Brazilian cruzeiros still in my pocket and feeling slightly better, I eventually dragged myself from bed and walked into town in the early evening, then spent my remaining cash on a wide-rimmed sombrero. Diarrhea had mostly depleted my insides, and now my pockets were empty as well. I kept walking, just wanting to be alone, but happened upon Joe Feinblatt and Yappi who invited me to join them for dinner. Joe's treat. How could I say no to that?

Yappi, aside from being black as night, had a strong build, deep voice, and was a great storyteller. He also flashed the biggest, whitest teeth I had ever seen—whiter than the tons of ivory pilfered from his country over the years. During dinner, he entertained Joe and me with stories from his homeland, starting first with his process of joining Oceanics.

He had heard about the program from a random source in the Ivory Coast. Having nothing better to do, nothing to look forward to, and nothing to lose, he decided to contact the Oceanics School by mail, hoping that he placed enough postage on the envelope to reach New York. After that, he gave it little thought.

"In Africa we haven't much opportunity for anything. Especially travel. So, if we hear of something, even if it's impossible, we must at least try. Things don't ever work out. We accept that. To protect ourselves from disappointment, we learn not to hope," he said. Then with a big smile lighting up his entire face, Yappi continued, "Within several weeks I received a response from Stephanie!" Extending his arms straight above his head and clasping his hands, he shouted, "I was accepted into the program with a full scholarship!"

His parents embraced the opportunity with nearly as much enthusiasm as he did. Listening to Yappi retell his story in that Brazilian café was an experience not soon to be forgotten, giving me goosebumps of appreciation.

Riverboat to Tome-Acu, Brazil

Dugout canoe on the Amazon River

Peter Poulsen and Janet Johnson at the wheel

Good winds heading northeast from Brazil

CHAPTER 16: TCHAU BELÉM

There was no send-off from folks on shore as we pulled away from the docks in Belém. No bums begging for money or prostitutes lining the dock, no vendors peddling their wares, and no attention from the press at the end of our eight-day visit. A Spanish cruise ship and a German freighter respectfully sounded their horns as we motored toward the Atlantic Ocean. Group C had standby watch, followed by four hours on duty as nightfall approached. The sky was filled with stars but void of the moon. It felt like home. I wrapped myself in a blanket and lay atop the galley, enjoying the freshness of the air and the amazing sky, despite my continued stomach issues.

For some reason after leaving Belém, galley food was lousy again. My room-mates and I discussed it and figured the budget must have been slashed. Food was our indicator of how well Chick and Stephanie's fundraising was going. The sometimes-tasty fluffy pancakes became nothing more than terrible-tasting shitty starch that sank quickly to the bottom of our stomachs like a ship's anchor in the sea. Frank and Arturo made light of the food situation, turning disgust into humor. That was surely better than complaining.

I opened the refrigerator door one day to pour myself a glass of water, just as the ship rocked hard to port side. The entire contents of the refrigerator crashed onto the floor - two full pitchers of milk, trays of cheese and lunch meats, mayon-naise, caviar, liverwurst, and more. It was a real seaman's mess! If ever there was a time for me to cuss, it was then. But I managed only an embarrassed, "Oh shit!"

The days once again had no beginning or end because of the sea schedule. Jaime started an early morning exercise class at 06:00 each day. Regular attend-ees included Jones, Todd, Willy, Gerry, and me, depending on our watch shifts. My stomach bug from Brazil lingered. Bouts of diarrhea, nausea, stomach cramps, and fever continued for several days. And sometimes I felt light-headed. Poulsen found out and wouldn't allow me to climb. I understood but it felt like an overre-action, a punishment for being sick.

Good winds carried the ship northwest at eight to ten knots. However, wind direction and currents were nearly perpendicular to the ship from the northeast, making it difficult to maintain directional coordinates without drifting toward the coast of Guyana. Schnitler calculated us to be going sideways at nearly two knots while listing strongly toward port. Several square sails had to be taken in to help correct the situation, but it also slowed our speed forward.

Lookout watch was great as the waves rolled and broke, shooting white foam high into the air and spraying mist onto the deck. Still in the tropics, I continued to wear as little clothing cover as possible, allowing the fresh mist to cool my skin. There was no better feeling on a hot day.

Ship's work and classes continued for nine days at sea. Complaints were minimal among the students, except about the food. Bones, fat, and gristle were served far too often. The stench lingered for a full day in the union mess and into the banjers after each serving. Maybe I was over-sensitive to the smell, but I made a habit of sleeping somewhere on deck.

One afternoon Todd and I were working together on the halfdeck, scraping and sanding varnish. It wasn't unusual for us to entertain thoughts of mischief. That day Todd suggested we count to three, then throw our scrapers as far as possible into the sea. Previously when we did something of the sort, we'd first agree on the act, then shake hands, sealing our deal to follow through. If one of us didn't do it, he owed the other two dollars. This time, however, the handshake didn't happen, and I wasn't certain either of us had fully committed to the toss.

Todd impatiently counted to three and lofted his good metal-blade scraper a mile into the sea. I stood frozen in place, momentarily stunned, then broke into a belly laugh on the halfdeck. It was too funny for words. But Todd wasn't laughing and demanded payment. We didn't settle our dispute that day or the next. In fact, it wasn't settled for a long time. Both of us were convinced we were right, and neither of us were willing to give in. There was one major difference, however: I was humored by it all while Todd was thoroughly pissed off. And he remained so.

My evenings off duty were often spent in the music room listening to piano concerts by Arturo or guitar duels between him and Dave Freedman. That room continued to be an escape for me from the activities above. I enjoyed low-key conversations there with my friends. Like Clark. He was one of the loners aboard who was blessed with a brilliant mind and who could intelligently discuss anything with anyone who seriously engaged him. On occasion he and I chose to discuss things we knew absolutely nothing about, calling it imaginative dialogue. Nonsensical by nature, it passed the time.

The haircut craze was long over, but one night, unprompted, Blake cut his hair. Wow, no one expected that! He was a very handsome guy. Not that cutting his hair made him more so, but it revealed his face and eyes, and broadened his occasional smile. Previously, his long, straggly, unkempt hair hid most of his expressive qualities. The haircut looked good.

Relationships aboard were constantly changing and developing. Lucy had a crush on First Mate Schnitler for a long while, maybe from the start. Eventually those feelings became mutual, although she and Hans both applied discretion; no one was sure when their romance started. Officers weren't necessarily held to higher standards than average sailors, but their circumstances were more complicated. Lucy was a cadet, not just a lady of the night at a foreign port. Although protocol for an officer-cadet relationship didn't apply in the same way as a teacher-student relationship in a regular school setting, guidelines would have suggested against it. Schnitler and Lucy's affair became public in Belém, and before we reached Trinidad a rumor had spread that they were planning to get married in Port of Spain. Lots of questions followed. Was she pregnant? How would Stephanie handle this situation? And what about the captain? Gossip circulated throughout the community onboard.

Yappi, me, Billy K, Birdman, Schnitler, Tim Harris

Steel drums

Mardi Gras costumes

160

CHAPTER 17: TRINIDAD

On Thursday, March 1, at 09:00 hours, a pilot boarded ship and ordered us to anchor a mile from the dock at the Gulf of Paria, which made little sense to us. Within minutes, two immigration officers came onboard checking everyone's passports and nationalities. Folks from the Office of Tourism then boarded and presented a quick verbal introduction to the island, suggesting things to see and do. They also helped arrange travel and tours for the next few days. Notably, it was Carnival time in Trinidad—the biggest, wildest celebration of the entire year. They explained details of the busy weekend ahead and the festivities leading up to the two biggest days of Carnival, next Monday and Tuesday.

"Things will get very crazy," one man explained, warning of pickpockets, rip-offs, drunks, drug dealers and the like. "Unfortunately, the city will not be safe for kids to walk alone, especially after dark. Make sure you are always in the company of at least one other person."

I thought to myself, "Why are we here at this time?" The forewarnings of thousands of folks getting crazy felt unnerving to me. But it also triggered excitement. Carnival in Trinidad was a big deal, and I wasn't one to shy away from new adventures. Birdman and Clark shared my mixed sentiments, but most students were thrilled beyond caution by the possibilities of this grandiose event.

George, Malcom, Alec, Katie, and I left the ship together at 18:30 to begin our exploration of Port of Spain. Although the written language in Trinidad is English, its spoken version is different from any English dialect I had heard before. The islanders speak fast, placing accents on different syllables than American English. I sometimes found it difficult to identify a single word in an entire sentence. Reading menus, street signs and billboards was fine, just not the verbal stuff.

In time, I separated from the group and eventually met up with Birdman, who also was wandering alone. We walked into a Portuguese club and shot several games of pool before having burgers at a local dive. It had been a long time since either of us ate a decent burger. We were not disappointed. Birdman was one of the kids who still hadn't cut his hair, appearing very much like an American freak. Maybe that had bearing on why we were approached several times by drug dealers. "Thanks, but no thanks," was my response. However, the temptations kept getting better.

We were solicited by two young charmers. The girls were good conversation-alists and aware of the school-ship anchored close to port. The taller one put her arm around my neck, kissed me on the cheek, smiled, then urged me to follow her to the upstairs apartment across the street. "Only ten dollars for one hour," she whispered, "I'll give you amazing pleasure." There was no chance of misinterpreting that. She was forthright and very sweet. I found it difficult to say no, mostly because I hated hurting her feelings. Seriously. (As crazy as that sounds!) But I had been through this before and knew I wasn't up for the emotional consequences.

CC was a beautiful dark-skinned street girl, probably younger than me, just trying to make a buck. Her sad eyes of rejection haunted me as I walked away. I wished I could befriend her beyond the services she offered. But I knew that wasn't possible. Some days I felt stronger, wiser, and seemed better able to apply lessons I had learned. This was one of those days.

Birdman grinned, not overly concerned about her feelings. "She's acting," he exclaimed, "She'll find someone else." He then suggested we get out of town for a few days. I agreed. However, our adventures in the city weren't over. Within minutes it was his turn to fend off the street freaks. A homely looking soul walked up to him and asked for a quarter. Rather than saying no, Birdman explained that he had only a twenty-dollar bill—certainly not the right thing to tell someone on the street. The guy insisted he could find a place to get change and led us to several retail stores. I'm still not sure why we followed. Even commercial vendors refused to break the twenty. Finally, Birdman and his new sidekick went into a Chinese restaurant. The manager explained he would trade two tens for the twenty but nothing smaller. That still didn't solve the problem, but Birdman did the exchange anyway.

As the man handed him the two tens, the other dude grabbed one from his hand, tearing it in half. Suddenly, the situation had gotten worse. Neither he nor Birdman were willing to give up their half. But the guy insisted he could find tape to repair the bill, then convinced Birdman to give up his half after he found a piece of tape. Big mistake. The guy quickly turned and ran across the street into a second-floor house of ill repute. I chased him to an upstairs landing where he disappeared down a narrow hallway into one of the rooms. He was fast. I wasn't crazy enough to start opening doors in that place for someone else's ten bucks.

Birdman was somber when I rejoined him on the sidewalk. Losing money was disheartening. Even more reason to leave town as soon as possible. The next morning, we wrote out a detailed field trip plan and presented it to administrators Steve and Mike. They approved it within fifteen minutes. After securing replacements for our scheduled watch shifts, we left ship with our packs, then invited Malcom to join us. But he couldn't find anyone to cover his shifts soon enough, and we decided not to wait.

Our plan was to spend a few days by the Caroni Swamp. That's what Steve and Mike approved. But after acquiring a map at the Tourist Office, we decided to head to the north coast instead. It was on the complete opposite side of the island from Port of Spain. We figured the further from the capital, the better. According to a map, there appeared to be a beach directly in front of the mountains on the north side.

Blanchisseuse (blan-chee-shears) is a small village located in the center of the north coast of Trinidad, accessible only by one narrow paved road from the south. We boarded a bus out of Port of Spain to Arima, after first fending off a pimp who insisted on hooking us up with two girls, supposedly nieces of a local banker who wanted desperately to meet American boys. The guy went as far as to order and pay for a taxi to the Danish Hotel across town. Birdman and I nodded to each other, then hopped in the taxi with the pimp. We were less naïve than it appeared; we had our own plan. I ordered the cabbie to take us to the bus depot, overriding prior instructions. The pimp became argumentative, but the cab driver was on our side from the start and paid him no mind. A few blocks further at a traffic light, Mr. Pimp jumped out, cursing, and shaking his fist at the cabbie and at us. Birdman didn't smile much on a regular basis, but he did this time. We had just managed to get a free cab ride.

In Arima we bought pastries at a corner bakery. Two eighteen-year-old guys sat down at our table, Reynold Williams and Herman Joshua. After realizing we came to Trinidad by ship, they insisted on stowing away with us on the *Statsraad Lehmkuhl*. They weren't kidding. I explained that wouldn't be possible. Then they politely asked to join us on our trek to the north coast. We both said no, kindly but firmly, making clear the purpose of our getaway. The island boys seemed to understand, nodded, and went their way.

While buying bus tickets for Blanchisseuse, I met a guy in line, also heading north to the same town. Frederick was friendly and decent, appearing to be someone we could trust. He planned to visit his aging father for a few days and thought it best to leave town during Carnival. Interestingly, he invited us to his father's house for the night. "The house is next to the beach. There is an extra room. My father will be honored to have you visit him."

By now we were growing weary of all the unwanted attention, demands of our time, and offers we didn't trust. Birdman and I were both set on camping without obligating ourselves to anyone. So, we declined his offer but continued talking with Frederick as we boarded the bus. Just then I turned to see Reynold and Herman sprinting down the street toward the ticket booth with packs over their shoulders. They boarded the bus to Blanchisseuse!

The twenty-four-mile ride over the mountain was beautiful, but not relaxing. Our bus driver was completely crazy. Thankfully, there was no opposing traffic as we bounced, rattled, and hummed through turns and rough terrain on the narrow mountainous road leading north. The smell of hot rubber permeated throughout the bus. At one point the brakes gave out completely. It felt to me like the bus could come apart at any moment. But the driver motored on with no concern for anything or anyone's comfort. His only task was to transport passengers to Blanchisseuse. And he did just that.

Upon arrival, we headed toward the beach. Reynold and Herman followed close behind, again explaining they wanted to join us for the night. They knew a good place to camp, and they had their own food. Also, they claimed they wouldn't be an imposition.

Although things hadn't gone exactly as planned, Birdman and I warmed up to the boys. The four of us walked along the beach and found a path leading up to a flat grassy area atop a small cliff overlooking the sea. That's where we set up camp. Palm trees towered above, swaying in the breeze. We ate bananas, cheese, and bread, then sipped red wine by the sea using coconut shells for cups. The best part was watching the crashing waves shoot white foam high into the air from the rocky shoreline as squawking seagulls dodged and weaved noisily overhead.

We gathered huge palm branches and laid them on the ground for bedding. I wrapped up in a sheet inside the small pup tent I borrowed from Sam, leaving the front flap open. The other three slept under the stars. Reynold and Herman again shared their desire to leave Trinidad, hoping to make a better life in the States. Birdman and I listened without comment while the boys discussed their future and smoked Trinidadian weed. My high came from the setting itself, from the beautiful sky, the soothing sounds of the sea, and from the warm breeze.

"It doesn't get better than this," I said aloud to no one in particular, before saying good night and closing the tent flap. It rained several times during the wee hours of morning, but the showers were brief, each lasting only minutes.

As the sun rose the next morning above the jungle to the east, birds sang beautifully, sometimes as soloists, sometimes in harmony with each other. Birdman, Reynold, and Herman shared a joint down by the water before breakfast. I enjoyed my quiet time of reflection high above them on the cliff's edge, in the non-smoking section.

The two native boys climbed coconut trees as fast and easily as most folks climb stairs. I watched enviously, wishing I could do the same, but knowing my feet weren't calloused enough for the task. They grabbed four coconuts, one for each of us, then cut holes in the tops for drinking. We had leftover bread, bananas, cheese, fresh mangos, and coconut for breakfast. Plenty for everyone. Then we stashed our packs behind several large rocks by the edge of the jungle and walked a kilometer along the rugged coast to a beautiful sandy area. The setting was perfectly situated with a freshwater pond surrounded by lush green plants 200 feet back from the sea. We had the entire place to ourselves, juggling time between the pond and sea.

I suppose the only thing missing for me was a quiet, gorgeous girl with whom to share this experience. The place was remarkably romantic. I thought of CC. If only she was as interested in adventure and fun as she was in hooking. Confusing thoughts meshed my ideals with her livelihood.

Instead, I spent my time with new friends enjoying the serenity of our natural surroundings. It was a great day and the perfect antidote to Carnival in the city. Birdman and I concluded that the north coast of Trinidad was absolutely the best kept secret of the entire island, without needing to prove our point to anyone. This is the true value of secrets—no one else knows.

By late afternoon the four of us started walking down the winding road toward Arima. After an hour, we heard the bus rumbling from behind. Cautiously, we flagged it down from the side of the road, not trusting the driver to stop. But he did and we quickly found seats in the back. That was a mistake—we should've known better. The continuous bouncing, tossing, and turning on our way south didn't win favors with any of the passengers. Two old ladies seated in the center section yelled at the driver, demanding that he slow down. But their words fell on deaf ears as he leaned forward, nose to the windshield and eyes glued to the road, never blinking. He stayed focused on things in front, with no regard for anything behind. Again, the bus brakes overheated and gave out, only to recover within several minutes. That appeared to be part of the daily routine on this route. I suppose it didn't matter because with or without brakes, the driver didn't change how he drove.

In Arima Birdman and I bid farewell to Reynold and Herman. They had proven themselves to be fun, decent guys after all. We didn't mind hanging out with them for two days. Again, we visited the little bakery in Arima for pastries and ice-cold milk.

After an hour's wait, the bus for Port of Spain pulled into the small terminal. Then, as we boarded, Reynold and Herman came bounding down the sidewalk, just like before! They again climbed aboard with their packs! "You've gotta be kidding me," I exclaimed to Birdman. This time it felt very strange and awkward. Their persistence to stow away with us was unbelievable! We determined not to take them anywhere close to the ship. Their behavior had become alarming. Although it was out of character for both of us, Birdman and I needed to be more assertive. No more giving in. No more being nice guys.

I became nervous and sullen. "Who are these guys? What do they want from us?" Something had changed. Both boys appeared desperate. Reynold was agitated about something after he found his seat. He began talking loudly and making fun of passengers sitting nearby. Then he hit on some guy's wife, and the situation became stranger by the minute. The guy stood up and pushed Reynold back, telling him to stay away from his lady and shut up.

A vicious fight broke out, as the two tussled back and forth in the aisle, fast and furious, cursing and throwing punches. Finally, the conductor and another guy broke it up, but the driver was shaken as he watched the scene unfold from the mirror above his windshield. Nervously, he high tailed full throttle down the road toward the capital, stopping for no one. Passengers yelled and rang the bell for their stops, but he paid them no mind.

As the bus barreled through villages, pedestrians scurried out of the way, shouting obscenities with raised fists. In one town there was a small police station by the side of the road. The driver slammed on the brakes, jumped out through the side door, and was immediately met by two officers who grabbed him by the shoulders, thrusting his arms behind his back. He pleaded with them to hear him out. After a brief conversation, the cops boarded the bus and cuffed both Reynold and the disgruntled husband, then hauled them off. Birdman and I said nothing at all but hung onto the seatback in front of us as the bus rumbled toward the capital. Despite our varying experiences with Trinidadian street behavior, we both were shocked by this latest episode.

After some time, the driver seemed to calm down slightly. Then someone lit up a joint in the back of the bus. That was it. He had had enough! The rest of the way to Port of Spain he again stopped for no one—no drop-offs and no pickups. Folks tried flagging him down along the way, but he shouted out the window repeatedly, "No more riders, defective bus!" He also yelled at passengers, now hostages, who wanted off, "SIT DOWN AND SHUT UP!" The locked-down locals inside the bus became furiously anxious. One woman, who was supposed to pick up her two small children started wailing uncontrollably as the bus passed by her stop. Few onboard were amused by the drama, aside from Birdman and me. For us, it was just another unbelievable adventure. We were indeed strangers in a very strange land.

The mile-long launch ride from the dock to the ship was particularly nice. Poulsen was at the helm, dependable, steady, and as proficient as anyone anywhere in the world. It was great to see a familiar face we could trust. And it was comforting to separate from the island crowds as we boarded the wonderfully quiet ship.

Just before crawling into bed, I was asked to cover Kovacik's two-hour watch. He had inadvertently left on a field trip without finding shift replacements. I understood how and why that could happen. I also understood the consequences of missing a watch. And after our recent experiences, covering someone's shift seemed like the easiest task in the world. It was after midnight when I finally flopped down on my bunk. It could have been worse.

At 04:00 hours I was awakened by Clark. He had just come off his two-hour fire watch and needed to find a replacement for Todd's two-hour gangway shift. Todd had also left town without filling his post. So, I did his shift as well. Sleep had a way of eluding me aboard ship.

Then came a much-needed blessing as I experienced the beautiful pre-dawn sky. I felt something so real, so promising, and so innocently hopeful about the start of this new day, even anchored a mile out in the Gulf of Paria. Maybe I was grasping at straws to stay positive, but a divine spirit seemed to be bursting from the atmosphere, bouncing up from the gangway, reflecting from the galley windows, and swooping down from the yards above in an indescribable sensory surround-sound silence.

Few kids showed up for breakfast that morning. I devoured eleven sunny-side-up eggs—that's right, eleven—and a ton of bacon, curing both hunger and emotional discomfort from my unplanned night on duty.

The US Ambassador to Trinidad and a few of his staff came aboard ship for lunch and to address the students. We were asked to dress up in our best formal attire. The Ambassador's speech emphasized the island's beauty and culture—all positive stuff for sure. But by now I had experienced the realities of Trinidad, including the scum of its undergarments. I suppose the real beauty of any place is not just visual but knowing its entirety. That includes a sense of its history, understanding its weaknesses, and celebrating its strengths. There wasn't a follow-up question and answer time to the Ambassador's presentation of praises for the island. Lucky for him. He was scheduled to dine with Captain Fossa, Mike, Steve and Debbie, and several officers.

After student lunch in the mess hall, shipmates headed in different directions. I considered joining Barry and Stein for a trip to the beach, but overheard Zoe and Linda discussing a place in the mountains—Blue Basin Falls. According to the literature, it was a two-hour drive from Port of Spain. The girls intended to hitchhike there together but invited me to go along at the last minute.

Zoe was one of the quietest students onboard, attractively so. She remained a low-key kid who avoided conflict and the spotlight whenever possible. Her gentle spirit complemented her soft confidence. But because of social cautions, and the fact that she was part of another work group onboard, I didn't know her well. Linda, along with being superstitious, was less shy than Zoe, but was also a girl with whom I had little interaction. They both appeared surprised that I agreed to join them. Admittedly, they were leery of hitchhiking by themselves.

After acquiring basic directions, the three of us walked north from the docks and stuck out our thumbs. Within minutes a taxi stopped. We were looking for a free ride, not a taxi, certain that his costs would be prohibitive. The driver kindly asked where we were headed.

"Blue Basin Falls," Linda answered, then quickly added that we couldn't afford a taxi.

The taxi driver Micah was a friendly guy with no apparent time constraints. It was Sunday. Despite the festivities of Carnival, the pace in town was more relaxed than previous days, and he was having a slow day. He responded with a shrug, then offered to take us there for four Trinidadian dollars—less than half the regular rate! That was a no-brainer. The girls each chipped in a dollar, I paid two.

Micah smiled when he realized we were from the tall ship anchored in the bay. By now most folks were aware of the school ship's visit to Port of Spain. He shared with us his dreams of sailing someday. Unfortunately, the opportunity never presented itself beyond riding on his grandpa's small fishing boat as a teenager. Although now in his 40s, Micah had never left the island except for a brief visit to Venezuela, seven miles across the bay, also with his grandpa. He told us about his two boys at home, ages eight and ten, both of whom he desired educational opportunities for in the States.

"Trinidad is too small for the next generation to all survive and have a good life here," he said with sad certainty. And he indicated a willingness to sacrifice his own dreams for his sons' chances of achieving theirs.

The drive along the west coast was beautiful, as the road curved and eventually climbed high above the sea, then turned inland toward the interior mountains. After a turn-off, we wound our way several kilometers to a small gravel parking area at the end of the narrow road. Micah pointed to a foot path leading into the forest. "The falls is that way," he said and bid us farewell.

The sun felt warm, but the cool mountain air was refreshing as we hiked to the pool basin surrounded by high rock walls on three sides. The water appeared blue but crystal clear. Several local kids had a nice fire crackling on the far side of the beach. Because my decision to join the girls was unplanned, I had no swimwear or towel. The girls came prepared. Before we entered the water, they both removed their shirts and shorts stripping down to bikinis. Then Linda asked me with a sly grin, "Are you taking anything off?"

"I've got nothing underneath," I replied as we waded along the edge of the pool and circled toward the 70-foot falls at the backside. The water became gradually deeper as we approached the front of the falls. So, I had a choice, either go back to the rocky beach and watch, or remove my clothes and continue. It became a group decision as the girls coerced me to be a sport and override my tendency for modesty. Zoe commented convincingly, "Marlie, we don't care what you're not wearing, we just want you to stay with us to the falls." She then smiled and waited for my response.

Without saying a word, I stripped down, folded my clothing, and stashed them under a rock, feeling more than a little self-conscious. But the clear refreshing mountain water redirected my attention as the three of us dove, swam, and played under the falls. My inhibitions vanished as well and my time with Zoe and Linda at Blue Basin Falls proved to be the best time I'd had since arriving in Trinidad.

After drying myself by the fire, I spotted Jill and Lilly approaching the pool from the trail. They had also found their way to this beautiful place. I dressed quickly.

By early evening, Zoe, Linda, and I hitched back to Port of Spain, needing just one ride.

Fully costumed Carnival dancers had already filled the streets as we ate burgers and watched the action from a sidewalk cafe. The orchestral sound of steelpans was amazing as the city came to life. But nothing in town could top my day at the Falls.

Ω

Bill Bacon had just finished his gangway shift as we boarded ship. He pulled me aside and asked me to join him, Tara, and Eiji at the Hilton in one hour. After changing into more formal clothes, the four of us hailed a taxi to midtown. The first-class Hilton was a contrast to our sailors' norm. A uniformed doorman welcomed us through opened glass doors, then escorted us into a plush lobby. From there, Tara led us up one level to a balcony bar overlooking the street below. She had been there before with Stephanie. We sipped creatively named drinks and caught up with the latest news concerning the Oceanics program.

Being a summer employee at the Oceanics office in New York, Tara was privy to information many of us were not. She told us that day that Mike was leaving ship for several weeks, maybe more. But more surprising, she explained that Eiji was taking over Mike's position onboard!

I looked at Eiji, who remained expressionless seated next to me, then I blurted out, "That's a joke, right?" He remained speechless, glancing momentarily at Tara, then nodded in agreement.

Faculty members were divided about some major issues on board. Money was at the core. Supposedly, the administration hadn't been paid for several months. Tara also explained that Captain Fossa was lonely and wanted to head back to Norway as soon as possible. Our conversation in the Hilton lounge was heavy, but as time passed, the mood lightened.

Bill had a knack for creating timely humor, regardless of what was at stake. He ordered another round of sophisticated drinks, and in time the four of us laughed our way out of the Hilton. We walked to The Savana near downtown where we all ate hot rotis. They were more mouth-burning hot than good, but never mind that, Carnival activities were now in full swing.

Downtown Port of Spain was packed with folks donning flamboyant, brilliantly colored costumes. Spikes and wings extended high and wide alongside exotic dancers, musicians, steel drums, drunks, topless men and women, and thousands of spectators-turned-participants. All were commemorating Carnival 1973 with little regard for time, noise, self-dignity, or the welfare of fellow celebrants. It was just one huge, wild, iniquitous party as the city proclaimed its sins of the flesh. I didn't need Uncle Dan's presence to determine that. Although incredibly fascinating and exciting, Carnival vibes stretched well beyond my nineteen years of Lancaster County Mennonite cultural teaching. And honestly, even beyond what I could now absorb as a partially seasoned Norwegian sailor.

After a night on the town, we slowly made our way back toward the ship, then joined several Norwegian crewmen for a beer at a dock-dive, Cowboy Jack's Ranch Bar. Although curfew was extended to 03:00 hours, we managed to make the 01:00 launch back to safety. As expected, the night was far from over, both in the city and aboard the *Statsraad Lehmkuhl*. At 03:00, I heard a terrible sound coming from the dayroom—blood-curdling screams and cursing. I jumped from my bunk to see what was happening. The scene was violent as Chuck and Emil were engaged in a vigorous fight, as if to kill each other.

Chuck was normally expressive, but not violent. No one aboard had seen him like this. His screams were uncharacteristic. Jones arrived in the dayroom seconds before me. Without assessing the situation, he attacked Emil in a rage, throwing punches, pulling his hair, and screaming, "YOU NO GOOD NIGGER!"

I stood paralyzed as others came on the scene. Able-bodied seaman Arne jumped in without throwing punches, truly trying to separate Jones and Emil. Meanwhile, Chuck backed away and regained his composure just as Mike bounded into the room and broke up the fight quickly. Without mincing words he exclaimed in a booming voice, "You're both going home!"

I was traumatized by it all. Emil was a friend who I cared deeply about. Jones was my roommate, a guy I had learned to know, accept, and better understand as the year went on. Chuck was a fellow-cadet, a neutral comrade who I always got along with. Not only was this incident confusing, but it was demoralizing. I absolutely hated violence. I despised conflicts. What I had just witnessed felt so wrong, so inhumane.

After processing my thoughts and emotions with Barry for half an hour, I went back to bed. We had a good talk, calculated and void of emotion, of course. I needed that. But sleep was slow in coming as my mind churned like a turbine and my heart pounded like a dry piston. Those guys would have killed each other if given the chance. Alcohol had destroyed their sanity, their ability to reason, their humanity.

Ω

06:30 came much too soon. My group went on duty after breakfast, which included raising a new mesan sail to replace the old one that had developed a tear. The rigging felt like a good place to be after the events of last night. Birdman and I engaged in serious conversation, discussing recent happenings within the community. He confessed that he and several others started smoking pot regularly during night watches on the foredeck, just to cope with the difficulties onboard. That was troubling to me, realizing the Oceanics program was in jeopardy if they got caught. Captain was already looking for reasons to take the ship home.

I began preparing for the worst. I received a letter from Dad and Mom that day sharing their plans to meet up with the ship in the Virgin Islands. I was surprised beyond words! How could they possibly do that? Financially or otherwise? The news only added to my apprehensions concerning everything else onboard. I needed time to sort things out.

I borrowed ten dollars from Stein and invited Eiji out for a beer, just to talk. He seemed best equipped to help process my anxieties concerning a possible parental visit. The last thing I wanted was for them to see the mess, to know the truth about what was happening onboard. I trusted Eiji for straight answers. Our evening proved to be the right prescription for my confusion. Discussions drifted from the serious stuff onboard, to past life issues, to plans after the program, to death itself.

Eiji explained that some of the staff wanted the program to end in the Caribbean before recrossing the Atlantic. The captain was wary of that, needing a full crew to sail the ship back to Norway. The recent breakdown in trust sparked uncertainties. My position was clear, however. I wasn't ready for this experience to end and was willing to deal with anything that might happen onboard. I wanted to keep sailing. Things didn't need to be perfect. I would adjust.

Despite everything going on, I was encouraged by Eiji's calm spirit. We sat on the second-floor deck of the Penthouse Restaurant overlooking the street below with intrigue, experiencing the parade of steel drums and another night of celebration on this unique Caribbean Island. I had never heard of steel drums, calypso music, or Carnival before this visit to Trinidad. My sheltered existence exposed my innocence. But during the past months, the dark shades of the world had knocked on my doors, broken through some windows, and infiltrated the shell of my soul. I had seen the Devil's playground. Experienced it. But still, my ingenuousness was not overcome. Still a teenager, I could only hope for enough time to become wise.

A faculty meeting was called to discuss the recent internal crisis among the staff. It was important to reach an agreement in the Caribbean before recrossing the Atlantic. Joe Feinblatt, discouraged by recent events, lack of pay, discord among the administration, and the fact that we were leaving town before the actual two days of Carnival, had already checked availability and costs for flights from Martinique to Los Angeles.

We were scheduled to leave the island on the morning of March 6. After ship cleanup, anchors were pulled, several sails were set, and the ship eased out of the bay at 10:00 hours with a northward heading toward Grenada. There was a new addition to the library—a ping pong table. Someone from the US embassy in Trinidad had donated it to the ship. After our work on deck was done, Billy K and I engaged in several spirited games of ping pong below deck, bringing back fabled memories of my Monday night lunatic experiences at my cousin Pooh's house in Smoketown.

Salty dogs Jacobsen and Johannsen (Morgan Kane)

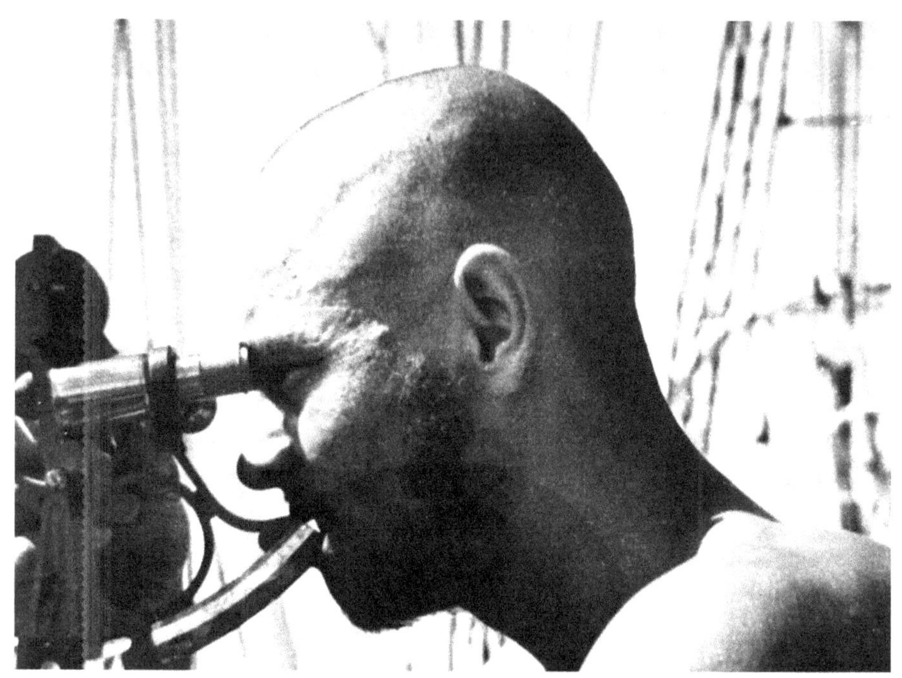

2nd mate Kjemtrup

1st mate Schnitler and Sailmaster Bernes

CHAPTER 18: LEEWARDS

Grenada is a small country made up of several islands in the southern part of the Lesser Antilles—a short one-hundred-mile sail from Trinidad. Its capital, St George's, has a beautiful natural harbor that serves as a central hub for yachts in the eastern Caribbean. Once a British colony, Grenada is also known as the Isle of Spice. Its main island is oval-shaped, thirty miles long and twelve miles wide, with a lush green mountainous interior.

I woke at 06:00 on March 7 as daylight beckoned through the cabin porthole. Being off duty, our group wasn't involved in ship's work. I was surprised after ascending the stairs to see the town of St George's less than a quarter mile off starboard. Again, we anchored and shuttled between ship and shore. But first I played several games of ping pong with Robert and Martin. The competition really wasn't great—I didn't lose a single match. Not that day or any day after.

Sam, Rick Goodfriend, and I spent several hours walking, first around a small bay, then to the marina where a host of beautiful yachts were docked. We engaged with several boat owners who were intrigued by the *Statsraad Lehmkuhl* anchored several thousand feet from shore. That was our ticket to privilege at the marina. We were permitted to go where we pleased and were treated with honor.

Sailing is highly respected in Grenada, so local folks felt fortunate to be visited by a square-rigger. We didn't turn down offers of free beer and food at the bar as we kicked back and answered silly questions. The three of us stayed mostly positive concerning our duties and life onboard ship and had an unexpectedly good time with several wealthy yacht owners who paid for absolutely everything. I didn't spend a dime.

As evening approached, we sat by the second-floor window of a small French restaurant in town overlooking the bay, eating simple teenagers' food: burgers, fries, and rum & Coke. The place was the best of the best in town, held in high esteem by local folks. Several shipmates found their way there as well.

Upon first arriving in Grenada, a handful of students called home and were told by their parents that someone from the Oceanics office contacted them soliciting additional funds to keep the school operational. News circulated quickly among the kids that the program was in trouble. And the reality of our school year ending soon became more probable. How quickly things had changed.

With no responsibilities onboard, I spent my second day in Grenada at the beach with friends. We first bought bananas, cookies, bread, peanut butter, and honey, then five of us hitched rides several miles down the beautiful palm-lined coast near the Holiday Inn. The water was crystal clear, by far the cleanest ocean water I had ever seen. Great for snorkeling, a great day in the sun.

Then in the mid-afternoon, we noticed a small, strange looking sailboat heading toward shore. Kjemtrup and five cadets from the ship had rigged up a small, single sail mast on one of the lifeboats, lowered it to the water, and sailed across the bay. Peter was proud of his new creation. In fact, he was so excited he and his crew forgot to pack any food. They hung out with us for a good while, then offered rides back to the ship in exchange for food. It was a fair trade. Those of us already at the beach combined our existing food, then bought, borrowed, and begged enough to provide a picnic for everyone. And Kjemtrup's sailboat was large enough to transport all ten of us safely back to the ship with the help of a stiff Caribbean breeze. The greatest thrill was sailing with Peter on this small boat adventure. His childlike exuberance was more refreshing than the water.

I joined Sam, Ellie, Zoe, and Amor for an early evening dinner in town. The problem was, none of us had money. Grenada proved to be more expensive than any place we had visited thus far. We could've eaten onboard, but that didn't appeal to any of us as we were becoming spoiled by the island's wealth.

Someone suggested bumming money on the streets. It was the best idea we could come up with. And it was something new. None of us had pan-handled before. After mutual encouraging words and back pats, we went our separate ways in town, agreeing to meet up half an hour later, hopefully with cash. Begging felt awkward but most folks on the streets were sympathetic. A few engaged us after realizing we were kids from the ship. And our pitch was simple but true: we needed money for dinner.

Ellie was a natural, being a great conversationalist and storyteller. The rest of us weren't privy to what she said, but she pocketed far more cash during that half hour than anyone else. She was known to sometimes embellish the truth and flat out lie if the situation called for it. And she could do it without flinching. Her tactics made up for the timidity demonstrated by Zoe and Amor. I wasn't convinced that Ellie had never done this before, but regardless, she was willing to share her proceeds with us fellow beggars. So, all five of us were able to buy full meals, including dessert, plus two rum & Cokes each.

Grenada wasn't exactly a great cultural experience, but it surely was a fun place to relax and enjoy rare luxuries. Richie was probably the only cadet who truly considered the all-white, rich man's yacht club to be an experience of culture.

At 23:00, an attendance muster was called to make sure everyone was onboard. The anchors were then raised, and we sailed into the night. Our destination was a deserted island further north. Again, Group C was off duty. Sometimes things just worked out that way.

Ω

After the 05:30 whistle, we all reported for cleaning stations, followed by a breakfast of beans, bacon, and corn flakes. We then dropped anchor a quarter mile offshore from a small island with no town, no dock, no buildings, no roads, no electricity, and no running water. We were told there were also no inhabitants. A sandy beach with small shrubs and trees gave way to a grassy meadow plateau high above the sea. I grabbed a towel, blanket, several snacks, and my recorder and jumped on the first launch ashore.

With no place to tie up, we hopped out of the launch into a small cove and waded the last fifteen feet to shore. Sam and I explored the island together, walking through patches of cactus and other prickly desert plants as we ascended the hill. We came upon a large grass field where several goats were grazing, tended by three boys sitting under a weathered three-sided shed. One of the boys, Diego, joined Sam and me for an hour. He led us to an overlook near the center of the island where we could see for miles in every direction. From there the Caribbean waters appeared incredibly blue.

Diego pointed out several coral reefs as we descended the opposite slope to the sea. I estimated the island to be about one mile wide. Fish swam freely in the clear waters by the shore. There were numerous, whole, unbroken conch shells on the beach. Their numbers made sense as no one was there to collect them. Sam and I behaved like little kids reliving our childhood days: building sandcastles, swimming, running, collecting shells then tossing them into the water, all the while basking in the warm March Caribbean sun.

We later met up with Bill Bacon, Rufus, Perry, and Frutchi, who added creative new slants to our already humor-filled conversations. It was a carefree day away from our normal responsibilities. No one knew what country we were in. That was a never mind. Without immigration officers, reporters, pilots, pickpockets, prostitutes, pimps, and bums, Bill Bacon figured there also were no rules. I agreed.

The galley cooks prepared a barbecue feast on the beach, shipside. They found plenty of rocks to build a fire pit, and enough scattered driftwood to burn. Burgo and Johnnie brought griddles and a big pot for beans from the ship, then constructed a grill. Their menu was simple, but a sailor's dream: beef steaks, beans, warm bread, fresh fruit, and beer. With plenty of everything. Suddenly, the moods and feelings within our community felt more positive than they had in a long time! Maybe the combination of good food, booze, and freedom is what our broken community needed. Back to basics!

Eiji brought a huge jug of cheap port wine ashore. After dinner, he, Sam, Kevin, and I walked to a secluded place on the beach, sat by the water and passed the open jug around and around and around. We had no cups, so we drank directly from the heavy jug. Initially, we needed assistance to lift it to our mouths. In time, after each round, the jug lightened. But before each swig, we named something we missed about home. The exercise was tearfully serious at first, but the wine circulated far too many times and eventually we were naming things like lima beans, Grandma's shoes, Uncle Ralph's beard, brother Ted's torn t-shirt, President Nixon's two dogs Pasha and Vicky, and Aunt Barb's bad breath. At some point we appropriately called ourselves 'Characters of the Caribbean.' No one kept track of the time or the laughter, but there was plenty of both. We ran out of things to name about the same time we were overcome with aphasia. Sadly, we all got smashed. Sam was first to stand up, but he couldn't walk. No one could. I passed out in the sand from my sitting position—certainly not one of my prouder moments.

Most of my shipmates slept somewhere on the island that night. A warm, steady breeze reduced bugs and mosquitoes, and the bright moonlight added favor to our setting. Unfortunately, I had no recollection of any of that.

The next morning, I woke in my bunk aboard ship with no clue how I had gotten there. Sand was ground into my forehead, cheeks, and hair. My eyes were bloodshot, and my skin burned from the previous day's unprotected rays. Worst of all was the taste of vomit in my mouth. After making my way to the bathroom, I was appalled by what I saw in the mirror.

Right then and there, I made a vow to never ever become so intoxicated again. With no one to blame but myself, I processed my self-disappointment. It was both depressing and humbling. Another sobering life experience, one for which I had little to say. I was a boy badly in need of grace.

After taking the 10 o'clock launch to the island, I sat alone by the sea, self-reflecting, watching small waves wash ashore, chasing tiny birds feeding by the water's edge. Occasionally fellow students passed by, nodding salutations. It was a mellow time. Clark sat two hundred feet further west, also deep in thought. That was normal for him. He and I didn't need many words to communicate. In that way, this day was no different than any other.

While the afternoon launch hauled cadets back onboard, it was pouring rain, a cleansing rain that required no need for shelter. After two days on the island, we felt like family—all of us, including the crew. It was a much-needed spring break. Now it was time to pull anchor and sail back to reality.

A soft breeze caught the bellies of several staysails as the ship slowly pulled away from nowhere land. I stood by the railing on starboard side, staring at the sea, at the distant islands, and at the beautiful puffy clouds floating effortlessly above, and realized I would never be able to recapture the beauty of this place nor this moment in time. I quietly hummed Joan Baez's song, "Donna Donna": *How the winds are laughing, they laugh with all their might. Laugh and laugh the whole day through, and half the summer's night. Donna, Donna, Donna...* It was nice to be at sea again.

James Thurber's movie, *The War Between Men and Women*, showed in the union that night. It was interesting, creative, and imaginative.

Ω

On Monday, March 11, I woke with the sound of Poulsen's whistle, followed by his booming, "Good morning, it's time to get up!" Everything seemed to be back to normal. Breakfast was great: fried eggs, bacon, fresh grapefruit, and corn flakes. While setting the morning sails, I felt an adrenaline rush as I climbed. More so than usual. I explained my excitement to Poulsen after coming down. He smiled and agreed, "That's why I am here." Although sailing wasn't my primary reason for joining the Oceanics, it was now the reason I didn't want the program to end.

Todd and I had dinner galley duty. We cut lots of vegetables while assisting Burgo, then enjoyed plenty of rewards in the form of grapefruit and pineapple slices. After dinner a German ship did a complete circle around the *Lehmkuhl*. Everyone was on the decks of both ships, waving and saluting. As the German vessel reset its course, it blasted a deep, funny sounding burp, then headed east.

My leisure time was spent playing chess, which had become a popular activity among students and faculty. No one totally dominated, certainly not me, but

Jaime probably won more games than anyone else. His poor English did not translate into poor chess. And as always, he was all smiles.

We docked in Fort-de-France, Martinique at 08:00 after a short forty-hour sail. A box full of student mail from the States awaited us, including a letter from Mom confirming her and Dad's flights to St. Maarten. They planned a short visit from March 14 to 17. It felt like a lot to digest with the uncertainty of our schedule as well as the situation onboard. Not to mention my parents' financial status. They were actively paying school tuition at Lancaster Mennonite High for my three younger sisters, in addition to the outstanding school debts of us older siblings.

Several shipmates also received letters from home concerning possible parental visits in St. Maarten, namely Bill Wright, Katie, and Gary—all of whom shared my concerns about the schedule. Most parents who planned to visit St. Maarten, however, intended to stay for an entire week, so the ship's schedule was less of an issue for them. I found out later that Grossmommie Smucker had offered to finance the trip for Dad and Mom. They certainly couldn't afford it on their own. In that sense, I suppose, the visit seemed a bit irresponsible. Both Dad and Mom knew what they were taught, and what they in turn taught each of us about needless spending. However, Mom desperately wanted to see me, fearing it might be her only opportunity for many months. Maybe forever. My letters home describing the storm, the riverboat experience in Gambia, working in the rigging, and other details, were not consoling. Justification for their trip was confirmed by friends and family who encouraged them to go, no matter the cost. I suppose they decided to make this trip for the right reasons.

Although Martinique was probably an interesting island, I was preoccupied by my parents' planned visit. On our second day there, I was standing on deck and saw three sailors from a Dutch Navy ship at the bottom of the gangway, eyeing the rigging and pointing. Poulsen invited them aboard, then asked me to show them around. The three Dutchmen were full of questions during their hour-long tour, mostly about the school and my routines as a cadet. But also, about the girls' role onboard, and stuff concerning our sea adventures. Before they left, the tallest of the three, Peter Verbeck, invited me to visit the Navy ship later that night. "Bring a few of your friends," he added. We shook hands and planned to meet up at twenty hundred hours.

After dinner, Fredrik invited me to join him, Tor, and Robert in his cabin. The school year had played out oddly with our activities, hectic schedules, and individual survival methods onboard. I could go for days, weeks, even months without having much contact with certain cadets, especially those who were not in my group. That's how it was for me and the Norwegian boys.

During sail training in Bergen, we had become friends. I enjoyed their company as well as their refreshing life perspectives. Finally, on this night in Martinique, the four of us reconnected, shared stories, and rekindled friendships. Tor pulled out a bottle of fine red wine which he poured into four goblets, then made a toast to our individual futures. The Norwegian boys knew their place and seemed committed to making the most of each phase of life, including their time aboard the *Statsraad Lehmkuhl*. I admired their quiet confidence.

Suddenly it became obvious who I should invite aboard the Dutch ship tonight—Tor, Robert, and Fredrik, of course! They smiled and readily accepted my invitation. I asked several other shipmates to join us as well. It was a proud honor to walk up the gangway and be saluted by the attending Naval officer at the gate. He clicked his heels together and stood at attention as we boarded. I was caught off guard by this formality and responded with a hearty "howdy," before realizing I should also salute. Which I did. A second deck officer paged Peter Verbeck over the PA system.

After brief introductions, Peter led our group into a large saloon where there must have been 150 people already in party mode, singing, drinking, smoking, and celebrating whatever the Dutch deemed important that day. The social atmosphere reminded me of the Hofbräuhaus in Munich, Germany. We were well received by the Dutch sailors who escorted us to a table with several other guests from the island. Peter then asked Tor and me to join him for a quick fifteen-minute introduction and guided tour of the chart room with all the latest technology, the ship's radar equipment, and the mounted guns on the foredeck. It was a massive ship towering high above the dock. The *Statsraad Lehmkuhl* appeared small and insignificant by comparison.

The experience felt a bit overwhelming to me, but the three Norwegian boys fit in comfortably and stayed for the evening. I dawdled with the Dutchmen for an hour, enjoyed the free food and beer but socialized guardedly, trying to find my comfort zone. This was a navy ship—unfamiliar territory for a Mennonite boy from Lancaster County. I chuckled at those thoughts as most everything I had experienced since leaving the States was unfamiliar territory.

Mom on the foredeck

Sailing away under staysail power

CHAPTER 19: PARENTAL VISIT

Yappi, Bill Wright, and I walked to the Western Union Telecommunications office in Fort-de-France in the early morning to call home. Mom was thrilled to hear my voice. And I hers. Our connection was impressively clear. Although the conversation lasted just three minutes, Mom told me their plan: she and Dad were flying to St. Maarten the following day. I explained that I'd try to get there somehow about the same time. The ship was scheduled to arrive a day or two later.

Several other students phoned home to arrange with parents as well, then six of us met at Liat Travel Service to book flights to St. Maarten for the next day—226 francs (50 dollars) per person. We each were required to get immigration forms from Captain Fossa because of arriving in Fort-de-France by ship but leaving by plane.

It felt strange standing on the dock with the others, watching the *Statsraad Lehmkuhl*, our home, sail away and head out to sea. For 20 francs, we hired a transport to Martinique Aimé Césaire International Airport where we settled in for the night, sprawled on cushioned benches in the airport lounge. All of us were physically and emotionally exhausted after a stressful day. But worse than that, the mosquitoes buzzing around our heads and the loud, rattling air conditioner prevented any possibility of a good night's sleep.

Airport maintenance woke us at 06:30. We were asked to sit up and make room for other travelers as the small airport was already alive with activity. We had café au lait and bread rolls for breakfast, then we hung out on the terrace watching two planes take off before our eleven o'clock departure. It was not a busy airport.

Our flight to St. Maarten was short. Juliana International Airport was just a few kilometers from the town of Philipsburg where Dad and Mom had hotel reservations. Gary's parents met us when we arrived. The rest of our parents were on a flight out of Puerto Rico which was scheduled to land within the hour.

Everything went as planned. I spotted Mom as soon as she and Dad cleared customs. We ran to each other and embraced for a long time. She was all smiles. At 48 years old, she had just survived her first flying experience. Dad, at 53, appeared relaxed, also smiling broadly as he offered me one of his rare hugs. The joy of the moment overrode my physical and emotional weariness. We caught up on news from home on the fifteen-minute taxi ride to the St. Maarten Isle Hotel. It was a nice reunion.

After checking in, we had dinner on the veranda overlooking the Philipsburg Bay. Views were spectacular from our hotel situated up the hill from the shore. We ate with several of my shipmates and their parents. After introductions, we excitedly shared travel stories and made toasts to our parents for planning this visit to the Caribbean. Dad and Mom connected well with Katie's parents from Minnesota. They seemed to share a similar ideology.

The food and accommodations at the hotel were secondary to our time together. Mom was talkative and happy. She explained how much she enjoyed her flights but seeing me here on an island in the Caribbean was beyond anything she could imagine. I smiled from my soul.

After dinner, we strolled the hotel grounds, relaxed by the pool, then sat on the terrace enjoying the soft sea breeze on this perfectly beautiful evening. None of us had previously experienced this sort of luxury. I felt honored to have my parents make this trip on my behalf. But my biggest thrill was seeing their joy.

While relaxing on our balcony, Mom pulled out the stash of food she brought along: homemade Jell-O, ham, and dried beef loaf sandwiches, three bags of hard pretzels, angel food cake, a slice of cousin Judy Lapp's wedding cake, and cookies from Aunt Sara Ann. Also, an envelope of cash from family and friends. It was all an unexpected treat.

The three of us stayed together in one spacious room at a cost of 80 dollars per night which included meals. The day quickly became a blur as we drifted off to sleep with smiles of contentment on each of our faces. Even Dad's.

Ω

St. Maarten has a total land area of just 37 square miles, divided and owned by both the Netherlands and France. Each side retains its own distinct culture, including language, signage, and food. The borders are opened, allowing easy access for visitors to all parts of the island. Both are blessed with beautiful beaches and landscape, and both recognize the US dollar as acceptable currency. There are several profound differences, however. The Dutch side uses 110 volts, same as the US, whereas the French side uses 220 volts, same as mainland Europe. Philipsburg is the Dutch capital, Marigot the French. Each side has its own international airport and separate country codes for phone usage. Making a call from one side of the island to the other is an international call.

It felt magical to be on our patio at the resort, peering out at the sea. A beautiful morning greeted us. While leaving the dining hall after lunch, I glanced across the bay and saw the *Statsraad Lehmkuhl* floating a half mile from shore! Excitedly, we walked down to the dock and waited. Katie's parents were already there, anticipating an onboard visit as well. Within minutes, Kjemtrup motored up to the dock in the launch with a dozen cadets. Katie and I then escorted our parents to the ship via the launch. Mom quietly dismissed her small boat apprehensions as we crossed the bay. Her biggest challenge was stepping onto the gangway while the launch tossed in the choppy waters. Dad steadied her from behind as I planted my feet on the gangway with outstretched arms, clutching her as she did her step of faith. She had done that step many times before, just not in this literal setting.

We spent the next two hours onboard touring the ship and satisfying my parents' curiosity. Both were fascinated beyond spoken words. Dad, being a small boat designer, was amazed at the size of everything. He was intrigued by the rigging and massive complicated structures above deck, as well as the diesel engine in the hull. He would've happily sailed for a few days if given the chance. Except for his occasional test runs in the Chesapeake Bay and a rare deep-sea fishing trip, he didn't have much opportunity to sail. Boats were his life, but boating was not.

He stood in awe by the big wheel at mid-ship, then checked out the navigation equipment. Mom wanted to see the sleeping quarters, mess hall, library, and galley. She wanted to know more about the program itself, class time, and field trips. But mostly she just wanted to be with me. That was nice. I introduced my parents to friends, faculty, and several officers before returning to Philipsburg. Mom, of course, was as polite as ever, totally trusting everyone's character as she had done throughout her entire life. I suddenly became aware of just how similar she and I were in that regard. I inherited many traits from her, some of which were learned, many of which were simply in our DNA.

We spent time at the beach, then I joined friends in town for several hours. Barry North and I discussed the program and what might happen in the coming weeks. I desperately hoped my parents wouldn't hear any rumblings about that. Mom would only worry. Barry was pragmatic concerning the program and its chances of continuing. He didn't seem to have a clear personal preference or conviction concerning what should happen, appearing to be emotionally removed from the tensions within the administration. I suppose that made sense; emotions can't be calculated.

After dinner, Dad, Mom, and I went shopping for souvenirs and meandered around town. We had a poolside chat during which Mom shared her deepest concerns at home. Like the fact that my sister Carolyn, at 16, was becoming entirely too involved with a guy named Phil. She told me that Dennis Smucker (no relation!), from Bart Mennonite Church, had eloped with his girlfriend, then added that she couldn't really blame him because of his home situation. Also, that John Kennel's brother stabbed his mother to death with a butcher knife. And that my brother Merv planned to go back to Germany the next week after he and cousin John finished helping Uncle Elmer plant shrubbery. It was a nice reminder that life was steadily on par back in PA, and that the world was still alive beyond the *Statsraad Lehmkuhl*. Except, of course, for John Kennel's mom.

It was impossible to share some of my off-ship experiences with them beyond riverboats and upbeat folks I met along the way in Tenerife, Gambia, and Tomé-Açu. How could parents from the spiritually and culturally protected little town of Bird-in-Hand understand my exposure to the wiles of Belém and Port of Spain? I was able to make them laugh with funny stories. That was important. And I managed to write several letters to my siblings for Mom to hand deliver. The evening passed quickly.

The next morning was sunny and nice, just like every day. St. Maarten proved to be the perfect setting for a parental visit. I suggested an island tour for the three of us. We probably wouldn't have another opportunity to be together in the Caribbean. Dad was fascinated by the fact that this small land area was shared by two countries. We booked a private three-hour tour through the hotel with a local driver. Mom laughed when I compared the VW minibus to the famed hippie transports in the US.

First stop was Marigot on the French side. We went to the marketplace before visiting the pier where fishermen unloaded small boats with their catch from the day. A variety of fish and sea creatures, including several lobsters, were thrown into tubs then sold to restaurateurs roaming the dock. Mom thought the fisher-men were rough characters until I reminded her that some of Jesus's disciples were fishermen. "Anyone can be transformed, Mom," I said with a smile.

"Oh Marlie, I guess you're right," she exclaimed with a doubtful look of knowing the truth but wishing it weren't so. I glanced over at Dad who was watching the fishermen with interest, his mouth watering. He loved seafood but seldom had the opportunity to eat it. Mom never learned how to cook fish at home. In fact, recipes for preparing seafood weren't in Amish cookbooks. Dad seldom vocalized his food preferences, humbly keeping those desires to himself and eating whatever was served. My perceptions of my parents had changed since I'd left home in the spring of 1971. I had never given much thought to their wishes and desires while I was growing up. I thoroughly enjoyed watching them in this foreign setting.

Dad was an avid reader. I could still picture him perched on his beloved recliner in the living room, absorbed in a James Michener novel. But now he was here, far from home on an island in the Caribbean experiencing things he had previously only read about. I was reminded how unselfish he and Mom really were. Both were content with what they had. Maybe when someone has lost so much, as both of them had, and when dreams have been shattered by tragedy, expectations change. Maybe they could no longer dream big or hope for things beyond their grasp for fear of more disappointment. All that to say, these three days in the Caribbean were for Dad and Mom to enjoy.

I made sure Dad ate some of the best seafood available. And I reassured Mom that I was safe aboard ship and would remain so for the remainder of the trip. That was most important for her. Having a visual of the ship and trusting the community onboard helped lessen her worry.

Dad was surprisingly engaged in conversation with our driver throughout the tour. Several times he initiated questions concerning the island's history and culture. And he comprehended most everything that was said despite the guide's broken English and heavy accent. Dad certainly wasn't racist, but I'd never seen him interact with a black Frenchman with such enthusiasm and interest. Mom and I did side glances and smiled several times, impressed and proud of his assertiveness. Neither of us said a word regarding his uncharacteristic chattiness.

After a snack at the hotel, we again walked to the wharf and caught the launch for a second visit to the ship. This time Eiji and Bill Bacon rode along. Our conversations continued in the mess hall. Mom genuinely enjoyed interacting with two of my closest friends. Like me, she valued relationships more than the physical things in life. But the sea was rough that day. Mom became seasick and needed to go up on deck for air. "Imagine that," I thought to myself, "Mom getting motion sickness aboard the *Statsraad Lehmkuhl*!" It felt surreal.

Alec took Dad down into the engine room again while I stayed with Mom. The two hours onboard passed quickly. Dad would've loved to stay longer, but as always, he accepted his reality, obviously more concerned about Mom than himself.

We again ate dinner with several cadets and their parents. Group interaction was exceptional that evening as the whole experience on St. Maarten continued to be orderly and sane. Students were on their best behavior. No one got drunk. No one broke curfew. No one was loud or obnoxious. It was the same for the crewmen, including Jacobsen. I developed deepened respect for my Oceanics community, even if just for three days. It provided encouragement and hope for the days and weeks ahead. We were better individuals than we sometimes appeared to be.

After a nice hot bath, surely my last for a while, I relaxed in the hotel room with my parents. It was a time to express my gratitude, thanking them for their visit, for all the food they brought, for their efforts in raising nine children, and for their guidance and patience with me over the years.

After hugs and goodbyes at 23:00 hours, I joined shipmates for a beer by the docks then caught the 00:30 launch back to the ship. Selfishly, I stashed two bags of hard pretzels and a large hunk of longhorn cheese in my locker, for my consumption only. If rationed carefully, I could enjoy it for a long while.

Early the next morning Eiji asked me to go ashore with him to buy perfume for his mother. He jokingly needed a second opinion. Neither of us knew anything about perfume but we came out of the shop smiling and smelling like a million bucks. Eiji proudly protected his eleven-dollar bottle of sweet sachet on the launch when we returned to the ship.

Dad and Mom headed back to the States as I prepared for another transatlantic adventure.

Pulling ropes/setting sails

Sailing into the North Atlantic

Joe "Cook" with cinnamon rolls

Jim Soja, History Prof

Joe Feinblatt, Photography & Calligraphy Prof

CHAPTER 20: NORTH ATLANTIC

Group C was on duty as the *Statsraad Lehmkuhl* sailed out of Philipsburg Harbor. Everyone came up on deck to help set sails, assuming that parents were watching proudly from shore as their sons and daughters sailed away. Winds were good, so all sails were set from the start, and St. Maarten soon became a speck on the horizon. Thank God for its memories, which lingered much longer than the three days we had there.

As the sea schedule kicked in, several crewmen changed their tones quickly. Maybe to balance the scale, so to speak, for their mandated civility in St. Maarten. Even Kjemtrup had a bug up his ass. I suppose being on one's best behavior can last only so long for sailors.

Officers and able-bodied seamen shouted orders as we dutifully responded. Life on deck returned to normal. Then after a long day of ship's work, we were rewarded with a movie in the union mess. Several crewmen joined us, including Burgo and Jacobsen. Both were drunk. Jacobsen had no authority over the students while off duty, but it was discomforting to have him on our turf, loud and irreverent. No one dared say a word in response to his disruptive behavior during the movie for fear of retaliatory consequences.

Two students left the ship in St. Maarten and returned home—Dave Pappas and Lucy. Dave's departure was planned in advance but Lucy was asked to leave because of her recent marriage to First Mate Schnitler. And as several of us assumed, she was pregnant. That changed everything. It was sad to see her leave. I liked Lucy. She was rough and straightforward at times, but also genuine and soft-hearted.

I smiled inwardly as I recalled leaving the theater together after watching *Fiddler on the Roof* with her in Bergen, when she had taken my arm and casually told me she was horny. At the time I didn't know what to do with that. I typically erred on the side of caution when facing tough battles between my spirit and flesh, and I was usually better off in the end when my spirit won out.

On our second day at sea, we again heard unofficial talk concerning the program's future. Issues that had haunted the school before we arrived in St.

Maarten resurfaced. Unrest among the faculty escalated, especially concerning their pay. But there were other problems as well. Some students were disgruntled, just tired of living in such close quarters onboard. Worse than that, I felt the crew was becoming less tolerant of the school and its purpose.

On the evening of our third day after leaving St. Maarten, an all-school meeting was held. Several crewmen attended as well. Unfortunately, talk preceded thought that night. Even Peter Kjemtrup's comments made no sense. A tense exchange between Schnitler and Poulsen quickly became personal, switching from moderate-toned English to high decibel Norwegian. I could only assume it had something to do with their female relationships onboard.

Students who tried to articulate their feelings at the meeting weren't taken seriously. Professor Soja was the only one who I thought understood the big picture. His words were unbiased and calming, helping to maintain some cordiality during the meeting. Difficult decisions needed to be made concerning our future. How should the program proceed? The administration formulated a questionnaire that was handed out to every student with the purpose of finding out where we all stood. The questions were simple and straightforward:

1. Would you like to see the program continue until June as originally planned?

2. Would you like to see the program end now and sail the ship directly back to Bergen?

3. Would you prefer the program to end in May, approximately one month earlier than planned?

Do you have any other ideas or suggestions as they pertain to the program? (Please give reasons for your preference concerning the questions above)

After some thought, I chose number 3, wanting the program to continue through May. I realized our community onboard wasn't going to get better with time. The inherent conflicts between school and crew couldn't be resolved. And the struggles for control would continue to the end. Tensions were mounting. How long before there'd be a major blowup? How long before students would rebel against perceived unfair treatment?

Helplessness and pessimistic thoughts began creeping into my psyche. All year I had done my best to be a solid cadet, giving in to ridiculous commands and discipline when my mind said otherwise. I accepted harsh words in silence and went out of my way to keep officers and crew happy. I never missed a watch, never missed a muster, never received a red-ring for anything. I did my utmost to encourage others and be a peacemaker. Now suddenly, it seemed all for naught.

In St. Maarten I had received a letter from Cousin Jerry concerning the Bird-in-Hand softball team back in PA. The team had officially been accepted into the Intercourse League for the coming season. Suddenly, going home became more attractive as I began removing myself emotionally from the Oceanics experience. But one thing remained certain: my underlying draw to the sea and my love for sailing was strong.

That night there was partying in the banjers. Several kids got drunk and no one seemed to care. I quietly sat on my bunk and ate leftover angel food cake, pretzels, grapes, and cheese from Mom. It felt like everyone onboard had suddenly become strangers. Later I watched the big orange full moon rise from the sea on the eastern horizon. The scene was breathtakingly beautiful! Nothing compared with a moonrise at sea. I suppose I was lucky that way. Something positive and good always seemed to come along at just the right time to lift my spiraling spirits.

Lifeboat drills replaced normal cleaning stations after muster the next morning. Chief Mate thought Rick Goodfriend was on drugs and sent him below to get checked out by the Doc. Strange things were happening; it was like suddenly the crew was looking for excuses to end the program.

Group C wasn't scheduled to go on duty until 17:00, but Timberman interrupted my mid-afternoon philosophy class and summoned me on deck. Surprised, I obeyed the order without protest after shooting a quick glance at Professor Frank who shrugged but said nothing at all. Varnishing railings wasn't difficult, and the weather was nice. It seemed odd however, that I was pulled from class to do it. Maybe Timberman liked my work.

Before Group C's shift ended, I helped take in three square sails on both masts, then joined fellow students in the union mess to view the posted results of the questionnaire. 45 kids voted.

1. Continue the program into June as scheduled—15 votes.

2. End the program now, sail the ship back to Bergen—3 votes.

3. End the program in May, one month early—27 votes.

The results were posted for everyone to see. No surprises. Barry North seemed to think our answers would have little or no bearing on the final decision. It wasn't up to us. He claimed the questionnaire was simply meant to appease the student body. To make us feel included.

♎︎

Alternating days between class time and ship duties continued at sea. Our lives again settled into a routine, with each group making efforts to keep things as mellow and hassle-free as possible. Ship's work was physical: painting, scrubbing the deck and its accessories, replacing ratlines, setting sails, and taking in sails.

Movies were shown in the union mess hall most evenings. I continued playing ping pong, mowing down all my opponents: Tom, Todd, Emil, Jaime, Yappi, Steve Hilbert, Zoe, and anyone else who challenged. Zoe was impressively competitive, however, and held her own in every match. When the idea of playing doubles was suggested, I chose her as my partner. We blew away every doubles combination we faced.

Of course, Todd was humiliated by losing to a girl. So, after some serious trash-talking, he invited her to a one-on-one match. She responded without a word or hesitation, then proceeded to beat him soundly. Zoe never flaunted her talents, but if given the chance, she exercised her abilities with action. I loved her quiet confidence.

During our second Atlantic crossing, I spent a significant amount of time in the music room, reflecting, thinking, reading, writing, and sometimes engaging friends in random conversations. When possible, I was on deck or in the rigging to experience every sunrise and sunset. The North Atlantic offered some of the most breathtaking skies of the entire trip.

One night I wandered toward the bow looking for Birdman, knowing I'd probably find him by the forecastle on port side. Sure enough, there he was, holding a joint, looking sheepish, standing with two faculty members. I wasn't surprised by what I found, and honestly, by now I didn't really care. The three were cautious as I approached, then chuckled nervously when I took three deep drags from the joint and left without saying a word. It was a strange encounter. One with neither forethought nor regret as I retreated from the shadows. Uncharacteristic? Yes, of course it was. An act of pride? Certainly not.

Meals were getting worse. I, along with others, surmised the ship steward purposely planned crappy food for the students. He had several run-ins with kids in the galley and consistently proved himself to be an arrogant, vengeful cuss. Steward was one person onboard who I really didn't like much. He temporarily disallowed any of us to work in the kitchen, even when we were assigned to galley duty. I suppose it didn't help that several cadets complained to the Doc about finding "fucking maggots" in the provisions one day. It was best not to piss off anyone with any authority onboard, especially not the person who plans meals.

The cooks were great, however. We got along fine with them. But they were under the steward's command and had little to say concerning the menu. Johnnie tried to explain to me one day the challenge of making bad food taste good.

Our ongoing complaints made things worse. Some of the food was impossible to describe, at least in the English language. Bones, fat, and gristle made from stinky old mutton was served too often. I took my plate up on deck one day and threw everything overboard. Willy witnessed the toss with humored surprise, then later testified that even sea creatures wouldn't touch the stuff. Except maybe the plate.

I must admit that good meals were served on very rare occasions. Like pork chops and watermelon. But in those cases, the mess hall became a free-for-all as we fought for seconds. Anyone attempting to sit down and eat peaceably had food scarfed from their plates. The only way to keep what we had was to flee the dining area and eat in the corridors or banjers, away from the masses. The dining hall sometimes became an arena for survival of the fittest. One night after not faring well in the feeding frenzy, I quietly went to my locker and finished off my stash of hard pretzels and cheese. I didn't share it with anyone.

Mike did a surprise locker check one morning, completely emptying out and sorting through every cadet's locker in search of contraband, namely booze and weed. Of course, the episode caused heated pushback from several students and plenty of cursing. No drugs were found, but two bottles of whiskey were pillaged from Bill Bacon's locker. Perry had a padlock on his and declared that unless a Norwegian officer accompanied Mike and demanded the locker to be opened, he wouldn't remove the lock. It wasn't a good start to anyone's day.

Mike then challenged Perry to an all-out, no rules, knock-down, knockout wrestling match on deck. Perry later admitted being scared silly as Mike was a tough guy—faster and stronger, even though much shorter, than he. Mike became the obvious aggressor as the furious tussle provided brief entertainment and shouts of excitement from the gathered audience. Meanwhile Perry went into defensive mode, just trying to somehow survive. Neither pinned the other to the deck.

During daylight hours when winds were good, the ship cruised nicely, slicing through the mid-Atlantic swells while manifesting the purpose of the *Statsraad Lehmkuhl* and providing contentment onboard. But sometimes we encountered rough seas, making it difficult to maintain accurate headings while the wheel compass varied ten degrees during the worst rolling and pitching. In such cases, it was a physical workout to steer the ship.

Nights became cold again as the tropical air of the Caribbean was long gone. I wore a coat and scarf on lookout and buoy watch. Although square sails were most times taken in before nightfall, the ship still maintained moderate speeds using only the stays.

One night the captain ordered three square sails on the main mast to be left up. And sure enough, winds picked up as a rain squall hit about the time Group C went on duty at 03:00 hours. We worked several hours bracing and taking in sails while fighting cold, driving rains. I had developed significant calluses from months of rope pulling, but that night the wet ropes tore skin from my hands. By the end of our shift, my palms and fingers were pink, bleeding, swollen and sore. I should have worn gloves.

Some nights, after the work was done, we had impromptu group gatherings with absorbing discussions concerning our individual futures beyond Oceanics. New bonds developed as we continued to grow our acceptance, respect, and support for each other. I continued to write every day, recording my thoughts, feelings, and experiences. The following is an excerpt from my journal written on March 23, 1973:

We're now approximately 1 week from the Azores, somewhere in the middle of the North Atlantic. The weather has changed drastically in the past week. Now, instead of just a pair of cut-offs on lookout watch, I wear long pants, a warm shirt, jacket, and I sometimes wrap up in a blanket. We're headed toward a region of the sea where there are frequent storms, rain, rough waters, and uncertainty. Few bare backs or bikinis are seen anymore. Our bodies are covered, tanning days are over, and sleeping on the deck is out of the question. Things are not great with the school—constant problems and hassles. There is talk of kids leaving when we reach Spain. Many are tired of feeling mistreated by the crew, and now by the steward. I plan to remain onboard to the end. I have found my place on the ship, and in this community. Thankfully, I'm able to make good of most situations. As this adventure continues, I want to experience every new day in its fullness. I'm realizing more and more that life is about relationships, no matter where one happens to be. People are more important to me than anything else, but I've still got stuff to figure out. And I desire more adventures before going home.

Ω

Finally, the food issue came to a head. Officers and crewmen continued being served well prepared food from good stock since leaving the Caribbean. We, the students, were not. Even the school administrators became concerned with the poor food quality. One evening the crew was served fish, chicken, baked potatoes and fresh fruit. Our dinner consisted of greasy lunchmeat, stale bread, and bruised apples. Administrators Mike and Steve decided enough was enough. So, Mike wrote a letter to Captain Fossa explaining the unacceptable food situation onboard and requested he have a conversation with the steward.

Word circulated among the officers concerning the letter, and it became a joke. Kjemtrup suggested laughingly that the cadets should throw the steward overboard. But his humor didn't sit well with anyone. It wasn't a never mind. Not this time.

The next day, lunch was terrible again. No improvement at all. Todd and I survived on corn flakes for all three meals. But it was a catch-22. The only corn flakes available were the boxes bought in Bergen many months before. By now, they were stale and soft, making it impossible to know for sure whether we were eating cereal or fragments of the cardboard box. It was that bad. But a spoonful of sugar helped the stuff go down. I doused my cereal with two.

Grumbling among the cadets continued, louder and more frequent. Group A was scheduled for duty at 19:00 on the evening of March 23 but didn't show for muster. That got the crew's attention. Then at 13:30 on Monday, March 26, Group A went on strike, refusing to work, completely ignoring orders from the officers and crew.

Word spread rapidly throughout the community as tensions mounted. It was anyone's guess what might happen next, or what the captain would do. Surprisingly, no immediate disciplinary action was taken during Group A's entire shift. Group C went on duty in the late afternoon. Although we supported Group A in theory, we agreed to perform our regular tasks. I helped set a few sails then followed with lookout watch. Earlier that day during Group A's stint, the winds died completely. In fact, it was so eerily calm and quiet that the ship couldn't maintain course, sometimes going sideways. Like in the doldrums. Twice, we floated backwards, like the winds were holding their breath, knowing trouble was brewing onboard.

Several of the younger crewmen were sympathetic to our food situation. Arne and others shared apples and candy bars with us from their stash. That evening we anticipated dinner like dogs anticipate treats after good behavior. But we were rewarded with bones, fat, and gristle with rotten strands of cabbage. Zoe sat next to me, smiled, and quietly handed me a pack of Marlboro smokes as an appeasement to my appetite.

We left the table together and went up on deck where we enjoyed an orange and two cigarettes each by the railing. I couldn't swallow one more morsel of that mutton stew. Zoe didn't discuss the food. Her even-tempered spirit didn't allow her to wallow in woe. And her encouraging words along with a few cigarettes went a long way for me.

By late evening there was a long line to make grilled cheese sandwiches on the single portable burner in the union mess. I was more tired than hungry, so Zoe and I shared another cigarette before bed. Although my fatigue and hunger lingered, her presence soothed my emotions. Jack shared some of his chicken noodle soup with us, then Birdman gave us each a cookie. Friends looking out for friends.

In philosophy class, Frank issued an assignment for each of us to write an essay concerning the dinner served on the previous night, but none of us bothered to do it. So, Frank walked out of the class, thoroughly pissed off. For me it was punishment enough to experience the bad food without writing about it.

Various responses to the lousy food began causing ill feelings among cadets toward each other. Gary became a self-appointed galley worker. Unlike the rest of us, he and the steward had developed some sort of friendship. Others became jealous, claiming Gary was kissing butt just to receive decent food, which was probably true. But he bragged about it, and that didn't sit well with anyone.

By now, The Brotherhood had morphed into a group called The Radicals, basically serving the same purpose as before, now under a different name. Their task, of course, was to right the wrongs onboard. Not surprisingly, The Radicals began harassing Gary, first verbally then physically. Gary's mattress was removed from his bed. Mark, Martin, Gerry, and Kavasic determined they no longer wanted to bunk with a traitor.

As a result, Gary and Kavasic got into a heated tussle in the banjers, which led to an instant court appearance. Gary was brought before The Radicals with Judge Perry presiding, found guilty of collusion with the steward, and banished from his room forever.

Several others were tried for unrelated infractions. Richie was accused of having sex with Ellie and was also found guilty. I don't recall anyone ever being tried and acquitted by this self-appointed prosecution and judge team. Nor did any of the accused ever have fair representation in court. After Richie's guilty verdict was read, but before sentencing, a fight broke out between him and Judge Perry.

The next day, spaghetti was served for breakfast. That and a glass of OJ sustained me throughout the day. Group A again refused to do ship's work. Kjemtrup, who was the crew leader in charge of tasks on deck, became angry this time, taking their declination personally. Fiery-eyed, he shouted at the "worthless cadets" (as he called them), claiming their refusal to obey orders was considered mutiny on the high seas, punishable by imprisonment under Norwegian law!

Off-duty cadets got involved in the standoff, openly supporting Group A, declaring it a strike, not mutiny. At 15:00 an emotional school meeting was held. Kids sounded off angrily but weren't orderly or articulate enough to make a coherent case. They interrupted each other incessantly which only added to the confusion. So little was accomplished except to get things off their chests. I remained silent, and sorely disappointed. Although no one was able to lead a united effort for the cause, work onboard came to a halt. And that received high-end attention.

Captain claimed the ship's safety was now being compromised. Several crewmen assumed the ship would go directly back to Bergen. But we, the students, finally felt empowered. We now had the captain's attention.

Many of us hung out on deck playing games: Red Light/Green Light, Mother May I, and Walking Tag (since running wasn't allowed). Zoe gave me another pack of cigarettes. I figured her kindness and the situation onboard was reason enough to continue smoking for a while. We sat together in the guest saloon feeling nervous about the uncertainty as the ship floated precariously in the North Atlantic. Interestingly, no one in authority seemed to care. That felt very odd.

Barry and Alec showed slides in the union mess, beautiful photos of Norway during what was labeled as the good old days. Several kids got their hands on hunks of cheese and bread, and again made grilled cheese sandwiches to supplement our crappy dinner. Maybe we were lacking proper nutrition, but no one was starving. And the growing bond within the student body became stronger than ever. Our core felt secure, at least for now.

Joe Feinblatt invited me to his room for a glass of sherry wine and a calm analysis of the situation. He talked while I listened and sipped wine. He had good things to say.

Ω

The next morning felt like a new day. We were served sunny-side-up eggs, bacon, new boxes of corn flakes, and orange juice! Several kids had already begun taking Geritol tablets and vitamins. Who knew where stuff like that came from in the middle of the Atlantic, but it did. Better still, the galley food improved 200 percent. There was no mention of any direct discussions between Captain Fossa and the steward, but good food was evidence enough. And the work strike ended. No need to report mutiny to the Norwegian maritime authorities.

Someone with clout (maybe it was Chief Mate?) suggested, for the sake of morale, that things should change concerning group composition and sea schedules. Four new groups were formed, triggering mixed feelings for me. I had become attached to my group. We had spent lots of time together working countless hours in the rigging, enduring long nights on duty, and covering each other's butts. We were also keen on each other's strengths and weaknesses and responded to ship's work accordingly. However, I agreed with the decision to restructure. It was time for a change.

The new groups consisted of 13 or 14 cadets each. Watch shifts and ship's work were scheduled to last six hours, twice a day, with two groups alternating over a 48-hour period. The other two off-duty groups were scheduled for class and study time. Every two days, we switched. I was now in Group B with Zoe, Jane, Tor, Jack, Randy, Todd, Tara, Mark, Emil, Clark, Sam, and Pisacano. It was a great team. And I believe we each were energized by the change. I heard zero complaints from anyone.

A violent movie showed in the mess hall, *Sitting Target*, about several prison escapees. The film was entertaining, but worst of all was Arturo smoking a stinky cigar during the show. Several of us asked him kindly to put it out, but he laughed and kept puffing with his head tilted back, exhaling through his whistle-holed lips, sending smoke straight up into the air. We warned him of severe consequences if he didn't stop, but to no avail. So, Jim Johnson, Alec, Sam, and I attacked him, slapping his pink belly and serving him with a well-deserved wedgie.

Frank, who was sitting nearby, defended his oversized friend. Then Todd joined in, also supporting the fat boys. The resulting rumble lasted only minutes. Although not outnumbered, us skinny boys were outweighed and forced to back off and declare a truce.

Ω

On the first day after reorganizing, the call went out just before lunch, "Alle mann pa deck!" The winds had picked up considerably, and the ship was listing strongly to port, racing along at nearly thirteen knots. It was raining heavily as well. The officers feared higher winds as radar picked up a storm close by. The high sails on both masts needed to be taken in, which required lots of manpower. We responded well and completed the task with ease before sitting down for a lunch worth waiting for: chicken, rice, peas, and carrots, with plenty of everything. Funny how good food makes everything better.

Just before nightfall, all square sails on both masts were furled, except the storm sails, as we prepared for the worst. Necessary adjustments were also made to the ship's course to avoid a direct hit by the storm while Bosun's booming voice could be heard clacking above the winds, "Heave… heave… heave… heave!" But we couldn't steer clear of the raging seas, strong winds, and cold rain. Once again, the sea unleashed its fury, tossing the ship like a toy amidst giant swells. Again, waves washed over the deck as we rocked dangerously from side to side, forcing cadets to run for cover in fear and excitement.

We had been through much worse, but still, this was a thrill, another adventure. I couldn't pull myself away from the enticement of the sea. Fierce winds and rain pelted my exposed skin, feeding my quest for more, daring the sea to throw its arsenal at us. I no longer felt anxious or vulnerable as before, craving whatever consequences this sea experience could provide. I wanted more.

By morning the storm had passed, and the seas calmed significantly. The banjers were due for a thorough cleaning, so after breakfast everything, including bedding, mattresses, clothing, and locker contents were hauled up on deck to be aired out and washed with hot water and Clorox. It was the most complete sanitizing project onboard since leaving Norway. The deck became a temporary mess with things strewn everywhere. Mattresses turned into gymnastic mats as cadets flipped, cart-wheeled, and jumped from the galley roof, making a romp-room out of the main deck. Great fun while it lasted.

Freshwater showers were then turned on. After two weeks in the North Atlantic, it was a race to the stalls. Like so many times before, there was no better feeling in the world than to be freshwater clean. But I suppose I could've said that about a whole raft of experiences onboard the *Statsraad Lehmkuhl*: the best feeling in the world.

Seawater shower on deck – alternative to fresh water

Rough seas

CHAPTER 21: AZORES

Early Sunday morning, April 1, the silhouette of São Miguel was sighted from the bow in the pre-dawn light. By 13:30 we docked in the town of Ponta Delgada. During the Atlantic crossing, I tried to familiarize myself with these Portuguese islands from books and periodicals in the library. Previously, I knew almost nothing about them.

The Azores are technically an archipelago, composed of nine volcanic islands in the North Atlantic, 850 miles west of Portugal, with nearly perfect year-round climate. Daytime temperatures average between 61-77 degrees Fahrenheit, attractive to a large influx of visitors from mainland Europe. Although officially governed by Portugal, the culture, language, foods, and traditions vary considerably because of mixed ethnic settlements over the span of two centuries.

The largest island, São Miguel, is known as The Green Island, and for good reason. Its landscape is made up of lush forests, natural floral gardens with vivid blooms, volcanic peaks, and beautiful lakes and calderas. Agriculture, fishing, and tourism are its main industries. There is no continental shelf surrounding the island, so the waters are deep, allowing deep-sea creatures to swim close to the coastline. Sperm whales and dolphins are often seen surfacing just offshore.

São Miguel is an exceptional place for any traveler to visit, but we felt incredibly privileged to land on the island after spending two weeks at sea. A bag of hard pretzels, a jar of Tang, and a letter from Mom were waiting for me in a box delivered to the ship.

Sam and I cruised through Ponta Delgada on our first shore leave, enjoying the town's beauty, cleanliness, and charm. It was so good to walk on solid ground again and experience a mix of culture and ethnicity. However, since food aboard ship had improved, and because our cash was dwindling, we returned to the mess hall for dinner. Most of our shipmates had dinner in town, leaving plenty of roast beef, potatoes, and fresh pineapple for those of us onboard. Sam and I then joined Eiji, George, and Malcom for a night on the town, making the most of our first night in port. Landlubbers who haven't sailed cannot possibly relate to the euphoria of that experience. And I could never explain it.

After we all eventually wandered home, the noise and banjer behavior seemed normal. Screaming kids ran through the corridors dousing each other with shaving cream. Barry was furious after being caught in the cream crossfire, demanding that Jack Wright and Bill Bacon be sent home. Unfortunately, his overreaction only added to cadet humor, with little consequence.

We were offered open shore leave during our entire stay in the Azores which was a huge gift from the staff and crew. And it proved to be fair for all of us because each group, in turn, was required to spend one day onboard for ship's work. Aside from that day, we came and went as we pleased, limited only by the midnight curfew. This new arrangement received high approval ratings from the entire community. I spent several hours alone one day, reflecting and writing letters in one of the beautiful city parks before taking a stroll through town. Inspired by the beauty of the late afternoon and the newness of this place, I headed to the east side of Ponta Delgada on foot with no thoughts of returning to the ship anytime soon. After reaching the edge of town, I continued up a slight grade by the sea, allowing full views of the shoreline. Without a moment's hesitation, I stuck out my thumb when I heard an approaching car. Franco, a mainlander from Lisbon, stopped, introduced himself in perfect English and told me to get in.

"Where are you going? he asked.

I responded quickly, "Lagoa," recalling the name of a town I had seen on a map downtown. I offered no further words of explanation. Truth was, I knew nothing about the place except that it was on the map.

Franco curiously asked with a side glance, "What do you want there?"

I smiled sheepishly, looked him in the eye, and answered honestly, "I have no plans except to explore the island. I'm from the tall ship that sailed into port two days ago."

Now intrigued, Franco asked several follow-up questions testing my authenticity and within minutes was convinced I was who I said I was. He didn't seem to be in a hurry as we headed along the coast for half an hour before pulling onto a winding gravel road leading down toward the sea. He parked the car by the side of the road, then we clambered several hundred feet down a rocky path to an oval-shaped natural sea-water pool nestled in a maze of rocks. The pool was about twenty-five feet wide in the center, and supposedly fifteen meters deep. He obviously was familiar with the place. Several smaller pools connected by concrete walkways were scattered nearby. Random diving points protruded from rock outcroppings around the large pool—some high, some low. Franco said it's a hangout for local folks, mostly teens.

"Few tourists know this place exists," he nodded toward three teenage boys diving from the high rocks. Back home a water park like this would've been packed with people! It was an amazing place.

Franco was a history buff and seemed knowledgeable about most everything in the Azores. He explained the belief held by some that civilization began on these islands thousands of years ago. There were seven ancient cities on São Miguel that were wiped out by volcanic eruptions. The few survivors escaped and left the island. After miraculously reaching the mainland, they began procreating, and in time populated the earth. End of story.

I smiled to myself, seriously questioning whether civilization began here. Then Franco shared another story as we climbed back up to the car, explaining the formation of the beautiful twin lakes at Sete Cidades caldera on the west side. One lake is blue, one green. According to legend, a green-eyed royal princess and a blue-eyed shepherd boy secretly fell in love. But when the king found out, he forbade his daughter from seeing the boy, breaking their hearts. The resulting tears of these star-crossed lovers formed two lakes matching their eyes. The scientific explanation for the varying-colored lakes was less interesting, and much less romantic. Franco didn't mention anything about that, but Barry North explained it to me later.

Except for the bright moonlight casting vivid shadows on the landscape, it got dark very quickly. Franco continued east, so I decided it was time for me to return to Ponta Delgado. He dropped me off by the side of the road and wished me well. From there I began walking toward the city at a moderate pace. It was a warm evening as a light sea breeze caressed my face. I was in no rush to get back, even if it meant walking the entire fifteen kilometers.

At one point two girls on bicycles rode past headed in the same direction. They appeared to be German from their accented "hello." I walked on, enjoying moonlight views of the sea and two ships on the distant horizon. After a sharp turn in the road, I came to a small house where a car sat waiting to merge onto the roadway. As I passed, I caught a quick glimpse of two girls in the car and wondered intuitively if it might be the cyclists who passed me minutes before. The car slowly pulled out heading in the same direction as me, so I stuck out my thumb. But they didn't stop until several hundred feet further on, then suddenly did a U-turn. As the car approached, the driver yelled through the open window, in English, "Do you know what time it is?"

I figured it was a linguistic test, to see if I knew English, so I answered quickly, "No I do not."

She stopped the car, smiled, and said in a quieter tone, "Get in." The driver was British, and the girl riding shotgun was Swiss. Both were in their early 20s, living and working on the island. After introductions, our first conversation was about international travel. They shared their story.

Sophie and Britta met in London several years earlier, became friends, stayed in touch, then decided to move to São Miguel on a whim. Neither had previously even visited the island. Obviously adventurous, both girls were also opportunists. I could relate. I told them about my time in Switzerland, and briefly about my life aboard the *Statsraad Lehmkuhl.* But mostly I listened, thoroughly enjoying their stories and experiences.

The girls willingly drove me all the way to the docks, claiming it wasn't much out of their way, then oohed and aahed when they saw the ship. I thanked them and said good night as they sped off. But I wasn't ready to call it a night. I joined Alec and George for screwdrivers and cake in a small café as we each shared highlights from the day. Relaxed times with fellow cadets were becoming more special to me. I felt connected as I boarded the ship at 23:00. This had been a very good day.

Joe then invited me to his room for a glass of Liquor de Oro. It was a weird drink with actual particles of gold floating inside the bottle, like high-end backwash. But it tasted good, and that's all that mattered. With gold in our guts, Joe shared with me his plan for the following day. I agreed to join him.

Ω

Mid-morning Joe drove up to the docks in a little Austin Mini that he had rented for two days. Kevin and I signed off ship at the gangway post and met him on the pier. Unfortunately, the only cars available to rent came with standard shift transmissions. Joe had not previously driven stick shift. But never mind that. He was determined to explore the island. Although the gears were clearly marked on the shift knob, they were close, allowing little room for error. Joe had a problem hitting the proper gears. He also had difficulty coordinating the clutch and throttle while shifting. And when he did manage a successful shift, he couldn't recall which gear the car was in.

The three of us headed out of town in what felt more like a bucking bronco than an Austin Mini. Once he shifted from fourth to first as the little engine screamed for mercy in high tenor. Thank God the car was blessed with durability and forgiveness. Kevin sat in the back seat smiling while I quietly cringed commiseratively in front. I felt badly for Joe. He was a good guy, kind, unselfish, and willing to take us along on his island exploration. And he paid for everything. But his driving was painful.

The first stop was the beach on the east side where we enjoyed wine and pastries. From there we climbed into the hills. The entire island felt like a national park filled with incredible natural beauty. Many roads were cobblestone, making it excusable for Joe to drive in third gear. The few cars going our direction tooted their horns and passed as they could. In time, it seemed like Joe was catching on to the little car. But as we passed the town of Provoação and headed into the interior, roads became overwhelmingly rough and narrow, prompting him to turn around and backtrack. We spotted a small ice cream shop along the way where we stopped to indulge—a nice break for the three of us, as well as for the Austin Mini.

After finishing my last few bites of black raspberry ice cream, I quietly offered to drive. Without a moment's hesitation, Joe nodded, seemingly relieved. I was thrilled to get behind the wheel of a car for the first time in a very long time. The Austin handled beautifully, with plenty of torque, as we sped through the countryside, hugging curves and powering up mountain roads. Kevin gave me a thumbs up in the rearview mirror from the back seat. Now relaxed, Joe began talking more. His knowledge of the island was amazing—stuff I'd never have found out on my own. It was better than geography class.

After visiting Furnas Valley and the hot springs, we turned off onto a road that climbed up the back side of a dormant volcano into the clouds and above. From the highest pull-off point, we viewed a crater lake in the shadows far below. Kevin insisted on hiking down, so I joined him. Actually, we ran down a switchback trail all the way to the water's edge. It felt good to breathe cool mountain air and feel the wind in our faces during the descent. But the climb back up was a serious workout—something we hadn't considered in our boyish eagerness to see the lake. We kept reminding each other that we are trained Norwegian cadets who can endure anything we set our minds to. We huffed and puffed our way to the top.

That night, back in Ponta Delgada, we befriended a curious Swiss couple standing on the dock near the ship. Peter and Liesl invited all three of us to join them for dinner at the best steakhouse in town. Hungry as a horse, I chowed down a huge slab of tender, medium rare roast beef with papas fritas. In exchange for the free food, we entertained the Swiss folks with stories from our experiences aboard ship.

At 03:00, long after I was in bed, Todd came into our room drunk off his ass. After puking twice, he fell out of his top bunk onto the floor with a deafening thud, then laid there moaning in vomit. My bunkmates and I paid him no mind, too irritated to be compassionate about his self-inflictions. He eventually crawled out of the room on all fours and didn't return.

Joe, Kevin, and I decided to get an early start for another sight-seeing trip the next morning. By 06:30 we were on the road again in the Austin Mini. Joe asked me to drive, which was fine by me.

Things were quiet as we made our way through Ponta Delgada toward the mountains on the west side of São Miguel. Farmers were already working in their fields as several folks rode donkeys by the side of the road. Others walked, carrying their wares. The morning was misty, cool, and refreshing as we climbed our way up to Sete Cidades and the twin lakes, the ones that legend declares were formed by tears from the princess and shepherd boy.

The setting was even more spectacular than the legend. Breathtakingly beautiful! And there was no denying the distinct colors. One lake was green, one was blue. We followed a dirt road leading down to a bridge between the two lakes. There we ate our bag breakfast from the ship: fresh pineapple and cookies. We met up with a few others from the ship—Mark, Gerry, and Kovacik—who had also managed to rent a car.

They unfortunately ran off the road into a dirt bank on their way home and mangled the front fender of their rental, causing a fiasco at the docks. The car rental agent came aboard and demanded 400 dollars in repairs. Arturo was called to the scene for interpretation purposes. After intense negotiations, the guys agreed to pay 333 dollars, much to the chagrin of both parties. From my perspective, it seemed like a fair compromise. When it was all settled, Arturo gave his best Puerto Rican sigh, threw his hands into the air in exasperation, and walked away.

After another day of experiencing São Miguel's beauty, I was convinced the Azores must be the sweetest place on earth next to Hershey, Pennsylvania, but for vastly different reasons. It was easy to understand why some folks thought civilization began here. The island matches biblical descriptions of the Garden of Eden, but without snakes. And no mosquitoes either.

Ω

Several visitors from town toured the ship later that evening. I had randomly invited some of my new acquaintances from the island to visit the ship at their convenience. The strange thing was, they all showed up at the same time. Eight of them! And even more surprising, they all knew each other! There was an explanation, however. After seeing my astonishment, John, the older guy, said it best: "Marlie, this is an island. Need I say more?"

The group of eight included fifty-five-year-old John (an American), Peter and Liesl (the Swiss couple), Sophie, the British girl who picked me up hitchhiking, Luana, the earth-shatteringly gorgeous Portuguese airline stewardess who I met one night in a café, and Amelia, the Brazilian server from the same café who also brought her two kids along. It was a diverse group, indicative of the random connections I had made on the island. But they interacted well, teasing and joking openly, and asking questions without reserve.

While touring the banjers, Luana smiled at me and asked about the living arrangements, seeing both male and female cadets casually meandering about. "Do boys and girls sleep in the same rooms?"

I eyed the group before answering, now feeling the attention of everyone. John, the socially conservative one of the bunch, scowled at the idea of co-ed bunk quarters. So, I chose my words carefully, "The community aboard is rather progressive minded." I hoped the questions concerning sleeping arrangements would stop, but John wasn't finished.

"The girls don't bunk with the guys, do they?" Then he mumbled something about that being unfathomable for an American-administered school.

Sensing the group's conflicted ideology, I answered honestly, "According to the rules, that is forbidden." John seemed okay with that and dropped the subject. However, Sophie and Luana responded simultaneously, "Aw, that's too bad," expressing their disappointment. Later when John was out of ear shot, I whispered to the girls, "There are rules onboard, as there are speed limits on roadways," then added, "but please go easy on John. He lives in a different world than you all."

The tour continued, upbeat and fun, without conflict. They all insisted that I climb into the rigging. I was in the mood to talk, not to climb, but I obliged. These folks had done a lot for me, welcomed me hospitably and contributed to my enjoyment of their island. Climbing was an easy thing for me to do. Kevin joined me. We scurried up the ratlines like seasoned sailors, maneuvering around the first platform then up to the second. We were probably showing off a trifle, but it was a proud moment with such an admiring audience.

It was harder saying goodbye to this group than any other folks I'd met along the way. The friends I met on São Miguel were special. I offered formal handshakes to each of them, but the four girls insisted on hugs and kisses. I was fine with that, especially from Luana, the bronze-toned, beautiful, black-haired stewardess. Her embrace would have been difficult for any red-blooded nineteen-year-old boy to forget.

The next day I visited the Botanical Gardens in Ponta Delgada, then had dinner with Eiji, Tara, and Kevin at the Atlántico. A wild-haired local guy joined our table for a few minutes and bought us all drinks. He was extremely happy about something, rambling nonstop in Portuguese like he was in a drunken stupor. None of us understood a word he said, but we responded in fast English of our own, not to mock him, but rather to keep pace. Before anyone's drinks were finished, he bought another round, then checked his watch.

The only thing we knew about the man was his first name. Alfred. The whole episode was bizarre. After the second round of drinks came, he held his glass high and proposed a toast in Portuguese. Finally, someone figured it out. Alfred was getting married that very afternoon! We all congratulated him with high-fives and as much exuberance as we could muster for a man we had just met and surely would never see again. He departed the scene and walked down the sidewalk at 15:00 hours, still on his pre-matrimonial high. The wedding was scheduled for an hour later.

Our conversation turned serious when Eiji reported that Malcom was heading home the following day.

"No way!" I exclaimed, "What happened?"

Eiji explained that Malcom was feeling sick for a while but didn't tell anyone. Finally, he talked to the doc who had him checked at the hospital in Ponta Delgada. After tests and bloodwork, it was determined that Malcom had nephrosis, a kidney disease. Medication was prescribed immediately, and he was told to get plenty of rest—not the type of rest one gets aboard a sail ship. Sadly, he had no choice but to go home.

George also planned to leave in Ponta Delgada. His departure had been scheduled from the beginning of the school year due to obligations in Minnesota. Although the administration knew, George kept his plans secret until the end of our stay in the Azores. That was another blow. Another one of my friends abandoning ship. George was a great guy, good-hearted, unselfish, friendly, genuinely positive, and a fun shipmate.

After Eiji and I returned to the ship, we invited George to an impromptu farewell party in Eiji's room along with Arturo, Joe, and Kevin. We shared a bottle of champagne, toasted George, then told stories that only sailors on a school ship could understand, both humorous and sad. We then offered good life blessings to our departing friend.

A large Portuguese ocean liner, which was moored at the dock several hundred feet behind the *Statsraad Lehmkuhl*, was scheduled to leave port that very evening for Lisbon. George had a one-way ticket to ride and had also reserved a flight from Lisbon to the States.

As he left ship with his belongings, fifteen of us accompanied him to the ocean liner. We then joined a multitude of others on the dock to see him off. Portuguese students lined the outer railings of the ocean liner's main deck, singing, chanting, and waving to their friends and families. Minutes after boarding, George appeared by the railing as well, already integrated with the Portuguese kids onboard. As we danced and yelled from the pier, someone started a "George, George, George" chant that could be heard above all the other noise. Several girls standing next to him on deck yelled back, blowing kisses, and shouting their cabin numbers, beckoning us aboard. It was an emotionally charged send-off for George who suddenly was the envy of every male cadet left behind.

When the ocean liner departed, we ran to the *Statsraad Lehmkuhl* and stood by the railing, yelling, whistling, and chanting, "George, George, George" as the ship passed by. Schnitler was in a foul mood and screamed for us to get away from the railing. We then climbed onto the halfdeck and continued our vocal send-off. Red-faced and angry, Schnitler ordered everyone below, triggering a barrage of loud, rousing, angry words in response, led by Perry and Alec. The tone on deck turned from festive to hostile. Amid the chaos, Johnnie the cook pushed Tom, and a fight broke out. Tom pulled a knife from his pocket, not necessarily intending to use it, but Johnnie went ballistic resulting in a fast and furious tussle before crewmen broke it up. It was a side of both Tom and Johnnie that none of us had seen before. External expressions resulting from internal tensions which had been brewing for a long while.

Then to cap off the action onboard, Charlie walked up the gangway drunk, followed by an irate taxi driver demanding payment for his fare. The incident was comical, prompting smiles on a night that had sadly turned sour. Charlie was adamant about not paying the cabby, and for good reason. After leaving a bar across town, he stuck out his thumb and hitchhiked back to the ship, unaware that he was picked up by a cab. His explanation was innocently simple, "Hitchhiking is free, right?"

The driver's argument was simple as well, "Taxi not free. You must pay."
I wasn't certain how the conflict was finally settled, but the disgruntled cabbie
left.

Then shortly past midnight, I heard loud, angry voices on deck. Perry, Tom,
Gerry, Mike, and a few others were in a heated argument with Schnitler and
Jacobsen. I was awake, still trying to calm my spirit from the events of the
evening. I made my way up and lingered on the fringes of the squabble for fifteen
minutes, unable to make any sense of it. There was a lot of shouting and very
little listening. And in the end, nothing was gained. The only thing that remained
important to me, that loomed larger than anything else, was the fact that two of
my friends were gone. I missed George and Malcom already.

The next day was amazingly quiet and peaceful, like nothing had happened.
Maybe the events and memories of the previous night were mysteriously wiped
out. Or maybe they were just a figment of my imagination. I only wished that was
true because George and Malcom were still gone.

Ω

I determined it was time for a self-evaluation. Not just a quick assessment, but
a deep heart, body, and soul-searching evaluation. Right after morning muster,
cadets reported to their assigned cleaning stations. But not me. I grabbed a
notebook and pen and headed ashore, alone. No one knew I left except Willy, the
gangway watchman, who smiled and nodded. He understood my tone without the
need for words. The fact was, I was extremely tired. Tired of cleaning the damn
toilets, tired of conflicts onboard, and tired of the uncertainty surrounding the
program.

Two days earlier I heard the ship was leaving the Azores and heading back to
Norway. The next day I had heard from Eiji that a rich donor came through with
250,000 dollars to keep the program afloat. Hopefully that would be enough to
allow several more port stops. I felt controlled by circumstantial chaos while my
own welfare was being jeopardized. It was time for me to face reality and change
my naïve hopes and expectations. And to figure out a way to cope with the challenges beyond my control.

I stood and watched a few early morning fishermen sitting at the pier. Their
lives appeared to be so simple. I exchanged nods with the guard at the station
near the dock entrance then strolled past the fortress and naval base by the bay.
From across the water, I heard a distant lone bugle and a few squawking gulls

above. In the plaza, I passed by four old ladies dressed in black sitting on wooden benches, then I slipped into the cathedral at the far side.

There I knelt behind several rows of empty benches while the organ played, resurrecting memories from Taizé—soothing, comforting, cleansing music. On this day in Ponta Delgada, I wanted to hear from God, if indeed He had anything to say. I wasn't there to ask Him for anything, or even to pray. I wanted only to listen, to hear His voice.

In time, a spirit of peace and assurance filled my soul, like a cool mist that moves in from the sea, humbling, covering, and protecting anything in its path. Beyond that, there were no words to describe what I felt.

Then, before leaving the church, I stood in silence, enjoying my transformative moments. Something deep inside had changed. I bought coffee at a nearby café, sat at a table in the corner, and wrote as the self-evaluation process continued. It was like gazing into a splintered mirror. I didn't like what I saw. My stomach was bloated, my lungs polluted, my liver ached from contamination, and I lacked discipline. Worst of all, I was becoming self-absorbed. Selfish.

I determined to make immediate changes concerning food, alcohol, and cigarettes. After pledging a cleansing to God and to myself, it felt like a new day, a fresh start.

Before returning to the ship, I walked to the far side of the dock and peered out over the water, enjoying my last minutes of solitude. A person appeared to be lying atop the wall at the far end of the dock, facing the sea. As I approached, I realized it was Eiji, basking in his own solitude. I stood quietly watching my friend, not wanting to interrupt. Suddenly a seagull flew from the water toward me, squawking about something. Eiji turned to watch the bird and saw me standing close by.

According to him, nothing happens by chance. Our conversation that day was deep, without time constraints. And he provided the encouragement I needed to stay positive amid our imposing surroundings. We walked into town without a destination.

By year's end each faculty member was required to do student evaluations. Eiji had broken his finger several days earlier, so he asked me to take notes while he talked. His dictation to me concerning other students probably breached protocol, but he trusted my sworn confidentiality. We wandered through the city for several hours while he verbally evaluated each student, and I wrote. We also took the time to spend our last Portuguese Escudos on snacks, peanut butter, canned soups, and fresh pineapples. So, a day that started with mountains of uncertainty turned into an inspirational day of reflection, transformation, and forgiveness.

Me heading off ship

Eiji Imamura, my encourager

George Kramer, furling the merse before leaving the ship

CHAPTER 22: GIBRALTAR

The ship's navigational itinerary had us heading southeast from the Azores, through the Strait of Gibraltar into the Mediterranean Sea, and up the east coast of Spain to the city of Malaga. Everyone was anxious to hit the mainland.

Saturday, April 7 started with Poulsen's crazy whistle followed by the Florida boys' curses. This was supposedly our final day for main deck cleaning stations. Thank God! The local milkman came aboard, selling raw milk for 25 cents a bottle. Most of us bought at least one. Anything was better than the diluted evaporated milk onboard. Then the car rental guy came onboard looking for Pisacano who was caught driving with an expired license during a routine traffic stop. The officer contacted the car rental agency, insisting they were responsible to collect the fifty-dollar fine. Arturo again got involved because of his linguistic abilities, and managed to negotiate a reduced fine, this time from fifty to thirty-five dollars.

Mooring lines were removed from the dock at 10:30, and a tug slowly pulled us into the harbor. Three long horn blasts from the tug, answered by three long blasts from the *Statsraad Lehmkuhl*, then a short toot from each as the open seas again welcomed Captain Fossa and his motley crew. On this day however, we had a surprise guest onboard—Chick Gallagher. According to word below deck, Chick wanted direct contact with all of us to hear first-hand what was really going on.

Students were again anxious to participate in formal class time after a break in the Azores. Professor Frank shared an anonymous letter in Philosophy class from a student/cadet to his mother describing life aboard. It was sad, articulate, and heartfelt explaining the student's struggles. Interestingly, the real hardships shared in the letter weren't about the work, climbing the rigging, polishing brass, night watches, discipline onboard, or about the food. Nor were they about being at sea for weeks, or about the curriculum or school-related activities. Rather, the real challenges expressed in the letter were concerning lack of unity and love within the community itself. Frank made several copies, then shared it with faculty and students outside his class. The letter's substance touched a deep chord within many of us. We could relate. Of course, everyone wanted to know who wrote it. Within two days, the letter's author was exposed: Alec.

I had several assignments due before reaching the next port. After finally finishing my credo for English class, I then chose a story for my next project: Samuel Beckett's tragicomedy *Waiting for Godot.* Just one year prior at Eastern Mennonite College, I had seen the play performed on campus. It seemed strange at the time, but now it resonated, depicting real life and the act of living, hope and waiting, proclaiming no generation better off than the prior one. Philosophically deep stuff, yet simplicity at its finest.

Kevin's birthday was April 8, our second day at sea. Several of his closest friends decided to throw a party for him in Eiji's room late that night. I helped drag Kevin from his bunk, but in doing so, I slipped by the hatch and cut my foot badly. The cut was painfully deep but appeared to be clean. After the bleeding slowed, I applied gauze and bandage, wrapped it well and paid it no more mind. Kevin's birthday party was festive and fun for a while but unfortunately, there was additional consequential fallout.

Amor drank too much brandy. After leaving the celebration, she fell down the metal steps from the deck to the banjers into an unconscious heap. Doc treated her cuts and bruises but was most concerned about her head injuries. Although Eiji accepted full responsibility for the incident, we all shared equal blame. There was plenty of guilt to go around. Mike was livid, making continual comments for several days about how Amor could've been paralyzed or killed, directly placing the blame on Eiji.

Yes, Eiji had messed up. That much was true. But by now there wasn't an officer, crewman, cadet, faculty member, or administrator aboard who had not mucked something up during the year. Even our seldom seen, dough-faced captain wasn't off the hook. It's a fact that grace and forgiveness are divine, not human. So, I suppose sailors and administrators aboard a ship in the North Atlantic could not be expected to demonstrate such attributes. And they didn't.

Ω

On our fifth day at sea, I decided to switch rooms for no reason except to make a change. Now, with four fewer cadets aboard, there were several empty bunks. So, I joined up with Tom, Clark, and Nancy Graham in cabin 14. Although it meant adjusting to all the little idiosyncrasies of three new roommates, I found the change refreshing. Also, it was closer to the showers. My security was now apparently found in change rather than in familiarity and routine.

The sail from Ponta Delgada to Spain was relatively short, so the freshwater showers were turned on every evening for two hours. That was a luxury we seldom enjoyed at sea, and we made the most of it. Someone suggested that clean cadets are next to godliness. I wouldn't have gone quite that far.

Chief Mate lectured us one morning at muster, naming three recurring infractions: smoking in the banjers, drinking on board, and reporting late for muster. Although his speech was general in nature, he was speaking directly to several cadets who regularly violated the rules. We all knew who they were. That same afternoon, Chick Gallagher called an all-school meeting in the union mess. It was quite different from meetings in the past, one that had the potential of actually accomplishing something positive.

Chick was cool, humble, and receptive to student suggestions and feelings. He was careful not to initially write anything off. That was a new response from the administration. As a result, there was optimism regarding immediate changes in student punishments. For instance, the red-ring policy was discarded. Any wrongdoings onboard would now result in corrections onboard as opposed to losing shore leave or infringing on cross-cultural experiences in port. That made sense. Penalizing education was in direct opposition to the purpose of Oceanics. Chick, being one of the founders, had helped define that objective. So, there was no one better to re-emphasize its importance than he.

Another suggestion at the meeting was to be more spontaneous while sailing, allowing the currents and winds to help dictate destinations, rather than scheduling specific ports too far in advance. Students finally felt like they were heard. Chick and Stephanie were masters at initiating alternative education, but the devil always seemed to be in the details. Chick's role in grinding out some of those details during these few days aboard ship produced a positive student response. No previous all-school meeting compared. Then to top it off, the best cake ever was served during mid-afternoon coffee break. Chick was credited for that as well. Things were improving!

My group went on duty at 21:00. Lookout watch was cold and exciting. Choppy, breaking waves forced a constant battle between the water being pushed from the ship's bow and the oncoming swells. Their head-on clashing shot mist high into the air, soaking both the forecastle and main deck. And me. We were now less than 300 miles from Gibraltar, crossing the same place in the sea as last December. When I hit the sack at 03:00 hours, my roommates were already asleep. No one was snoring, no one was drunk, and no one was having sex. Thank God for my new cabin!

The next day arrived in ordinary fashion. We were served an acceptable breakfast, average lunch, and above average dinner. I enjoyed the spring weather, good conversations, ship's work, watches, coffee breaks, and musters. My shipmates and I shared the mild joys of the day without major incident. It was Friday the 13th.

I finished my English project—fourteen handwritten pages. It felt like a personal accomplishment to complete the project with little interruption in this most unusual ocean setting.

Four days had passed since Kevin's party and my foot had become badly infected. My entire lower right leg was red and swollen, oozing with pus from the wound. Doc used a hot knife to recut, then squeezed out gobs of ugly discolored crap—excruciating pain! Then he redressed the cut with a large bandage and prescribed antibiotics. The infection had spread up my leg and settled in lymph nodes at my groin. He instructed me to keep my leg elevated as much as possible. No ship's work and no climbing. I was painfully restricted and seriously concerned enough to take care.

Doc repeated the cutting, squeezing, cleaning, and redressing procedure daily until the abrasion healed.

Several kids informed me, confidentially, that they were planning to leave ship in Malaga. The idea of reaching the mainland became an invitation for unrestricted travel, away from the program's control and discipline. Robert and Tor, the Norwegian cadets, and Birdman all planned to leave. None of the three were controversial figures onboard, but each felt they had endured enough. I was saddened by their decisions to abandon ship but understood full well. I didn't try to change their minds. However, I reminded them that this unique opportunity aboard the *Statsraad Lehmkuhl* was a once in a lifetime experience that could never be replicated. Only time would tell if they were serious about leaving.

The night was remarkably clear and beautiful at 21:00 as I went on duty for the next six hours. I sometimes think the words "totally awesome" are overused. But not on this night. The stars, the sky, the air, and the dispositions of both sea and sailors appeared unusually great. It was a night that could've lasted forever! Until Kjemtrup, who suddenly turned sour, mustered us off at 03:00 hours. Instead of saying his usual, "Good night, go to bed," he looked at each of us standing at attention, then casually said, "Good night, go to hell." With that I quietly slipped down into the banjers, cabin 14, and sat on someone sleeping in my bed. I was too tired to find out who or why, male or female, so I retreated to my old bunk for the remainder of the night. There wasn't much sleep time left.

Ω

Fried hotdogs and orange juice for breakfast and no ship's work for me. Doc again cut and drained pus from my infected foot. I still had lots of pain, but noticeably less swelling.

Willy, Clark, and I shared a late evening theology class with Eiji in the large guest saloon in the officers' quarters. Normally that room played host to ambassadors and special guests and was off limits to off-duty cadets at night. Our discussion centered around insanity, which led to a debate about who of us might slowly be going insane. Willy figured he probably was, Clark wasn't sure, and Eiji claimed it was too soon to tell. I explained that since my self-evaluation in Ponta Delgada, I was doing just fine. Before that? Maybe. It was a great discussion drowned heavily in humor.

Clark monotoned, "I am a pillar of this program," then chugged several sips of red wine directly from a bottle that magically appeared from under someone's coat. Willy grinned and grabbed the bottle, gulped twice, then passed it to me. We debated the consequences of being caught drinking in the guest cabin, then laughed hysterically at the thought of Captain Fossa walking in. However, we sobered quickly imagining the possibility of Mate Schnitler finding us.

After Eiji left at 23:00, the three of us stayed in the guest cabin, daring ourselves to stay the night. Willy turned philosophical, as he had done so often before, concluding that the challenge alone was worth the risk. He somehow convinced Clark and I of the same. So, we talked past 01:00 hours, afraid to fall asleep but unable to prevent it. Willy's group went on duty at 03:00, so he took it upon himself to wake Clark and me at 06:00. It was then that we quietly got up and slipped back into our own cabins before morning muster.

The easterly winds remained strong, as did the head currents in the Strait. That condition continued throughout the night and the entire next day, allowing no progress forward into the Mediterranean. For hours the ship remained several miles off the coast of Morocco, sailing back and forth, fighting the elements, and waiting for the winds to subside. It was an exciting time on deck prompted by strong winds and an agitated sea causing huge waves to wash over the railing. Several of us stood by the side rail near mid-ship in awe of nature's power. When a wave approached, we quickly ducked under the railing shelf and watched the water crash onto the deck behind us. It was a crazy fun time! But no one stayed dry as the water sloshed on the deck's surface before finding its way out the side drains.

Things didn't improve weather-wise as evening approached. For a while, the ship floated out of control with the distress flag hoisted. Strong winds and high seas were relentless. But the captain wasn't ready to give up on sailing through the Strait toward Malaga. That tested our patience and endurance. The only thing we could figure was that maybe Captain had a mistress waiting for him in port.

Much larger ships swept past us into the Strait. Freighters and tankers with powerful engines were better equipped to overcome the elements than we. Tacking our way through the strait under these conditions was impossible. So, we lingered outside the gates waiting for our opportunity. Some of us whiled away the hours by playing chess, ping pong, or Monopoly. Others hung out in the music room or wrote letters. We heard rumors that we might return to the Canary Islands. Ship's work was minimal except for occasional bracing as we sailed up and down the North African coast waiting for the winds to change. Another day passed and still we waited.

As dawn was breaking early the next morning, we again tried to sail into the mouth of the Strait. But again, we found the sea and the winds overzealous. There was just no way the *Statsraad Lehmkuhl* could go through. We became increasingly more restless. Land was so close, yet so far away. Conversations deteriorated stupidly. Clark, Eric, and I discussed how cool it would be if our ship sank—strange dialogue to have aboard a ship in distress. But on the other hand, maybe it was the best time to discuss it. Capsizing would surely be a cure-all for everything else that was going wrong onboard. And there'd be no question about when or how to end the program. As for survivors, if indeed there were any, they'd have lots to say and write about for a very long time. We agreed that sinking the ship would be the ultimate excitement. Then grinning at each other, Clark and I acknowledged the fact we could no longer deny evidence of our insanity.

Something unusual happened in the mess hall during breakfast. I saw gentle Joe Feinblatt get really angry for the first time ever. He, Tom, and I were seated on the back bench, with Tom at the end, me in the middle, and Joe against the wall with no exit. He wanted a slice of bread from the next table and politely asked someone to pass the bread plate. But there was no response. After five seconds or so he said directly to Tom, without calling his name, "Can you please get me a piece of bread from the next table." Again, no response. Now, becoming noticeably irritated, Joe raised his voice, "Tom, do you hear me?!"

Fully aware of what was happening, Tom casually looked Joe's way and answered, "Yes Joe." Then he immediately turned his head and resumed his conversation with Tor.

Joe became frustrated by the blatant disrespect. Now noticeably angry, he yelled, "Would you PLEASE get me a slice of bread!"

Tom was still in dialogue with Tor, but after a few seconds turned casually to Joe and asked, "Oh, you want some bread?"

This was too much to take for even a calm guy like Joe. With fists clenched by the side of his face, he thundered, "YEEESSSSS!!!!!"

Students seated at both tables were unaware of the drama unfolding until that moment. Joe's outburst surprised everyone. Several leaned back and sniggered. But Tom, still cool as a cucumber, said in his deep monotone, "Marlie, Joe wants a piece of bread. Let's kindly let him out so he can get it."

Joe came undone! His face turned white with anger, setting a firm jaw like I had never seen. His beard stood on end. "SHUT UP!!!" he screamed with lividity, then stood up and made a violent move to get out from behind the table. Tom calmly picked up the plate of bread and handed it to him. Joe stood there seething, awkwardly holding the plate, much too exasperated to know what to do with it, now obviously more angry than hungry!

Todd nearly fell off his bench backward from hysterics. Maybe it was indeed time for the program to end. Such humor at the expense of a faculty member wasn't conducive to positive community life. But neither was sailing to nowhere for three days. Everyone onboard, except maybe the captain, knew it was time to move on from outside the gates of Gibraltar. Or as several kids now called it, the gates of Hell.

Finally, Captain decided to take the ship further north along the west coast of Spain to the city of Cádiz. Winds remained strong as we set several additional square sails, increasing our speed to eleven knots. It was great to finally have an attainable destination. And there was only mild disappointment about not going into the Mediterranean. We all knew full well it wasn't for lack of effort. I suppose some things in life are just not meant to be. Captain's mythical mistress would have to wait for another time.

Goodbye to shipmates in Cadiz, Spain

Chief mate Kavanvik left ship in Spain as well

Departing professors Frank and Arturo

CHAPTER 23: SPAIN

We docked at the port of Cádiz at 16:00 hours on Wednesday, April 18, but our group had no shore leave until the next day. Unlike in the Azores, ship's work continued after reaching the mainland. Several things of significance happened on arrival. The new Chief Mate came aboard. Actually, it was the return of Mr. Alv Gronningen. The memory of his discipline straightened my spine. He prided himself in running a tight ship. "To put it bluntly," Mike so eloquently stated, "the new Chief will not take shit from anyone."

Mr. Gronningen's wife, Captain's wife, and Stephanie Gallagher also came onboard. As usual, Stephanie brought a box of mail from the States. Funny, at this juncture of the trip, mail seemed less important than before. Life at home was now far removed, like on a different planet. And honestly, it was difficult to relate to, or care about anything in the States. My feelings and emotions fluctuated daily.

Someone ripped off the money box from the school store. As a result, no one had shore leave until it was found, negating the positive sentiments of our meeting with Chick. No details were shared about the incident, but first liberty was finally granted in the late afternoon after a long, very frustrating day onboard. Life was slowly deteriorating into nautical hell. I developed a tension headache from thinking too much. My heart felt sad while my soul felt empty and wall-less.

Clark and I left the ship as soon as we were able, just to get away. We hadn't researched the city before going ashore and were surprised by the festivities in town. Parades, drum and bugle bands, and folks in white hooded costumes filled the streets, bearing an unsettling resemblance to the KKK back in the States. This was Holy Week in Spain. The issues on ship were soon forgotten as we indulged in pastries, hot dogs, and beer at a sidewalk café, enjoying the celebrations in town as a welcomed distraction. We discussed field trip possibilities for the next few days, acknowledging our need to be away from the negative vibes that were spreading contagiously throughout the ship.

Early the next morning we quietly spoke with Chick, asking permission to visit the ancient city of Granada near the Sierra Nevada Mountain range in southern Spain. Granada is famous for its medieval architecture and Spanish-Islamic art, not that I cared much about that, but it seemed like a nice place to go. Chick was obviously on the side of the students as it pertained to educational opportunities within the program. He not only supported our idea, but smiled and gave us each five dollars to boot.

Clark and I exited the ship quickly before anything could go wrong. We took no sleeping bags or luggage, and weren't certain where we were headed, despite what we told Chick. We hopped the first bus leaving town after reaching the terminal, which happened to be going to Algeciras. After finding two empty seats near the front, Clark looked at me and smiled, "This is how field trips should be done."

We arrived at the port city by Gibraltar after a three-hour bus trip through the south of Spain. From there we had great views of the famous rock. Ferries to Morocco departed regularly from the port. We considered that, but in our haste to leave, we both forgot our passports. Bummer. Stupid. We wandered through Algeciras for several hours, just enjoying our freedom. But we found nothing of interest to keep us there for the night. Spontaneity led us back to the terminal where we bought bus tickets to Seville. Clark grinned and said it was a place he always wanted to go. "Why didn't you tell me that before?" I asked, doubting him. He just smiled. Clark was a boy of few words.

Bus transportation in Spain was cheap and surprisingly comfortable. From our seats we enjoyed rolling hills of grazing land scattered with small towns and villages, areas of barren desert, and mountainous terrain during our five-hour ride to Seville. In the early evening, we pulled into the downtown terminal. Like in Cádiz, Holy Week festivities were in full swing. The city hosted thousands of out-of-towners, negating any possibility of us finding an affordable hotel room or hostel. So, we prepared ourselves for a long night on the streets, agreeing it was still better than being aboard ship.

The city buzzed with activity and entertainment—parades, musicians, artists, and dancers in the streets. And of course, swindlers of all kinds trying to make a buck. I considered with a smile the possibility of being approached by a girl named DD, keeping up with the international hookers alphabetically. But it was not to be. The night action continued until 04:00. We walked plenty, hung out in cafés, interacted with local teens, then enjoyed a glass of red wine with a small group of Spanish students. And we drank far too much coffee. It was the cheapest and most purposeful drink of the night as we wrote post cards to pass time.

Seville is an impressively beautiful city. At one point we walked along the river in the early morning haze as the reflections of city lights and stone bridges carved a tone of medieval mystique. We passed through a dimly lit railroad underpass where orgasmic sounds of young lovers echoed from an elevated ledge above. Neither of us felt inspired to make comments concerning sex in Seville. Or to even look at each other. It wasn't about naivete or feelings of awkwardness. There simply was no need for words. I sometimes found humor in Clark's quiet, expressionless responses to life situations. We walked on in silence.

The eventual mid-morning sun warmed the city as we managed to stay alert during stints of random sightseeing. It was a new day, but it didn't feel new. Pulling an all-nighter certainly wasn't high on my list of favorite pastimes.

We found the old Gothic Seville Cathedral architecturally impressive, even in our weary state. By contrast, the tomb of Christopher Columbus was moderately interesting, but not impressive. I thought him to have more discredits than credits, despite what I was taught in elementary school. We relaxed in the sun at the beautiful Alcazar Castle Complex, watched people, and succumbed to a short powernap. By afternoon we had become robotic functioning humans without brains, wired by caffeine, numbed by lack of sleep.

Ω

Back aboard the *Statsraad Lehmkuhl*, we caught up with the goings-on there. It was Saturday night. During our brief time away, Mark completely flipped out and threatened to leave the ship. Blake and Debbie had already left. Several cadets were caught climbing down the mooring lines on Friday night. As a result, Emil, Kovacik, and Kevin were sentenced to ship's work for the duration of their time in Spain, a sure confirmation of the wonderful new methods of educational punishment. Alec, just tired of everything, made plans to leave the ship on Sunday. Birdman, who'd been contemplating leaving for quite a while, finally made up his mind to leave on Monday. Chuck and Lilly decided to go home on Monday as well. Both Clark and I had ship's duties starting at midnight. Neither of us were going anywhere.

The most difficult news for me was the fact that two faculty members, Professors Frank and Arturo, also left the ship. Both had been vocal concerning their declining support for the program. But their sudden departure was a surprise, no matter how or why it happened. Also, very sad. Not only were they my friends, but they were integral members of our community. Their departure felt much too final—I had no time to say goodbye, like when my father died suddenly in 1956.

That night I lay in bed, physically exhausted, with a million questions churning in my soul. Logic was no longer relevant. I cried for inner strength as the outer walls seemed to be crumbling in the darkness of the night, a night that was blacker than black. The Oceanics program as I knew it was falling apart, and nothing I might do or say could stop it. I understood that life wasn't intended to be easy or fair. I didn't expect it to be. God knew I had survived tough times before. Surely His mercy would secure my way forward now. I wanted to believe that. It felt like the only thing I had to hold onto.

Easter Sunday was a workday for me. I was on mess duty for breakfast and lunch, then I also had several regular watch shifts until mid-afternoon. Stephanie was hoping to connect with each student concerning class credits, upcoming projects, program evaluations, and plans after Oceanics. She felt an urgency to deal with the current challenges onboard as well. But I wasn't emotionally prepared to talk, with still too many unanswered questions rolling around in my head. I worked diligently that day, taking extra watch shifts, finding ship's work, anything to avoid the possibility of having time to meet with her.

Sadly, I watched Alec carry his stuff down the gangway to the waiting taxi. I wished him well. Sudden farewells were difficult. I remained somber throughout the afternoon, standing quietly on deck talking to no one. Then Gary invited me along with him to an early evening bullfight in San Fernando. Someone had given him free tickets. I decided to go, as anything was better than pouting onboard.

San Fernando was a short twenty-minute bus ride from Cádiz. We arrived in time for the last of three scheduled fights. Supposedly, this event was an Easter Sunday tradition in San Fernando. But we were there for the novelty of the experience, having no knowledge of or interest in the regional matadors. The fight seemed important to the locals, with plenty of crowd enthusiasm. Neither Gary nor I were impressed. And as expected, the bull did not win.

We stayed in town for the entire evening. The weather was great. Plazas and sidewalks were oozing with activities for young and old. Music filled the air as dancing bodies filled the streets. Several teenage girls flirted with us, but unfortunately language became a deterrent to any serious conversations. Still, it was nice to be hit on by cute Latinas. I tried not to show my excitement, but Gary was ecstatic.

Back on the ship, Emil tuned in to a transistor radio on deck—the Celtics-Knicks basketball playoff game, in English. He was thrilled because New York won in double overtime to go up three games to one. Also, on Sunday afternoon, a group of about seven students returned by bus from an adventurous trip to Seville.

I heard their story from Jim Soja and David Freedman who had also traveled from Cádiz to Seville, not necessarily as group leaders, but as advisors. By this time of our voyage, most students were making their own decisions concerning field trips and onshore activities, just as Clark and I had.

I wasn't told who all was part of the group, but it included Tor, Rick Good-friend, Zoe, and several others all carrying backpacks for their two-day overnight excursion. One planned activity was to see a bullfight. After arriving in Seville, the group found an affordable hotel. The kids piled into one room, which they negotiated themselves, while Soja and Freedman shared another. Later they all wandered into a lovely sidewalk café with outdoor tables covered by broad, colorful umbrellas. While they enjoyed the street activities, a girl in her 20s approached the group and introduced herself as Benta Blues, then kindly asked if she could join them for drinks.

Benta was Danish, a Gypsy girl with temporary employment training horses just outside Seville. Or so she said. Her unorthodox nature fit well with the Oceanics kids from the get-go, and she quickly earned their trust. After hanging with the group into the evening, she asked permission to crash in their hotel room for the night. No one seemed bothered by her request. What was one more body in an already crowded room?

The next morning the Oceanics kids went out for breakfast, including Soja and Freedman. But before they left, a guy friend of Benta's showed up at the hotel. Neither he nor Benta joined the others for breakfast. It was Easter Sunday morning, and the students planned to be back in Cádiz onboard ship by the after-noon. So immediately after breakfast, they returned to the hotel to checkout.

Big surprise! They found their room totally empty! Everything was cleared out! No trace of their packs, no Benta, no guy friend, no nothing! Several of the kids had left passports, personal items, wallets, even cash in their packs. It was all gone.

Soja and Freedman supplied the students with enough pesetas to buy bus tickets back to Cádiz with the assurance that they'd try their best to track down Benta and their belongings. It seemed like a tough task, however, to find a female Scandinavian horse trainer-turned-swindler, in a foreign city!

Freedman went to the hotel front desk and explained the whole story to the clerk. But the guy wasn't cooperative or interested in helping. Several police guards were standing outside the hotel entrance, so Freedman suggested report-ing the incident to them. Suddenly the clerk changed his tone, remembering a girl fitting Benta's description getting into a taxi with multiple packs. "No, no involucres a la policia," he exclaimed. He also remembered which taxi service had picked her up and offered to make a follow-up call. Sure enough, the cabby who transported Benta remembered her well. How could he forget? He had helped load a lot of stuff into his cab. The taxista escorted Soja and Freedman to another hotel where he had dropped her off. Fortunately, Benta was registered there for the night but was out of the room when they arrived.

The hotel manager was fearful, not wanting any trouble at his facility. However, he promised to do his best to hold her if and when she returned. Feeling somewhat relieved, the two profs then decided to go to the bullfight, as previously planned, feeding their naïve sense of adventure. When they returned to the hotel several hours later, they found Benta alone in her room!

Soja and Freedman firmly explained they wouldn't press charges or involve the police if all the packs, passports, and money were returned in good faith. Benta was nervous as they hailed a cab. She led them to a stucco building in town, through a large arched entrance leading into a courtyard landscaped with plants and shrubs. There, stashed behind several bushes was all the stolen stuff! It appeared that everything was intact, including passports and cash. Meanwhile, guards with Uzis were patrolling just outside the grounds, guaranteeing Benta's full cooperation.

Soja later tried to analyze the bizarre incident. Maybe Benta Blues was simply an opportunist. Perhaps she was no horse trainer at all but had acquired the brains of a horse. But for sure, she was perfectly formulated to be a player in Stephanie Gallagher's experiential Oceanics handbook.

Ω

Things remained rather chaotic onboard as the crew and administration prepared for departure from Spain on Monday morning. Only a few students were permitted to go ashore for any reason. I was one of them, given the responsibility of carrying everyone's outgoing mail to the post office. On my return, I met up with Tom who was obviously distraught. He went ashore intending to reach his parents by phone, desperately hoping to get their permission to leave the ship. Sullen faced, he informed me that before breakfast Chief Mate Gronningen and Mike told Perry to gather his things and leave the ship immediately. I wasn't privy to the details, but it seemed incredibly unfair. Tom was out of sorts, of course. Perry was his best friend. They were part of The Brotherhood for crying out loud, righting the wrongs onboard. But not this time. This situation was extremely unsettling, another blow to the community adding to the spiraling sadness.

I sat under the half-deck with Chuck and Lilly before they left. Lilly was eager to discuss their travel plans and wanted advice concerning a few things. I was surprised they came to me, but willingly obliged. I then shook Birdman's hand and wished him well. In a flash, all our experiences together came back to me. We had always connected cerebrally, often with few words. But the memories we created together were priceless. I knew our paths would not cross again. This was goodbye. No need for bumbling words, our eyes said it all. In total, nine of my friends left the ship in Cádiz.

As the *Statsraad Lehmkuhl* pulled away from the dock, I stood by the railing and waved to Frank and Arturo. They showed up to see us off along with Birdman, Chuck, Lilly, Perry, and the ghosts of Alec, Blake, and Debbie. Seeing Frank and Arturo on the dock was only slightly consoling. I suppose the fact they were there indicated smatterings of sentimental concern for the rest of us. Maybe that's how I wanted to interpret it. Several kids on deck threw matchboxes filled with cash to Perry as he stood in anticipation of his next steps. He had no money except for help from his friends. And he had no time to plan or process. Suddenly, and without warning, he was tossed from the ship with his few meager belongings and no ticket home. Perry was scared. He didn't want to leave. But without question, he had pushed the administrative limits, broken rules, bullied, and hadn't taken enough care to secure his place onboard. Still, it was sad.

As I stood quietly, processing my feelings and confusion, a strange sense of peace and contentment came over me from somewhere within. It didn't come from the dock.

When we reached the open sea, I helped set sails, climbed the rigging to unleash sizings, then helped pull the appropriate ropes on deck, burning up an abundance of anxious, nervous energy. The physical work countered my emotional anguish.

Stephanie brought a copy of the documentary film about the Oceanics experience along when she came onboard in Cádiz—the one narrated by David Wayne. So, as a distraction we watched it on our first night at sea. It felt strange viewing a story about the school, the ship, and about us while the drama was still playing out. David Wayne appeared better on film than in real life. We all did. We looked so innocent, so young, and had so much hair! The film over-romanticized our experience, giving skewed positive impressions of life onboard. Maybe at the time, things were better. But most of us watching the finished product understood the deeper truth. Nevertheless, it was a nice morale boost and proud entertainment. A day that started badly ultimately ended well.

I crawled into my bunk, happy to be alive, and thrilled to still be a cadet aboard the *Statsraad Lehmkuhl*. That night, I felt very, very lucky. My appreciation for life continued for the next few days. I seized every opportunity to set sails, work in the rigging, stand watch, and do menial ship's work. I even spent one entire day painting. Nothing seemed like a chore anymore, like maybe I was finally committed to my true purpose aboard, wanting to make the most of my last weeks as a sailor.

One morning after setting all the sails, Jack Wright and I stood at the end of the royl yard for half an hour enjoying the beauty of the world displayed around us, 360 degrees. The ocean spilled to the horizon in every direction, blending magically with the blue sky above. Suddenly what seemed like a million white doves appeared overhead. That moment best articulated my deepest feelings of peace, without words. Jack wasn't a heady-feely type of guy, but I could tell he sensed something magical about the moment as well.

We returned to the deck and greeted Mrs. Gronningen who was busy washing hatch doors. Her smile was enough to melt any lingering fears concerning her husband. I had to admit that Chief Mate was a fair family man who already had made a significant impact onboard. Best of all, the crewmen seemed to be on their best behavior under his command. Life aboard felt more refined, like the evil was gone. Things had changed.

Early the next morning on lookout watch, I again witnessed nature's splendor revealed through a magnificent sunrise, as the big red shining ball rose up from the sea behind a thin cloud-laced horizon. Then reaching upwards into the welcoming sky, it proudly cast reflections on the calm, glass-like waters. Within minutes the sun turned from deep red to bright yellow. But during those moments of awe, the ship, the wind, the sea, and everything in sight seemed to be under its command, standing at attention, waiting for the drum roll to carry on. Or maybe for Bosun's call for all hands on deck. "Wow," I whispered to myself. "How can I ever share this experience of magnificent beauty with anyone back home?"

Ω

Mike and the Doc picked up classes that were previously taught by Frank and Arturo. New energy was applied to school time as a noticeably positive tone emerged from the rubble. Students seemed more motivated than before. Again, groups needed to reorganize to accommodate the decreasing number of cadets. Emil and Pisacano were switched from my group to another. With smaller groups, each cadet had more responsibility and purpose. Our work was focused, and my hands again looked like the hands of a sailor, rough and calloused. I routinely did pull-ups and muscle-ups on the rings between morning muster and ship's tasks. Some days I ran up and down the rigging just for exercise, enjoying the same thrills as before but with more confidence and ease as my body, mind and soul jived in perfect sync, like a wind-up toy (just like Poulsen).

I latched onto an excerpt from the book, *Life At Its Best,* by Meyer Baba: "Keep your mind quiet, steady, and firm. Do not submit to desires, but rather, control them. One who cannot restrain his tongue cannot restrain his mind. One who cannot restrain his mind cannot restrain his actions. One who cannot restrain his actions cannot restrain himself. And one who cannot restrain himself cannot attain the real infinite self." I found those words both challenging and encouraging, in the worst of times and in the best of times.

We sailed west from southern Spain, then turned directly north past the coast of Portugal. On the evening of April 27, we passed Cape Finisterre and entered the Bay of Biscay. Almost immediately the winds increased as sea swells grew. None of us needed a reminder of what happened last time we were here. As evening approached, we experienced cold rain, but also favorable winds. The captain ordered five large square sails on the fore and main masts to remain set as we powered north at eight knots throughout the night. I spotted several ships close by from lookout watch, one passing less than 100 feet off port side. That hour was exciting and dangerous with so many ships, especially in dreary weather with poor visibility.

I remembered Franco's words concerning the Bay of Biscay, "It is a chilling fact that more than 5,000 ships have been lost in the bay during the past 150 years. Most of them are still on the ocean floor." At one point during the night, two lookout watchmen were positioned on the bow because of heavy traffic.

I played several games of ping pong with Jack after going off duty. Suddenly, ping pong at sea became much more challenging with the increased motion. During one volley, I made an errant shot that was headed off the table on Jack's side. But just at that moment the ship lurched straight up and toward starboard, knocking both of us off our feet but allowing the ball to catch the far corner of the table. It drew an "Oh shit!" from Jack, and a laugh of luck from me. It was game point. But win or lose, Jack and I were enjoying the novel experience and unpredictability of ping pong at sea. It was just one more peculiarity added to the ever-growing list of unusual things aboard the *Statsraad Lehmkuhl.*

Student interaction was great during our sail to France, with lots of talk concerning travel and personal dreams. And there was little horseplay in the banjers. No one skipped out of ship's work, and for the first in a very long time, life aboard was pleasant with everyone pulling their weight. Clark replaced Arturo as the music room pianist. One day we all helped give the ship a thorough cleaning, scrubbing the deck from front to back. And the best part of it all, no one complained! Our community felt amazingly different. Could it really have been about the nine who left ship? Or should it be credited to the new Chief Mate? Or just maybe the positive spirit demonstrated by several cadets onboard had become contagious enough to negate the negative.

Me playing my recorder on buoy watch

CHAPTER 24: FRANCE

Because of its protected bay area in the northwestern quadrant of France, Brest was and is an important commercial seaport with direct access to the North Atlantic. The city hosts a Naval Base and the French Naval Academy as well. Notably, its surroundings have rich Celtic history with medieval towns scattered throughout its hills and countryside.

We docked in the early evening. Temperatures were cold as Clark, Gary, and I went exploring after first grabbing some cookies and chocolate bars from a local store near the docks. Several commercial ships were also moored, so plenty of sailors slogged through town mingling with the usual riffraff. By now we were better at avoiding dives, swindlers, hookers, and undesirables. We kept walking, paying little mind to winks and requests for cash in exchange for services we did not need.

Before bed, I discussed a potential field trip with Clark for the following day. But again, we knew so little about the surrounding area. He suggested we wing it like before, and figure things out as we go. I agreed. After the hassles of plan documentation, pulling our passports from the safe, and acquiring administrative permission, we headed to the train station. Destination: Belle-Isle-en-Terre, a small village that appeared to be in the hilly countryside, as we could best determine from the map.

We exited the train at a small station in the middle of nowhere between Belle-Isle and Bégard but it wasn't at all what we expected. No matter, it was a cool sunny day, and our packs were light. We walked four kilometers to Bégard rather than to Belle-Isle. The town proved to be no more than a small community of old brown stucco houses with barns to match, no attractions, no points of interest, no restaurants, and no hotels. Our plans changed again.

Guingamp, we were told, was a larger town sixteen kilometers southeast. Limited cash dictated our means of transportation. So of course, hitchhiking was our best option. We got a ride in an old Peugeot with three French hippies, two of whom spoke English. But they were in a serious debate about something political and continued talking among themselves in French. So, the fifteen-minute ride to

Guingamp didn't necessitate any obligatory small talk from Clark or me. That was just fine. We needed a ride, nothing more.

The guys dropped us off at a beautiful central plaza in town. Guingamp was filled with medieval charm, well-preserved old buildings, and narrow cobblestone streets. We rented a room at Hotel de L' Avenue Guingamp for 17 francs (3 US dollars). From there, everything was accessible by foot. Just east of the square was the old Fontaine de la Plomée which served as the main water source for several hundred years. We then walked up to the old castle built in the 12th century, Chateau de Pierre II, and visited the basilica Notre-Dame-de-Bon-Secours from the 11th century. I was fascinated by the challenges involved in constructing these old buildings, and the time required to build them. Many laborers spent their entire lives working on just one structure without seeing its completion. I was amazed by that fact, knowing our lives now are so easy and good by comparison. And complaint free, right?

We shared a bottle of red wine and cookies in a café by the square. As in Spain, Clark was a fun traveling partner. His personality became increasingly more intriguing as he shared insights, opinions, dreams, and reflections, important things that I hadn't heard from him before. And he provided humor beyond what I thought possible. We laughed hysterically several times.

Two older gentlemen were seated at a nearby table. They had obviously already consumed enough alcohol to remove any social inhibitions. One of them attempted to strike up a conversation with me in French. The only English word he knew was beer. And of course, my French was almost nil, as was Clark's. But that didn't stop the Frenchman from continuing to talk. Once he went on a solid three-minute spiel with hand motions, eyebrow contortions and spit flying from his mouth before I responded with a story of my own in English. That started a hilarious fifteen-minute verbal exchange between him, Clark, and me.

The guy continued in French, while Clark and I did our best to keep pace in English. We were amused by the stupidity of our exchange, and by how much we enjoyed it. Completely void of intellectualism. Clark appeared to be entertained by my fictional stories. Like the one I told the Frenchman of my parents swimming with dolphins in the Indian Ocean near the port city of Columbo, Sri Lanka, wearing rubber flippers. The guy didn't understand anything I said. But no matter, Clark did.

We had plenty of time to discuss the latest changes within the Oceanics program. Clark shared the same awareness and understanding of things onboard as me and acknowledged the fact that both of us had been personally blessed

with endurance and acceptance beyond the norm. I listened and nodded but
wasn't convinced I was as patient and accepting as he. Clark appeared to have
come through the onboard drama unscathed, emotionally undaunted, giving no
indication otherwise. As for me, at times I felt derailed and wrecked despite my
random shots of optimism. Thankfully however, I had always been able to bounce
back from down times. Maybe that was my blessing.

It was easy to change the subject with Clark. His long lulls of silence during our
conversations allowed me to interpose. So that's what I did. I started talking about
French bread, one of France's greatest cultural attributes, until our mouths began
to water.

The next morning, we each bought a loaf of bread and topped it with honey.
That and a shared can of fruit cocktail was breakfast in our hotel room. Blue skies,
white puffy clouds, and cool temps greeted us as we walked to the west side of
town and stuck out our thumbs. We had no particular destination in mind, again
allowing spontaneity and fate to be our guides.

A little old lady, probably in her 50s, picked us up and invited us to her home
in a small country village several kilometers away. Her house was filled with
excessive numbers of potted flowers and cats. The air composition inside was an
unsavory mix of sour milk, cat pee, and fresh flower fragrance.

Delphine was obviously lonely, starving for human interaction. She insisted
on feeding us after first serving red wine in white coffee mugs. Although she
spoke not a word of English, she never stopped talking during our entire visit.
I tried my best to communicate with her, to respond with hand motions and facial
expressions to her gibberish. But I finally decided to just listen. She obviously had
plenty to say. Clark sat expressionless. That would've probably been the case even
if Delphine spoke English. I glanced at him several times, chuckling, as he quietly
sipped wine and chewed her pancakes.

The cakes had a texture of soft leather, pliable but tough. In one of his rare
comments, Clark determined that it might be better to wear them than eat them.
His comment brought hysterical laughs from us both. Meanwhile, Delphine just
kept chattering away. Truth was, without wine, those pancakes could not have
been swallowed. No way!

I explained to her that we were going to Morlaix, a town I'd seen on the map.
She wanted to know if we planned to hitchhike. Using sign language, she stuck
out her thumb sideways then shrugged with both hands facing up, indicating a
question. We nodded. She then left the room and returned minutes later, allowing
us time to secretly feed the remaining remnants of our pancakes to the cats.

Smiling broadly, she handed me an 8"x 10" piece of white cardboard complete with black print in the center, "MORLAIX." It was a nice gesture, but the print was too small to be of much use. "Merci beaucoup," I said just before I was overcome with a sneezing fit. I've always been plagued with cat allergies. It was long past time to get my butt out of that house.

Ω

From Delphine's, we walked several kilometers along a beautiful country road by a stream, then relaxed on the grounds of a colorful, flower-adorned graveyard and wrote letters among the dead. It was peaceful and quiet, as it should have been in such company, far from the chaotic community aboard ship. We agreed that the closest commonality between life onboard ship and this experience in western France was the leather pancakes.

With Morlaix just thirty-five kilometers away, we stuck out our thumbs, without using Delphine's sign, and promptly got a ride with a twenty-five-year-old girl eager to practice her English. I asked how she knew we spoke English. Her response was a look of surprise, "What kind of question is that?" Followed by a smile and a simple comment, "You look so American."

We found no reason to stay in Morlaix. Nothing interested us there. Our next ride was with a well-dressed middle-aged lady in a Mercedes Benz heading south toward Quimper, but she went only as far as Carhaix-Plouguer. Then a guy in an old, dilapidated Citroen 2CV picked us up. My last ride in one of those post-World War II cars was with a nun at Taizé, one year prior. Like then, this ride was rattly. But our conversation with Oliver was great. His English was better than anyone we'd met thus far. He even treated us to sodas and pastries at a small bakery while listening to our sea adventures. I couldn't remember meeting a friendlier, more well-mannered young man. We exchanged contact information before parting ways in Quimper.

Clark and I were both running low on cash. Before each field trip, I determined how much I could spend. Rationing funds wasn't fun, but I had no choice, relying on creativity to stretch my dollars whenever possible. So, I seldom turned down free food offers, even leather pancakes in a feline haven. Hotel costs were always problematic. Renting a room meant that something else had to be cut. Usually food. And when there wasn't enough cash to buy food and I was hungry, the situation sometimes called for more drastic measures. Compromised ethics.

We rented a third-floor room near the train station in Quimper for fifteen francs, less than 3 US dollars. We also bought milk and cookies at a small grocery store, then borrowed a hunk of cheese, salami, fruit cookies, and a jar of baby food. The baby food was Clark's doing, as he explained with a grin that it was the easiest thing to stuff inside his coat. We sat by our room window and ate dinner while enjoying the activities below. I suppose it was guilt that prompted our discussion concerning parental teaching. Neither of us were lacking in that department. And we both determined that someday we'd more than make up for the things we borrowed. I was completely serious about that. The commitment to someday pay back, or pay forward didn't totally remove my guilt, but it did give me a shot of humility and helped me better understand the needs of a broken world. Our efforts stretched the borrowed food enough to include breakfast. As a result of rationing, I was still hungry when I went to bed. The baby food wasn't overly satisfying.

After checking out, we visited the beautiful, soaring twin-spired Gothic cathedral in the town square. We also spent time at the fine arts museum before again sticking out our thumbs. Western France proved to be an easy place to hitchhike. We seldom waited more than two or three minutes for rides.

During the warmest time of the day, we explored the lovely little town of Châteaulin. From there we were able to secure a ride all the way back to Brest with an English-speaking travel agent. Jean-Pierre Strowski was a man of French-Polish origin who had traveled the world and was a gem to talk to. He asked questions, told stories, and prompted interesting dialogue during the entire trip back to the coast. Even Clark was inspired by his personality, openly engaging without any of his trademark aloofness. We invited Jean-Pierre to visit the ship during the next couple days, at his convenience. I knew he would. He was a relational guy, sincerely fascinated by our stories, and in love with sailing.

Our first night back onboard was a reminder of the realities at port. We watched a movie in the library, *Dr. Jekyll and Sister Hyde*, which was strangely entertaining but not all that great. There were disturbances in the banjers as drunk cadets slithered in, provoking a visit from Mate Schnitler. He didn't do much to address the issues at hand, but complained openly about the program itself to anyone who would listen. None of us were interested in hearing anything he had to say. "Sorry Schnitler, no disrespect, we just don't want to hear it," several of us thought aloud.

Late arrival field-trippers meandered back onboard. Eiji returned from a quick solo trip across the Channel to England, and a brief visit to Paris.

Ship's work consumed my entire next day after morning muster. Again, I painted, helping Evenson paint the brown stripe completely around the outside of the ship. It was probably my most enjoyable task all year. Evenson was a low-key able-bodied seaman, often seen but seldom heard. We all liked him. This was the first time I worked directly with him for an entire shift. What a nice, unexpected treat. But the night activities again hindered my sleep.

The next day after lunch, the fire watchman found me and said there was a visitor on deck asking for me by name. Sure enough, it was Jean-Pierre Strowski, accompanied by his wife, young son, and three friends from the travel agency. I spent the next hour showing them the ship. Jean-Pierre was awestruck. At the end of their time onboard, he invited me to join his group for a drink at a nearby café. Oddly, it felt like we had been friends for a long time. We shared past travel experiences, family history, and present-day life. I expounded on my Amish community of Bird-in-Hand and told stories about Pop and Grossmommie Smucker. Although it was unlikely that we'd ever meet again, we made the most of our time together that day. I was convinced again that everything else in life is secondary to relationships.

Ω

Due to inclement weather, the ship couldn't leave Brest as scheduled. To pass the time, cadets on duty did ship's work—mostly easy stuff. One thing that always amused me was the leather-lunged Bosun's role during shift changes. He stood on deck and yelled down through the hatch to the banjers in a booming voice and his best English, "Vatch und schtandby vatch on dekk fer schips verk," followed by a long blast from his whistle. His voice could be heard in every nook and cranny of the banjers, echoing below deck. We had no excuse not to show up. He then waited by the hatch door grinning like a hyena chewing bones, as cadets made their way to the deck and lined up for muster. That scenario happened three times a day, every day while at sea. And it was one of those routines that never got old nor lost its luster.

On our last day in port, Todd and I worked together. He had long since gotten over the two dollars he thought I owed him. Our discussions covered a lot of subjects that day, including the fact that Michelangelo wrote backwards in his diary. I was so intrigued by that, I decided to do the same. So, on Monday, May 7, 1973, I recorded the day's events in my journal writing from right to left. It wasn't as difficult as expected. When I held it up to the mirror checking for accuracy,

I was impressed! Without sounding boastful, my writing was nearly flawless, and with decent penmanship!

Later, Schnitler asked Todd and me to meet him on the deck after dark. He explained there was one additional task that he needed assistance with. At 22:00 we reported to the foredeck as commanded. Schnitler's tone seemed strangely low key. He spoke in a hushed voice as he led us to the bay side of the foredeck where garbage bags were piled near the side rail. From there he instructed us to quietly transfer the trash up to the half-deck and throw it overboard. I knew he wasn't kidding, but wished he was. I was under the impression that throwing garbage into the harbor of any port is illegal. He assured us it was OK, however, as he explained, "This happens all over the world. It doesn't hurt anything, especially not here in Brest where the harbor is deep." With that he glanced in all directions, then added nonchalantly, "But it's important that no one sees you. Keep this to yourselves." Then he disappeared.

"Wow!" I wondered aloud, "Does the captain know about this?" We concluded that we'd never find out because of the personal risk involved in asking.

Todd rubbed his hands together, pretending to wash them clean. "We're just obeying orders," he exclaimed. But still, it was difficult to completely remove our guilt because we were having too much fun tossing the trash overboard. It soon became a competition. I told him I could throw my bags farther into the bay than he could, as the whispered trash talking overshadowed the trash chucking.

Bosun giving orders on deck

Poulsen handling the wheel in rough seas

Buoy watch at night

CHAPTER 25: THE LAST SAIL

Despite strong winds from the west, Captain decided to attempt departure. At 10:00 the ship pulled away from the dock with its 450-horsepower engine running full throttle. He hoped to overcome the head winds long enough to get into the Bay of Biscay then turn north toward the English Channel. And he had enough confidence in the ship and crew to muscle our way through another challenge. By this time, the physical test of sailing in these conditions seemed smaller than Captain's desire to go home and the emotional repercussions of staying in port. Morale onboard was deteriorating again. It was time to get everyone back to Bergen.

After sunset, the ship navigated through large sea swells and cold winds. My group went on watch at midnight. First off, I helped Jane clean hordes of dirty dishes in the union mess before setting sails. At 02:00 I reported for lookout watch—it was a quiet night at sea. Then I joined Todd, Mark, Gary, Randy, and Tor in the guest saloon for an amusing hour of laughs, reminiscing, and bantering.

The six of us shared memories from the year. We started talking about the Sargent for some unknown reason, and agreed he was an impressive character—definitely one of the saltiest dogs onboard. He understood his place among the crew and somehow managed to avoid conflict, unlike some of the others. With little knowledge of the English language, he seldom spoke to us, but he was friendly. We all liked him.

One of Sargent's daily tasks was ensuring punctual mealtimes. He stood just outside the entrance to the mess hall fifteen minutes before each meal, keeping order. After the food was brought from the galley and placed on the dining tables, he blew a long whistle blast followed by a short toot, signaling the students to find their seats and start eating. After the whistle, he vanished, taking no further responsibility. This routine happened before every meal, every day during the entire year. I believe that no one onboard was more committed to executing his task than he.

Tor and I recalled the time Jacobsen did a balancing act spread-eagle on top of the fore mast while anchored off the coast of Gambia. It was a crazy stunt. The fact that Jacobsen had been drinking only multiplied the degree of foolishness. But no matter, it was one of the craziest, most impressive performances any of us had ever seen. He supposedly did it on a cash-rewarding dare, most of which he lost to the captain in fines. Although little more was said concerning the incident, the memory would live on for a very long time in the minds of all of us who witnessed it. Someone took a photo from the deck as documented proof against any naysayers.

I had climbed to the top of the rig often. I knew the level of difficulty involved, the balance, the degree of care and focus required, as well as the trust and confidence one must have in his own strength and agility to maneuver 155 feet up. But for the life of me I couldn't imagine climbing atop the mast and balancing on my stomach. Nor could I fathom anyone else doing it, had I not seen it with my own eyes. Jacobsen was one of a kind: a mule, both in body and mind.

We also discussed head games and things we did during night watch shifts to stay awake, like pacing and bouncing. Or pretending to be the captain of a pirate ship, allowing our imaginations to run wild. Smoking cigarettes, although less exciting, helped pass the time. And we all confessed to dozing off on buoy watch.

Kjemtrup interrupted our discussion at 05:00, ordering us on deck to set the bram and royl sails on both masts. What a cold, ungodly time to set the highest sails on the ship. But I decided it was better to respond than to think or complain. Jane and I were the first climbers to the top of the foremast. Within fifteen minutes the sails were set. Our new group worked with great proficiency that night. Even Kjemtrup thought so, nodding his squinty-eyed approval. Earning the endorsement of Second Mate at this point of the voyage wasn't as important as it had been before, but still it was nice. Better yet was the feeling of crawling into bed at 06:00. Even the wool blankets and feather pillows, both of which caused skin irritations for me, were acceptable that morning.

Ω

Between ship's work, watch shifts, meals, and classes, I read *The Catcher in the Rye* by J.D. Salinger. Although the dayroom was cold enough to see our breath during the final leg north, it's where I hung out to read, write, and socialize. It was one of those cold mornings, as the ship entered the English Channel, that I became aware of just how intrigued I was becoming with my friend Zoe. Always pleasant, amazingly accepting, soft-spoken, adaptable, cute, and sweet, she had quietly soared to the top of my radar. Before coffee break that day, she walked into the mess hall and gave me the biggest smile ever. "Only ten more minutes till goodies," she exclaimed while softly touching my arm.

Zoe had been one of my favorite female cadets for many months, but on this day, I realized my feelings had catapulted beyond sisterly sentiments. I found her innocence refreshingly attractive. She was fun. And her presence made it difficult to go negative about anything. Our three-year age difference no longer mattered to me. However, considering a romantic relationship onboard now felt preposterous, as this psychodrama was nearing its end. But I felt conflicted because my heart said otherwise.

"No," I kept telling myself. "Our friendship needs to remain pure and simple. Don't complicate things now." Honestly, I was probably too shy to start any sort of romance with Zoe anyway, but timidity didn't negate my feelings.

One evening, we were served bones, fat, and gristle for dinner again. As before, the putrid stench drifted into the banjers. Zoe sat quietly next to me, smiled, and offered me a portion of her raisin-topped sweet soup and big juicy orange. We chose not to talk about the bad food. Her acceptance of life was extraordinary.

My watch shift started at midnight. Our group had little down time as we set stay sails, braced yards, then again set top sails at 04:00. It was an exciting night as we sped along at 10–14 knots, skirting past other ships. In fact, during a course change, the *Statsraad Lehmkuhl* nearly got clipped off by a large Libyan tanker. Never mind that we had the right-of-way. Sailing vessels supposedly always have preference in the open seas. But I looked up with trembling as the huge tanker passed much too close for comfort heading south, blasting a deep, ear-splitting horn that matched its size.

I manned the wheel from 03:00 to 04:00, struggling to keep the compass needle on course. Our headings varied significantly, starting from 010' east to 015' then 025', and finally by the end of my hour-long shift the needle was at 028' east. Schnitler shouted heading changes from the chart room as Poulsen relayed them to me. It was my job to respond quickly. Ships appeared from everywhere—tankers, freighters, cargo, and passenger ships. We were the only ship with sails, but our right-of-way seemed to matter little. Never on this voyage had we encountered so much traffic. It was discomforting, especially at the helm. But our sails stayed up and the winds remained strong—adventurous sailing for sure!

As soon as my wheel duty ended, the command went out to set the top sails for those who dared to climb that night. It was dark, windy, and cold as the ship listed heavily toward starboard. But the task was brutally exhilarating! Both Jane and I expressed a deep sense of relief when we safely planted our feet on deck after the work was done. Finally off duty at 06:00 hours, I sat on my bed for ten solid minutes, totally exhausted but with adrenaline still pumping through my veins. My calloused hands were bleeding, my thighs were thumping, and my cheeks were numbed from the cold. The taste of sea salt on my cold lips was familiar and strangely consoling. I liked salt in most any form, even in a case like this.

It was an extremely proud and humbling moment, despite the contrast of those two words. I knew with certainty that I was a qualified sailor. I had earned my place. It felt soulfully satisfying as I lay down and drifted off to sleep, still fully clothed. The blood on my sheets authenticated everything I had done the night before, and everything I felt. Well, maybe not everything. I still didn't know what to do about my feelings for Zoe. Hard work, fatigue and sailing was only a temporary distraction.

♌

Classes officially ended on May 10. Aside from several formal written exams, most final grades were determined by our progress throughout the year and by student/professor interviews in the final week. One class required a year-end essay, but as intended, our educational experience went well beyond the classroom. Real-life stuff. Not that it mattered much, but I aced everything except marine biology, where I received hard-earned B. Final grades weren't as important to me as were the achievements of emotional and physical survival.

My last days aboard were devoted to sailing. They provided some of the best sailing weather of the entire trip. When not on watch or standby, we were free to sleep, read, hang out in the music room, or do whatever we wanted. But I chose to stay on deck and help with ship's work, making the most of my waning hours at sea. The excitement of sailing was now at a ten for me and for many of my shipmates. Even those who were previously less enthused.

Conversations centered around our next steps. What to do after Oceanics. Most of us planned to fly back to New York on the charter flight. Several hoped to travel in Europe. Eiji, Clark, and I actively explored the possibility of working aboard an Asian freighter making biweekly trips between Norway and Japan. Chief Mate advised us on the details. We'd need to travel to Oslo to interview, but the chances were slim that all three of us would be hired on the same ship. My motivation was to be with Eiji and Clark. Otherwise, the job was much less appealing.

Tim Harris named his plans to become a general in the Salvation Army. He loved collecting old coins, especially Indian head nickels, and figured the Salvation Army would give him the means to do that. With all the seriousness he could muster, Tim presented his plan, only to bring hoots of laughter from his friends.

As galley supplies dwindled, so did the food quality. I suppose stuff needed to be used up from the pantry bottom. I understood that but didn't like it. One morning we were served the worst tasting pancakes ever, for lunch no less. No one could figure out what could've possibly made them taste so badly. I stuffed my mouth with a few tomato slices, then gulped milk, just to get them down. Thankfully, I had oranges from Brest, and the company of my friend Zoe with whom to share the experience.

I came across an English newspaper in the library from our recent visit to France. Being in touch with the outside world wasn't a common occurrence, but I read with interest the news on Watergate. According to one reporter, President Nixon was still trying to convince the American public of his innocence. One night on prime-time TV, he stated emphatically, "Let me make myself perfectly clear. I did nothing wrong."

The article explained that many folks still trusted and supported him despite overwhelming evidence of guilt. I shook my head in disgust, hoping those who supported him were not naïve plain folks from my hometown. But I feared they were.

It was difficult for me to believe how easily people could be swayed by a political scoundrel—good people who allowed ignorance and wishful thinking to defy truth. It's always been that way. Being an idealist, however, I still had hope that truth would prevail, and that Congress would impeach his ass. Nixon was a smart politician, but was corrupt, obsessed with power, divisive, dishonest, and lacked ethics. I suppose my nineteen-year-old ideals came with expectations. No apologies for that. Meanwhile, the country remained mired in seemingly insurmountable challenges: disparity of wealth, the Vietnam war, foreign policy, nuclear weapons, healthcare, and civil rights.

I also read articles concerning the atrocities of Romanian dictator Ceaușescu, about Arab oil, and about the Panamanians protesting ongoing US control of the canal. Their sentiments were expressed at a recent UN meeting in New York. I paused in quiet reflection—the real world was going to hell. I was glad to still be at sea, still aboard the *Statsraad Lehmkuhl*, even though our community onboard was indeed just a microcosm of that real world I was about to reenter.

Suddenly at 14:00 hours the winds kicked up as the ship sailed into a small storm, causing it to list seriously toward starboard. Portholes on that side of the ship stayed completely submerged while the deck stood at a constant 30 degrees. Quickly, the bram and royl on both masts were furled, as well as several high staysails in an effort to correct the issue. The squall lasted just 15 minutes but was impressively violent before taming itself. We encountered several squalls reaching force-nine during the course of the evening, causing unexpected provocations for the crew on deck.

Freshwater showers were turned on from 12:00 to 24:00, but it was difficult for anyone to stay vertical as the ship rocked and pitched. Naked bodies were thrown from shower stalls below, while clothed excitement on deck continued into the night.

I had the first lookout shift when my group went on duty at midnight. After staggering my way to the foredeck, I was alarmed to find no one there. Someone was always on lookout, 24/7. This was strange!

I yelled into the howling wind, "LOOKOUT… LOOKOUT WATCH… IS ANYONE HERE?" I repeated my plea several times in every direction but got no response. A cold chill, colder than the wet night air, ascended through my spine. Did the watchman fall overboard? My mind raced. Who could it be—Amor, Katie, or maybe Kevin? "OH GOD, PLEASE NO," I cried heavenward.

Group A was just finishing their shift. The only sounds came from the driving wind and rain whipping and rattling the rigging, and from the violent sea slapping the ship's hull. I knew with certainty that a sea rescue was impossible in these conditions. The night was pitch black. With my face stinging and my heart pounding, I left the foredeck to report the missing cadet, emotionally numbed. It was then I heard a voice from the halfdeck shouting through cupped hands into the wind, "ARE YOU THE NEW WATCHMAN?" I looked up to see Mark Kaiser. Stunned, overjoyed, and relieved, I realized what happened. Lookout watch was relocated to the halfdeck because of imminent dangers on the bow.

I shouted back, "I THOUGHT YOU FELL OVERBOARD!"

Boosted by the fact that no one was lost, I climbed onto the halfdeck. All I wanted to do was give Mark a bear hug, but I restrained my joy. He would've looked at me sideways and made an unrepeatable comment. So instead, I planted my feet securely on the halfdeck to maintain balance in hopes of a clear view forward and to both sides for the next hour. Mark stayed only long enough to slap me on the back and offer a huge boyish grin, "Did you really think I fell over?"

I didn't answer. The stiff, cold wind and rain pelted my face, biting into my exposed skin like slivers of ice. The abusive elements continued for a solid hour. Again, I tasted salt on my lips, painfully so. I had unequivocally become a salty dog. I had become like my surroundings.

We sailed north at a brisk thirteen knots along the coast of Holland, passing several stationary oil rigs. Maybe they belonged to Karlson, the Dutch oil guru whose home Eli, Leamie, and I had innocently crashed in the fall of 1971. It was an amusing, passing thought, bringing back head-shaking memories.

Our night on duty competed with the excitement of previous adventures aboard the *Statsraad Lehmkuhl.* And best of all, I found myself in the rigging at 04:00 hours setting the merse and main sails. Climbing at night was no longer scary, even in these conditions. I had full confidence in my abilities to work safely on all parts of the ship, high or low. At 05:45, Rick Goodfriend gave me a piping hot bowl of mushroom soup. I chuckled quietly to myself, realizing that he was absolutely a good friend. Cadets were again making their own food. It appeared like many kids had hidden stashes, having now effectively mastered their techniques of personal survival. But more importantly, it was evident that we all had learned to share. Much of the selfishness from earlier days had dissipated.

I slept from 06:30 to 11:30, then reported for standby muster. Sleep came in small increments with the new watch schedule, sometimes twice a day, sometimes only once. But my body could now effectively operate on five hours of sleep in a 24-hour period. I sat with Eiji and Clark during lunch, again discussing the possibility of hiring onto a freighter traveling between Norway and Japan. I also shared my thoughts of going home and playing softball with the Bird-in-Hand boys and working at the Bird-in-Hand Restaurant for the summer. Honestly, I wasn't prepared to make decisions concerning my future. There was just too much to consider.

Mutton bones, fat, and gristle for dinner. This time it was served with rotten cabbage. I sneaked several apples from the galley, then joined Eiji, Tara, Kevin, Amor, and Barry for pickled mackerel, flatbread, blue cheese, and canned noodles from Tomé-Açu. The so-called gourmet grub wasn't great either, but the company was.

While eating mackerel, which included the whole kit and kaboodle, we discussed in detail each part we bit into, like the ovaries, guts, kidneys, eyes, head, scales, and tail. It was gross conversation to accentuate the gross food, raising a seriously legitimate question—where did the expression "holy mackerel" come from? No part of that fish was holy!

The winds calmed considerably as we entered the North Sea, slowing the ship to seven knots. My group anticipated a long, difficult watch shift starting at midnight, but lucked out except for the fact that it was frigid cold. And we had to cover Sam's watches. All was quiet on deck, but the North Sea remained eerie, even in calm waters. Something about the thick darkness looming overhead and the deep green sea couldn't be trusted. Kjemtrup reminded us that the North Sea could unleash its fury on anyone or anything at any time, like a pot of water on the brink of boiling, only multiplied a million times over. The crewmen on duty were uncharacteristically quiet, keeping a watchful eye, aware of how quickly things can change. They understood what history confirmed with the likes of 400 lost ships still sitting on its bottom.

To pass time, Gary started playing his harmonica in the middle of the night. Someone made a snide remark, then another, and soon our entire group began harassing him outside the guest saloon. We hadn't totally forgiven him for his arrogance during the food crisis in the mid-Atlantic.

Several cadets began mimicking his mother's New York accent. Gary had rented a motor bike in Grenada and wrecked it, costing his parents a large sum of money. So, in St. Maarten as his mother bid him farewell at the dock, she gave him some parental advice. Her departing words brought sniggers and smiles from those of us within earshot, "Galry, please don't rent no moir motacycles—we can't affoid it." Of course, we couldn't leave her comments alone.

So, that night on duty in the North Sea, our group exaggerated her accent and motherly advice: "Galry, listen to ya motha," and "Galry, be careful with ya harmonica, we can't affoid to have it fall overboid." He wasn't amused by our teasing but grinned ever so slightly at the "listen to ya motha" verbiage. Our efforts paid off. No longer wanting to be the center of attention, he stopped playing his annoying harmonica, which is precisely what we wanted.

At 04:00 I again went high to untie sizings on both the bram and royl sails. That had become my routine. Every morning when Poulsen gave orders, he looked directly at Jane and me, then nodded his head upwards, indicating what he wanted us to do without words. We usually gave a quick thumbs-up and headed for Jacob's ladder. Jane was always positive, a real morale boost for anyone fortunate enough to work alongside her. I believe there were times I fed off her spirit.

On this day I remained on the royl yard alone for fifteen minutes in the pre-dawn light, reflecting on what Eiji had shared with me several days earlier. "My favorite proverb to come out of the west, and the wisest quote from scripture is this," he said. "Blessed are the meek for they shall inherit the earth." So, that morning despite being cold, I stayed aloft trying to figure out its meaning.

Ω

Jones made a Jolly Roger flag from a large piece of black fabric, complete with the white skull and crossbones, like those flown on pirate ships in the past. It was an impressive replica. After lunch and standby muster, the students and faculty were called on deck for a short dedication commemorating our last day at sea. During the ceremony but unseen by crewmen, Jones raised the Jolly Roger flag, quietly hoisting it at the tip of the main mast where it flew proudly in the breeze for fifteen minutes. His pre-meditated action wasn't discussed with anyone of ranking importance beforehand. It wouldn't have been allowed. Pirates were perceived as nothing more than terrorists on the high seas. So, the flag wasn't welcome on any merchant ship. But it seemed fitting for the *Statsraad Lehmkuhl* in 1973, a year filled with extraordinary, unusual, and unlawful activities from the start. Chief Mate ordered the flag to be taken down, but not before photographs, mock salutes, and humor accentuated the event. There was no reprimand or punishment ordered from the captain. By now, I believe he was just glad to be going home.

Coffee break after the flag incident was insane. Jones brought a tray filled with cookies into the mess hall from the galley, but before ever reaching the bottom of the hatch stairs, the tray was attacked by the mob. Cookies flew everywhere as we scarfed up whatever we could, even crumbs from the floor, resembling hungry seagulls fighting for food on a crowded beach. The squawking was similar as well.

We had plenty to eat for dinner. Obviously, the steward cleared out more stuff from the storage pantry: hamburgers, fried eggs, spaghetti, peas, carrots, several types of soup, and an interesting fruit goop concoction served with milk. The cadet animal behavior continued as the mess hall lived up to its name. Unfortunately, I was on cleanup duty. But it came with a silver lining—Zoe was my assistant.

After dinner, all the sails were furled and taken in for the last time at sea. When the cry went out, "Alle mann pa dekk," I was still cleaning up, so I wasn't available to help with that final task. I heard the action above as orders were shouted from the halfdeck, followed by familiar chants, "Heave... heave... heave," and the thumping of running feet. I paused for a minute, then smiled, feeling a sense of security from the unabated familiarity triggered by this routine during the past months. I knew without being on deck where Jacobsen was positioned, and Poulsen, Bosun, and Peter Kjemtrup. And I knew who was surely in the rigging.

Zoe looked at me and smiled, sharing my sentiments as the sounds from above continued. Although we had agreed it was time for the program to end, on this night we felt secure, protected, proud, and fortunate to have been part of this experience.

My group went on its last sea watch shift starting at midnight. It was frigid cold with vicious winds and rain that stung my face and hands. I was happy not to climb. But I did relieve Zoe fifteen minutes early from buoy watch, then enjoyed her reward of piping hot chocolate which she prepared when my shift ended. Warming up with her felt special. She was princess-cute that night, sitting with her knees pulled tightly to her chest, wrapped in a winter coat, trying to survive one last night on duty just like me. Best of all was her smile. After swallowing our last drops of hot chocolate, we shared a cigarette as a token of our kindred spirits.

The *Statsraad Lehmkuhl* headed east into the fjord, away from the North Sea. Scheduled dock time in Bergen was set for 11:00 hours, allowing plenty of time to drift and float in the fjord. It was just 03:00. Pre-dawn light from the early sunrise already filled the eastern sky. This was Norway in May: land of the midnight sun with spring solstice just weeks away. The fjord's amazing beauty had a calming effect on everyone who was awake to experience it. Distant lights were scattered throughout the mountainous landscape. For many of the crew and the Norwegian cadets, this was home. For the rest of us, well, it certainly felt like home. But we had digested a lifetime of experiences during our time away, which had not only painted the lining of our souls but had pierced them as well. We were not the same cadets as before.

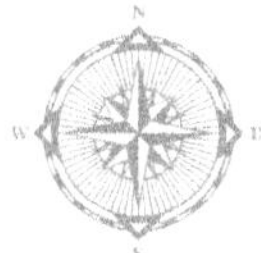

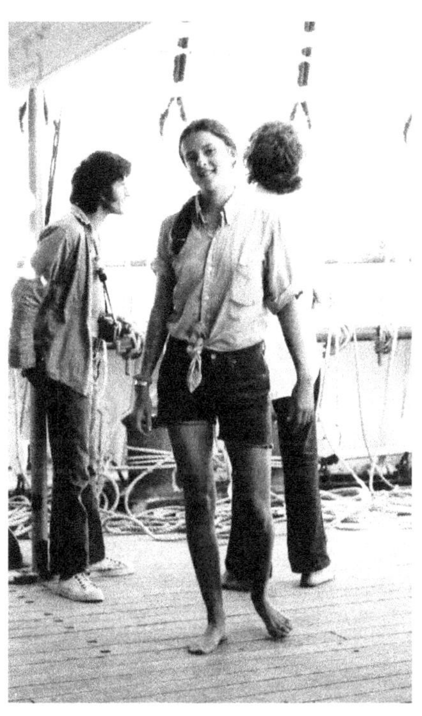

Zoe on deck

Me at the helm

Night sailing in the North Sea

Jones' Jolly Roger flag hoisted atop the main mast

Crewmen Arne and Eigl

CHAPTER 26: FINALE

I was awakened after three hours of sleep by several long blasts of the horn. Then someone yelled: "The bridge!" As we approached the Sotra Bridge, most everyone aboard went up on deck to watch the ship pass underneath. It appeared like the masts would surely hit its underside. Then we all clapped, hooted, and hollered after we cleared. Cadets and crewmen alike seemed ready to celebrate anything. The mood remained festive as we maneuvered toward the docks.

A small boat approached starboard side with several folks waving. Tor's father and a few friends of Tor, Robert, and Frederik traveled alongside the ship all the way into the harbor. I was pleased the Norwegian boys had changed their minds about leaving ship in Spain. Our community needed them onboard more than Spain needed them passing through.

No one thought much about the cold rain that greeted us in the harbor until Schnitler responded sarcastically looking skyward, "Welcome to Bergen."

The next days in Norway scattered my emotions. Ship's work continued, as did port watch schedules—gangway, fire watch, and a new position called gate-watch, stationed at the guard house by the entrance to the BMV. We washed all three masts from top to bottom, scrubbed the deck, polished brass, cleaned the banjers, and more. But with less intensity than before. Even the crewmen seemed relaxed. On the first sunny day, all square sails were dropped from their respective yards and hung to dry, like bed sheets from an Amish clothesline stretching from house to barn.

Despite school being officially over, we continued interacting educationally with the faculty. When not scheduled for ship's work, our free time was often spent in town at coffee shops, restaurants, museums, the library, or on Mt. Fløyen. Some days were remarkably gorgeous as springtime in Bergen proved to be spectacular. Evening hours were stretched, with actual daylight lasting well after 22:00. It never grew totally dark, resembling early dawn or late dusk even in the wee hours of the night.

One day I joined Joe, Clark, and Gary at the theater to see the film *Harold &
Maude*. The humor was great, but the movie ended strangely with Maude commit-
ting suicide on her 80th birthday. She had gotten from life what she wanted
during her eighty years, realizing that things would never get better. Old age
wasn't something I could remotely relate to, convinced that I'd never live long
enough to deal with Maude's dilemma of choice. Living to eighty years of age
seemed unfathomable, and really wasn't a goal of mine.

With each passing day, crew members bid farewell one by one, then headed
off for their next sea adventures. It was neither joyous nor sad as the community
began disbanding. Poulsen and Janet headed to Denmark, obviously in love. Their
relationship appeared to be respectfully serious enough to move from the paint
locker onboard to a life together onshore.

Constitution Day is celebrated in Norway on May 17, in similar fashion as July
4th in the States. Bergen buzzed with activity as folks had the day off. Children
blew insane little horns and squirted each other with water guns. Families enjoyed
picnics by the lake. Women dressed in colorful traditional costumes from years
past, and of course, there was an abundance of alcohol. Bergen became one big
party city. I met up with Zoe and Nancy Graham in town, then the three of us hung
out and spent time by the lake. But Zoe had agreed to cover someone's watch at
18:00 so needed to return to the ship. Bummer, I would've loved to spend the rest
of the day with her.

I then joined up with Gary, Katie, Sue, and Rufus who were just heading into
town. We spotted a small motorboat idling several hundred feet offshore with two
guys aboard and motioned them over for a ride. The Brits, with nothing better to
do, were happy to oblige. It was a fun ride all the way around to the fish market,
except when a hydrofoil sped past creating a wake large enough to crest into
our boat. Fjord water in May is really cold. In fact, fjord water is always cold, no
matter the time of year. Norwegians are known to be some of the toughest, most
element-tolerant folks in the world, but that wasn't necessarily the case for us
as we were nearly startled out of our pants by the unwelcome splash of icy cold.
Katie, who was sitting in front, took the brunt of the splash. Being from Minnesota, she handled it better than I would have. Minnesotans are Scandinavians
once removed.

Gary and I eventually split off from the others. He invited me to just carouse,
since the city was still filled with young folks. He suggested we try to pick up girls.
That was always his thing. I wasn't much interested in that but said nothing in
response. He interpreted my silence as a yes.

Teenage girls were everywhere, many hanging out in pairs, which was perfect for Gary's agenda. Hooking up proved to be as easy as eating a slice of Grossmommie Smucker's shoofly pie on a summer evening, as we wandered into a small café.

Anette and Sissel were having ice cream on the crowded deck just outside the café as we searched for a seat to eat the hotdogs and french fries we were carrying. Both girls were attractive, one blonde and one brunette, appearing to be seventeen or eighteen years old. As we entered the patio, they both smiled and made eye contact with us. That's all it took. Gary headed straight for their table with me trailing behind. "May we join you?" he asked.

"Yes, of course," was Sissel's response in perfect English. They were local girls from just outside the city. Anette and I hit it off from the start. She was bright, friendly, and a good conversationalist. And she knew about the American school aboard the *Statsraad Lehmkuhl*. In fact, one of her first questions was whether we were students from the ship. Suddenly, my sluggish interest in Gary's dumb idea of finding girls did a 180. I was all in. Not that it mattered much to me, but Gary and Sissel seemed to be doing fine as well.

After a few beers we walked to a nearby park where a rock band was performing on stage, prompting dancing on the lawn. By now, I had shed most of my Mennonite inhibitions. Firstly, I had acquired a taste for beer, and secondly, I could hold my own on the dance floor. Or in this case, the yard. Anette was a spirited girl, not at all shy. She had quickly taken hold of my arm when we left the café. I loved that about European girls. For some reason, I always had difficulty initiating romantic touch for fear of appearing too forward. Even holding hands. But I was quick to respond.

Our evening together ended too soon, but I needed to get back to the ship for gate-watch at midnight. She walked me to the BMV at 23:30 before saying goodnight. Our conversation remained light and sweet, and we made no plans to see each other again. I suppose we both were just out for a good time on Norwegian Constitution Day. For me, it was unexpected fun. I smiled and shook my head while reflecting on the evening, not certain who had picked up whom.

Ω

The next day was designated as a full day of work for all the cadets. Everyone onboard participated, including the remaining crewmen. Our group worked alongside Timberman taking down the mesan sail and several staysails, plus we removed sizings, guarding blocks, and other sail-related materials. It was warm and sunny, perfect for our last task in the rigging. But also, very sad. I tried to downplay that part, convincing myself it was time to move on. My biggest fear about going home was the emotional adjustment of melting back into the lifestyle and culture that no longer fit my character. I wasn't the same person who had left home in the fall of 1972.

Eiji, Bill Wright, Doc, and I went to a clinic in town for X-rays. Eiji's broken finger was bothering him, Bill had a head injury, and Doc was doing his duty, so I went along just to be in their company. But the clinic had a long waiting line, so we left, unchecked and untreated. What's a broken finger and broken head to sailors anyway? Instead, we went to the theater and saw a Burt Reynolds movie— by far a better prescription than the clinic could have provided. If given enough time, most injuries would surely heal themselves under theatrical care.

After our return to Bergen from the high seas, I assumed the morning routines would change. Like maybe there'd be no more ungodly wakeup whistles, musters, and workstations. But that wasn't so. I came to hate the sound of whistles. And ship's work was as unnecessary as a two-dollar bill. It made no difference if the chart room was cleaned, the deck was scrubbed, or the brass was polished. However, we were still living aboard ship under the captain's command. The ship needed to be maintained.

One afternoon Chick and Stephanie hosted an Oceanics picnic on top of Mt. Fløyen. Everyone was responsible for their own transportation. That shouldn't have been a big deal, but several of the faculty got lost on the way. There was plenty to eat, plenty to drink, and lichens to pick. A few kids tried to identify which ones were hallucinogenic and became irritated when Eiji wouldn't tell them. And Eiji was perturbed that anyone wanted to get high on lichens in the first place. But by now, Oceanics student behavior shouldn't have surprised anyone. We were all finding our way, our joy, and our place in a world that hadn't always been kind, loving, just, or safe. Some kids needed to get high. It was 1973.

Eiji and I rode a city bus back to Laksevåg. At the BMV we met up with Jaime, who wasn't smiling. That seemed odd until he explained that his Mexican passport had expired four days earlier. A serious oversight. Chief Mate said his only option was to go to the Mexican Embassy in Oslo, but it could take days to resolve. Jaime was seriously considering flying to New York on the charter flight and taking his chances at Kennedy Airport without current documentation. Eiji and I convinced him otherwise. A Mexican arriving in the States without a valid passport would certainly be problematic.

Ω

Stephanie scheduled hour-long interviews with each of the students during our last week in Bergen. I respected her efforts, energy, time, and the commitment she poured into the program. And I was grateful for the scholarship and the opportunity she gifted me. After discussing my academic work for the year, she encouraged me to continue my education creatively.

"I have connections with the director of a school community in northern India where lost arts are taught. I can get any information you need if you're interested," she explained. The Gallaghers were on the cutting edge of alternative education, and the world was their campus. I admired them for that.

She shared reflections on the past year from her perspective, both good and bad. "It was a tough year for everyone," she said. "But much more successful than last year on the *Antarna*. There were some things we could've done better, especially onboard, but we did a lot of things right as well. No one expected this experience to be easy. We set our sights high despite a multitude of unknowns. Education was at the core. In that respect, I hope we succeeded." I nodded in agreement, knowing little of the Oceanics experience aboard the *Antarna* the prior year. Stephanie continued, "Your transcripts will be sent by mail within the next weeks."

We formally shook hands and wished each other well. But I had one last question, "Will the program continue for another year?" Then added, "I hope so. This has been an experience I'll never forget. I've learned so much. And I believe I'm more accepting, more balanced, and maybe a little crazier because of it."

Stephanie paused, smiled, then answered carefully, "Thank you Marlie, you've been a quiet asset to the community onboard, as I expected you would be. And you will do just fine as you deal with life's unknown challenges that lie ahead. Your foundation is solid. And yes, the program will probably continue but with a different approach and a shorter time frame."

Obviously, there were lessons learned all around and things that should not be repeated. Funding and costs to run a program of this magnitude were nearly prohibitive. The dual challenge of simultaneously devoting time to sailing responsibilities and classes was tougher than anyone expected. Fatigue compounded by little sleep, dietary issues, stressful community life aboard, and constant motion at sea added uncalculated dimensions of difficulty. We were fortunate that no one fell overboard, died, or totally went berserk. However, there were differing opinions concerning the emotional survival of a few.

My last day aboard was a blur. Some students had already left ship. Tor, Robert, and Frederik returned to their homes in Norway. Jim Johnson and Sue Nelson returned to Minnesota. Others had left as well, but those who stayed had to deal with wakeup whistles, morning musters, and cleaning stations to the very end.

Eiji invited Bill Bacon and me for a nice dinner at an expensive restaurant in town on our final night. The décor was nicely done with ship memorabilia, ropes, pulleys, and photos throughout, including one of the *Statsraad Lehmkuhl*. We all ate charbroiled chateaubriand steaks and downed two bottles of red wine during our two-hour dinner. It was great to close this incredible chapter with two of my dearest friends. I suppose the one thing that would have made it better was for the evening not to end.

Zoe was on gangway watch when we returned to the ship. I stayed with her for the remaining forty-five minutes of her shift. We divulged things about ourselves that we hadn't shared before—our hopes, dreams, and desires. Zoe quietly articulated her personal feelings and perceptions of this Oceanics experience—the good, the bad, and the crazy. Like me, she had survived this adventure and was still very much alive. Notably, she had earned a tender place in my heart, as I believe I had in hers—places that we'd never have opportunity to explore. She was a special girl who someday would surely bless a very lucky man. We shared an orange and one last cigarette, and for the second time that evening, I wished time would stand still.

I finally crawled into my bunk in cabin 8 at 02:00 after hours of relaxing in the music room one last time, listening to Loggins and Messina. It was only fitting that I slept in my original cabin. Jones and Nancy were already asleep above me, Todd was snoring noisily on the opposite top bunk, and Birdman's bed was filled with junk, unimportant, random unclaimed stuff that had gathered there since he left ship. I wore a reflective smile on my face as I lay awake thinking, filled with a million questions. But I knew one thing for sure—I was a survivor. And that was good enough for me.

Morning came quickly. Zoe and I ate breakfast with Eiji and Amor. Our conversation was spirited and upbeat, nothing sad or sentimental.

By mid-morning it was discovered that the big Hilmar Reksten flag that flew from the mesan mast was missing. Apparently, someone had ripped it off. Chief Mate declared that no one would receive their sail training documents until the culprit fessed up, or until the flag was found. Even in our final hours there was discord, a continuation of the daunting realities that plagued our community throughout the year. But in this case, we cadets still aboard became the accused as this bizarre drama played out. Most anyone could have taken the flag, including a crewman. Many had already left ship. The fact that the flag was discovered to be missing on that day didn't mean it was taken that day. Finally, Chief Mate was forced to give in, realizing the truth: no one presently on board knew anything of its whereabouts. And the flag never showed up. We were each given our merchant sail training papers with congratulatory smiles.

Mr. Gronningen recovered from the incident quickly and delivered a nice, late morning farewell speech. We then gathered our belongings and marched down the gangway single file, dressed in our best outfits, sky-blue shirts and navy-blue blazers. We were a handsome, refined looking bunch, quite a contrast from the day we arrived. I was one of the last to leave ship. I turned and gave Jane a huge hug and kiss before my final exit. She was hands-down the most extraordinary cadet throughout the entire year, and her work ethic influenced me immeasurably. She chose to stay onboard and work for an indefinite period rather than fly home with the rest of us.

This class of cadets appeared fully seasoned, physically and emotionally, as we boarded buses waiting on the pier to transport us to the airport.

Jaime had decided to travel to Oslo to resolve his passport issue just one day before departure. The Oceanics transatlantic flight was scheduled to leave Bergen at 12:10. Jaime managed to acquire his legal documents quickly and was on a flight from Oslo arriving in Bergen at 12:05, just in time to catch our flight to New York. Of course, Jaime was all smiles as he boarded to an audience of clapping cadets.

I sat with Eiji as SAS flight 903 took off smoothly. From my window seat I watched the fjords fade quickly from sight. It all felt very much like a scene from the last chapter of an enchanting novel.

Me, front row, 2nd from right

Leaving the ship for the last time

CHAPTER 27: HOMEWARD BOUND

Seven hours later in New York, I experienced heartfelt hugs, handshakes, and goodbyes: Eiji, Bill Bacon, Jaime, Tara, the Wright brothers, Gary, Kevin, Emil, Nancy Graham, Amor, and so many more. But the most difficult goodbye was Zoe. As we embraced and kissed, my eyes became moist. How could this budding friendship be ending?

Minutes later she came back with her mother and sister for brief introductions. Again, we embraced without words, just holding each other. Our farewell was innocently sweet and sad. Indeed, it was goodbye. We never saw each other again.

Uncle Johnnie pulled up to the curb as I exited the baggage claim area. My last friend was still there on the sidewalk. Eiji. He and I had said everything we needed to say. Our final goodbye was quick with a wave and nod of assurance that we'd both be okay.

My Smucker cousins Dennis, Carl, Woody, and Joy were there to greet me, all excitedly talking at once. I could barely smile, emotionally numb, empty, and terribly lost. I wasn't prepared for the questions nor equipped for this fast reentry.

We had chicken, rice, and beans for dinner, followed by a time of romping with Joy and Woody in the family room, then an hour of seemingly unimportant TV news with Uncle Johnnie. New York's Mayor Lindsey had instructed the EPA to remove thousands of campaign posters and literature affixed to public property in the city and charge the offending candidates for removal costs in his effort to clean up "the unsightly litter." Also in the news, Julie Nixon Eisenhower, during an interview with *The New York Times*, suggested that although the Watergate scandal bothered her father, he would never resign his presidency. None of that had any bearing on what I felt inside, but it allowed me the opportunity to quietly go through the motions in the South Bronx without having to talk. My body, mind, and soul were in three different places, far removed from each other and far removed from everyone else.

The next morning, I took a bus from Southern Boulevard to 74th Street then boarded the subway train to Penn Station. The nine-dollar train ride from there to Lancaster was emotionally mellow as I drifted in and out of consciousness, consumed by recent hopes and fears. Mostly I was just scared. Now, as a twenty-year-old, it was time to find my direction, time to grow up. The storms in my mind felt more daunting than the Bay of Biscay or any challenges I had encountered on the *Statsraad Lehmkuhl.*

As the train sped through New Jersey into Pennsylvania, a tear appeared on my cheek. I replayed the adventures, the emotions, the pain, and the secrets of my voyage, knowing I could never share them with anyone. And I knew with certainty that I was extraordinarily blessed, living by the grace of God, and still very much on borrowed time.

Statsraad Lehmkuhl - the sail ship I came to love and would never forget

EPILOGUE

After several years of international travel, adventures, and love, I finally settled in my hometown of Bird-in Hand, Pennsylvania where I married, raised three wonderfully gifted children, and found my way into the business world. I didn't necessarily plan it that way. Nor was it an easy road. But additionally, I found joy, security, and happiness beyond what money could buy. I shared very few of my Oceanics experiences with anyone, even the folks I dearly loved. I didn't know how. Maybe I was still sorting it all out myself—the drama, the joys, the secrets, and the pain.

I had two surprise visits from Bill Bacon—once in 1982, and a second time in 2016 after his initial bout with throat cancer. Our brief time together was as good, but not nearly as exciting, as our time in 1972-1973. He always brought a positive charge into our friendship. And I was saddened to hear that he died in June of 2023 after recurring health issues that plagued him at the end after moving to the islands.

I also met up with Clark Shores in Portland, Oregon, in 1975 while he was in college. At the time I was living in Oregon for several months during a personal sabbatical while seeking direction and traveling the States. But we didn't stay in touch after that.

Joe Feinblatt was gracious enough to plan a visit to Bird-in-Hand, my cultural home, with his wife, Pepe, while traveling east in the early 1980s. I was managing a hotel at the time, which afforded him and Pepe the opportunity to visit Amish Country and stay in the quaint village of Intercourse, PA.

Eiji and I spoke again only once, in 1979, but sadly, we didn't meet up in person.

My phone rang one day in 2010 from a number in New Jersey. I don't habitually answer unrecognized callers, but on this day I did. A male voice on the other end asked anxiously, "Marlie? … Marlie Smucker? This is Jack Wright—remember me?" Before I could say anything except to confirm it was me, he continued, "Hold on, I'm gonna put my girlfriend on the phone. She doesn't believe I ever sailed on a Norwegian sail ship to Africa and South America as a teenager. Tell her we were shipmates and sailed across the damn Atlantic Ocean twice. And that we climbed 150 feet into the rigging and survived a hurricane. She doesn't believe a word I tell her."

I had no time to respond before I heard a female voice in the background, "No Jack, I don't want to talk to him," followed by some bantering between them. Then suddenly she spoke directly into the phone, "Hello… hello, we're having a silly argument here, but Jack tells me a lot of things about his past that I'm not sure he's telling the truth. This all sounds pretty far out."

I hesitated for a moment then spoke, "I don't know what Jack has told you, but we did live together on a square-rigged sail ship from Norway and shared some incredible travel adventures during our time aboard. Yes, we climbed the rigging. Yes, we encountered a hurricane in the Bay of Biscay, and yes, we sailed to Africa and South America. That much is true."

"Oh, so he's telling the truth?" Then I heard her say, away from the phone, "Oh shit Jack, I'm sorry." I expected Jack to pick up the phone and finish our conversation, but he didn't. Next thing I knew, I was holding the phone buzzing with dial tone. It was a strange encounter—a blast from the past. I never spoke with Jack again. Years later I heard he was killed in a motorcycle crash and that his brother, Bill, also died unexpectedly.

Others passed as well: both Chick and Stephanie Gallagher, Nancy Graham, Martin Schipper, Leslie Strong, Arturo Rivera, Mary Leeder, Steve Kovacik, Lucy Rodgers, Richie Yusem, Jacobsen and many of the older crewmen, including Captain Fossa, who supposedly died of a heart attack aboard ship— a fitting ending for an unusual captain who spent many years aboard an unusual ship.

My friend, Steve Paulus (Rufus), did an amazing job through his efforts to find and reconnect the student-cadets, faculty, and crew. His countless hours of work were an incredible gift to all of us. He created a website (Oceanics 1972–73) sharing photos, biographies, memories, obituaries, and videos, including the documentary filmed onboard and narrated by David Wayne. It was he who orchestrated our first Oceanics reunion in the fall of 2023 in Minneapolis after fifty years. Steve has also stayed actively involved with the ongoing enterprises of the *Statsraad Lehmkuhl* and has done several personal sails onboard in recent years. His initiative created the desire for some of us to do the same.

My greatest thrill after fifty years has been to reconnect with Steve and other shipmates in person, including Jim Johnson, Janet and Peter Poulsen, Katie Houck, Sue Nelson, Nancy Mair, Marc Alexander Frutchi, and Joe Feinblatt, plus many more via Zoom and email. I enjoyed hearing stories, reliving memories, and understanding varied perspectives of our shared experiences as teenagers aboard ship in times very different from the world we know today. Our four days together in Minneapolis were an incredible gift, reaffirming my love, trust, and appreciation for life, and for the valued efforts of maintaining relationships.

In January of 2025, I took the notion to contact several of the Florida boys in Miami. Without understanding exactly why, I felt the urge to reconnect with The Brotherhood, the boys who bantered in the banjers, were defiant, unfiltered and loud, bullying shipmates and testing the boundaries of the administration and officers aboard ship in 1972-73.

Perry Alexander, Tom Thornton, and Rick Goodfriend responded to my email expressing interest in getting together. I bought an airline ticket and flew with my wife to Miami for five days. Although Rick couldn't join us, Perry, Tom, and I spent an entire afternoon reminiscing, storytelling and becoming reacquainted at a marina near City Hall in Coconut Grove. Our reunion was extraordinary as the memories, feelings, fears, and emotions from 52 years ago were rekindled. Some things had changed drastically—we had all lost our hair! Aside from that, we had all become respectable citizens. Tom was a successful lawyer (now retired), Perry had become a bank vice-president (on the verge of retiring), and I was still involved in the businesses back in Pennsylvania. I found out that day that Bill Bacon was the one who stole the flag from the mesan mast after returning to Bergen in the spring of 1973.

The following day Perry invited my wife and me to have dinner with him and his Peruvian wife of 13 years at his home in Miami Shores. Perry and I shared unexpected emotion as he painfully relived his story of being thrown off the ship in Spain. I listened as he masterfully articulated what he felt as a 17-year-old boy standing on the pier watching the *Statsraad Lehmkuhl* pull away without him. My previous perceptions of Perry changed that day. For 52 years I had considered him to be a crazy, brash, unfiltered shipmate. That day he became my friend.

In early April of 2025 I returned to Bergen with the intention of seeing the *Statsraad Lehmkuhl* for the first time in 52 years. And with hopes of meeting and sailing with two old shipmates—Steve Paulus and Peter Kjemtrup. The ship was about to begin its second year-long voyage of the One Ocean Expedition. We each had signed up for the first leg—a 10-day sail in the North Sea to Tromso, Norway (above the Arctic Circle) with a stopover in Lerwick, Shetland.

I experienced an indescribable feeling as I stepped from the bus at the pier in Bryggen, directly across from the *Statsraad Lehmkuhl*, majestically displaying her beauty and charm, towering skyward. I could only speak in a whisper as tears formed on my cheeks. My eyes followed her fore mast upwards to the fokke yard, to the stumpe, the merse, the bram and the royl, flooding my mind with memories while ballooning my soul with excitement for this new experience.

My reunion with Steve and Peter followed in dream-like fashion during the next days as our shared experiences from 52 years ago created a new bond, absent of past roles as cadets and mate. Peter opened a large pack of black and white photos from our time onboard and scattered them on a table in his hotel room, then poured us each a shot of Danish rum. We couldn't stop talking. Although the years had taken their toll on our physical bodies, we each had also been blessed with experiential wisdom and humility.

All three of us were treated royally onboard ship as shipmates and crewmen became aware of our unique 52-year reunion. Andre, the social media guy, was fascinated with our story, of course, and followed up with interviews, photos, and videos which he posted on Instagram and Facebook. Peter told me several times that he wishes he'd had some training in dealing with teenagers before his time onboard as a mate with the Oceanics School. He appeared smaller now, more refined, intentional, and more appreciative of the simple pleasures in life.

Six months before the sail I had rotator cuff surgery on my left shoulder. My bicep was cut as well. The surgeon explained that I'd need ten months or more to achieve 90% recovery but unfortunately, my shoulder would never have the motion or the strength it once had. And I'd need three to four months of intense physical therapy, followed by another four months of daily exercise just to regain the 90%.

Inspired by a billboard that read, "PAIN DOESN'T LAST FOREVER, BUT ACHIEVE-MENT DOES," I determined to do what I feared I could not. I wanted to sail on the *Statsraad Lehmkuhl* in April and climb into the rigging, not just to the fokke yard but all the way to the royl. To do that, however, I'd need to do a pull-up, something I hadn't done since my mid-fifties. I was now approaching 72 years of age, and with my body in decline, plagued with 25 pounds of excess weight, a pull-up seemed like a long shot. The pain in my shoulder persisted for months after the surgery but I continued to exercise beyond what my therapist suggested, deter-mined to recover. If he told me to do 20 reps, I did 30 or 40.

This unique opportunity aboard ship in April 2025 was no less than a personal fairytale dream come true. I helped brace yards, pulled gardings and skortes and recoiled ropes on deck, then miraculously did a pull-up on our second day at sea. I gained favor with ABS Christine Thoresen, my watch leader who not only encouraged me but also enabled my wish to climb along with social media director, Andre Marton Pedersen. It was they who accompanied me to the royl yard. My legs, arms, shoulders, hands, and mind were in sync as I ascended Jacob's ladder, climbed up and over the platforms, and achieved my grandest thrill of the entire voyage—reaching the royl yard! I felt like the luckiest man in the world as I slid across foot cables to the very end, threw my hands into the air, and relived an experience I hadn't felt in 52 years: the sea, the sky, and the wind in my face, riding fearlessly high above the deck of the ship I had come to love. I enjoyed every pitch and sway on this wonderfully cold day in the North Sea, now as an old sailor alongside my new friends, Christine and Andre. It felt surreal knowing full well there is no place on earth that compares.

My story could have ended there, but it didn't. In early July 2025 I again toted my duffle bag up the gangway of the *Statsraad Lehmkuhl* in Ponta Delgada, Azores, in preparation for another voyage. This time I again joined my friend Steve Paulus for a sail across the North Atlantic to Nuuk, Greenland. I was in better shape than before and was determined to perform tasks in the rig. My White Watch group of 21 trainees spent eight hours a day on duty pulling and coiling ropes, taking turns on the various watches, cleaning banjers, scrubbing decks, and climbing to set and furl sails. During our three weeks at sea, we were fortunate enough to encounter two low-pressure cyclones which caused plenty of excitement amid six meter waves with wind gusts of 60 mph. I quietly smiled to myself, enjoying the thrill of another sea adventure while harnessed to the railing and lifelines on deck, fulfilling an old sailor's best dreams. It could not have been scripted better.

Since the Minneapolis reunion in 2023, I've stayed in touch with Oceanics shipmates with hopes of meeting up again in other settings, possibly aboard the *Statsraad Lehmkuhl* at ports in the USA. And I did just that in late October 2025, in Seattle, at a reunion that brought 14 shipmates from 1972-73 together—including four faculty and numerous family members. I was thrilled to have my wife and children plus several cousins join me there.

The ship remains an amazing vessel, still serving a great purpose while inspiring educators, scientists, cadets, adventure seekers, and expats to sail and learn more about the science and mysteries of our oceans. On January 14, 2026, the *Statsraad Lehmkuhl* quietly turned 112 years old in Cartagena, Columbia, and—like me—is still sailing. May God grant fair winds to us both!

As a grandpa of eight, I've been involved in the lives of three granddaughters and five grandsons. Until now, I haven't shared my Oceanics experiences with any of them, aside from an occasional comment in reference to the large, framed photo of the *Statsraad Lehmkuhl* hanging on my living room wall. I suppose the stories in this book will be a start.

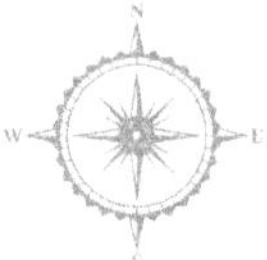

Dave Pappas, Chuck Vinson, Billy King (L to R)

APPENDIX

Me on deck

During my time aboard, I interacted with nearly 100 characters of varying personalities, cultures, and dispositions, all of whom made up our community and became my shipmates in the fall of 1972. Friendships developed randomly, initially with bunkmates followed by those in the same task group as me with whom I shared assigned watches and work details. Officers and crewmen became part of my everyday life as well, especially those who were involved directly in sail training. And of course, the Oceanics faculty and administration were each significant players in this experience from my first day aboard ship.

As this story unfolds, names of shipmates sometimes appear without prior introduction of who they are. The purpose of this appendix is to give brief background information of those persons. I've used first names for some, first and last for others keeping in compliance with permission granted. Although the list of names isn't complete, it does include those with whom I most interacted. In addition to my three roommates, Birdman, Jones and Todd, here are the names and personalities.

Ω

Alec McMullen was a tall, slender, sober-faced boy with long straight brown hair and big eyes peering from behind black framed glasses. He initially came across as loud and brash with a chip of anger that could ignite quickly. However, I realized that behind the front he posed there was a soft, sensitive, thoughtful side to Alec that I came to appreciate in time.

Amor, ethnically Philippine, was one of the youngest students in the program, probably the smallest, and maybe the bravest because of everything she endured in the rough environment aboard ship. She cautiously found her place of survival among several young peers and faculty members within the community. When on duty, her tasks were safely defined on deck. She wasn't comfortable climbing, nor was her upper body strength sufficient to maneuver up and over the first platform. Amor was a cute girl who smiled as much from her big beautiful brown eyes as she did with her mouth. She responsibly obeyed ship's rules, performed her tasks within the community, and applied herself scholastically.

Amor

Bill Bacon joined Oceanics from New Haven, Connecticut. He was a thin boy of moderate height with wavy, thick, black, longish hair and a short black beard matching his eyebrows and hair. Bill maintained an upbeat, spirited, independent personality. He wasn't shy, and fearlessly partici-pated in both ship's work and mischief onboard and off. As an adventure seeker who wasn't afraid of challenges or conflict, he sometimes crossed lines that led him into trouble with the administration, crewmen, and peers.

Bill and **Jack Wright** were brothers from New Jersey. Bill was a year older than Jack. Both were of average build, strong, physically fit, and able to climb and do ship's work with ease when they wanted to. Bill had thick, straight, shoul-der-length hair, and was easy going, confident, and romantically assertive when it came to meeting girls in port. Jack also had very thick, long brown hair that frizzed out from his head. He wasn't a heady guy, lived very much in the moment, and cared mostly about the things that affected him directly.

Billy King was yet another Bill onboard but one with whom I had little contact. His Boston accent and his longish blonde curly hair defined my impression of him more than his behavior. I seldom worked alongside him on deck or in the rig, and I wasn't assigned any field trips with him. However, we competed at the ping pong table on several occasions after its arrival in Trinidad. He and Linda were a couple for at least part of our voyage. And I learned that Billy was in the program mostly on scholarship, like many of us. Stephanie set his tuition at just $1,500 which he had to borrow from an aunt. (He told me much later that it took him 10 years to pay back.)

Blake, Chick Gallagher's son, was maybe the least seen cadet onboard through-out the Oceanics experience. His time was mostly spent in the engine room at the bottom of the hull with the crew commonly known as "the grease monkeys." Although his thin build, long brown straggly hair, quiet mannerism, and grease-stained coveralls defined him, he was more than that. Blake played an important role within the community onboard. He had been a student/cadet the prior year and was indeed part of the reason the school existed in the first place.

Charlie Samuels fit into the Oceanics program like the little finger of a leather glove, important but not prominent, staying mostly behind the scenes. He was a small-featured, handsome boy from Minnesota with short-cropped curly hair and confident eyes. His smiles, laughter, and responses to most everything were contained without drama. Charlie appeared to be more socially cautious than most, even after a few drinks. I suppose he got excited sometimes but I never saw it, as his exuberance was seldom displayed. He found solace in his romantic relationship with Mary. I was told they were a couple before ever coming onboard.

Chuck Vinson came aboard ship with short dark hair. His loud, sometimes brash personality defined him from the start while he quickly found his way into the center of life onboard. Chuck wore his feelings on his shoulders, so to speak, and was never at a loss for words among fellow cadets. He was a bright kid. However, I was surprised by his reliance on Lilly, who notably became his emotional support throughout their time onboard. Chuck's father had been killed in Vietnam several years earlier, which dramatically affected his life as a teen, especially concerning his role in the family.

Clark Shores might have been the quietest student in the entire program and he remained so throughout the duration of our voyage. Often seen but seldom heard, he performed his duties without show or pride. He also very well might have been the most intelligent kid onboard. Obviously a deep thinker, his mind was constantly churning. However, if there was no reason or need to say something, he didn't. His silence felt awkward at times. Clark certainly wasn't a trouble-maker, but he could entertain creative mischief and question authority with the best and worst of us. If only in theory.

Clark Shores (R) in Gambia

Ellie didn't necessarily possess the physique of a trainee aboard a tall ship but her knowledge and determined spirit was to her credit. She read a lot, stayed well-informed, and probably stored more information in her brain than most of us. From what I knew she was a good student. I believe she knew the ropes aboard the *Statsraad Lehmkuhl* better than many but climbed with caution, without ever admitting fear. Ellie wasn't one to discuss her faults or weaknesses. Notably, her understanding of tasks onboard surpassed her ability to perform them. She was a smooth talker, often to her detriment. Some of her stories were hard to believe. Unfortunately, she was perceived as a social misfit by the rowdy bunch and received undeserved taunting.

Emil Tompkins, one of only two black cadets onboard, sometimes was forced to defend his dignity amid racist behavior and racial slurs by fellow cadets and crewmen. He was bright, mild-mannered, athletic, and soft-spoken most of the time. But he didn't roll over and play dead when challenged. He was a competitor. And he held his place among peers both scholastically and in task performance. Emil could climb and set sails with the best of us. But more importantly, he earned my friendship, and I earned his.

Emil

Fredrick Dahl (Kiki) was one of three Norwegian cadets aboard ship for the 1972–73 Oceanics school year along with **Tor Hambre** and **Robert Larsen**. All three were strong, well-adjusted, responsible, hard-working, socially confident cadets who added stability to the conglomerate of trainees onboard. They of course were in their homeland during sail training but spoke fluent English, sometimes serving as communicators between the paid crewmen and the American cadets. Each earned his individual respect within the community among fellow students, crewmen, and school administrators alike. I considered all three to be the most well-rounded, well-adapted cadets aboard ship.

Tor (L) and Robert

Frutchi was a mild-mannered boy from Palo Alto, California who seemed to epitomize the purpose of Oceanics. He was tall, lean and suitably built for sailing a square-rigged ship, whether on deck or working high in the rigging. Adventure was truly his education as he sought personal acceptance within the community. And he quietly found a way to fit in with the more vocal guys in his work group. Perry was his roommate. The mischief Frutchi dallied in was usually downplayed because of the more boisterous guys he hung with. One night while drinking, he began smashing furniture in the dayroom. Interestingly, it wasn't he who received the blame.

Gary Pollard was a curly-haired boy with long locks who confidently planted his feet within the community after arriving in Bergen. Sometimes quiet, sometimes outspoken, sometimes proud, he was able to hold his own socially as a cadet and student both onboard and onshore. He had a great smile. Although shorter than most of the guys, he was a handsome boy, strong, and walked with a jerky bounce. Gary was not afraid to climb in the rigging nor meet girls in port, with the latter being his passion.

Gary

George Kramer, one of the students from Minnesota, was friendly, bright, hardworking, level-headed, and appeared to come from good stock. He was onboard to learn. George contributed well to the good of the community and proved to be an encourager while exercising integrity in every aspect of life onboard. He got along well with everyone as far as I could tell and avoided conflict. Like me. Of moderate strength and build, also like me, he stayed upbeat no matter the task. I was told he and Katie had a dating relationship in Minnesota before Oceanics but chose not to continue as a couple onboard.

Gerry Del Hagen was a "git 'er done" and "do things right" sort of guy with a solid, muscular build. His long, straight brown hair rested on his shoulders. He took his tasks and assignments onboard seriously, applying those same expectations to his fellow cadets. He smiled sparingly and wasn't afraid to call kids out on subpar performance. Gerry was a strong, obedient, able cadet during his Oceanics experience, seemingly primed for a life in civil service.

Jane proved to be the model cadet aboard ship in 1972-73 if there ever was one. She set high standards for all of us with her tireless efforts to learn the ropes, do the work, and sail the ship. Her focus from the beginning was sailing. I'm not sure how many actual classes or college credits she signed up for, but it didn't matter. She was a sailor to the core and very much part of the crew. Through prior research, Jane came onboard with more knowledge and understanding of the *Statsraad Lehmkuhl* than any of us. And she hit the deck running, literally, as an exceptional girl who never shied away from hard work. That included climbing high to set sails, polishing brass, scrubbing the deck, and everything in between. All without complaint. The officers and crew loved her for obvious reasons. I was fortunate enough to share many onboard work tasks with her. I found out much later that Jane had been onboard the ill-fated *Antarna* the prior year — the Oceanics vessel whose crew and students were forced to abandon ship in Panama. She never mentioned that to me. I'm not sure why, except that she lived very much in the present and chose not to discuss things from her past.

Jane

Jill Wyllie, also from Minnesota, was short in stature, cute, friendly, kind, trust-worthy, and a willing no-nonsense worker both on deck and below. As the saying goes, she was small but mighty. Like many of the female cadets aboard, Jill found her places of comfort, often behind the scenes, while dealing with the unpredict-able unknowns both onboard and off.

Jim and **Janet Johnson** were the only brother and sister cadets onboard. They were part of the Minnesota contingency who arrived in Bergen several days after the charter flight from New York. Both Jim and Janet were tall, blonde, fair-skinned, and of Swedish descent. Jim had long flowing hair that lay on his shoulders, like his sister. Both were quiet, cooperative, and cautiously found their places within the student body and the sail training program. The Johnsons were both easy to like.

John Goan, a moderately tall, quiet, all-American appearing boy, also hailed from Minnesota. I unfortunately had little interaction with him throughout the year, as we were never part of the same watch group onboard, or on the same field trips onshore. Nor did we bunk in the same section of the banjers. From my observations, John was a capable, cooperative cadet who climbed with confidence and contributed to the workload while sharing his reserved smile and trust sparingly. Definitely a straight shooter.

Katie Houck hailed from Minnesota as well and made a good first impression on me and most everyone else

Katie

onboard, especially the crew. She was bright, friendly, kind, easy to talk to, and appeared to come from a culturally sound family. Out of all the cadets onboard, Katie most exemplified the characteristics of someone from my home community of Bird-in-Hand, Pennsylvania: positive, steady, humble, modest, hardworking, and filled with applicable common sense. She understood her purpose onboard and contributed to the program from the start.

Kevin O'Donovan was a happy student, young, innocent, and eager to learn. He wore glasses which helped to redirect his long bangs away from his eyes. His time onboard exposed him to many first-time experiences. I suppose the same could be said for all of us, but Kevin spilled with questions of innocence. He was a curious boy. I sometimes felt more like his big brother than his fellow cadet.

Lilly Reitzel and Chuck became a couple only weeks after arriving in Norway, although she appeared to be an independent girl — quiet, confident, and self-assured. It was she who gave many of us haircuts during our voyage. I'm not certain that she had hair-cutting experience before, but she did it with authority. Lilly was a no-nonsense girl who could perform most of the tasks on deck and in the rigging with anyone, without discussion or complaint.

Kjemtrup and Lilly at the helm

Linda Peters didn't initially strike me as a girl who would sign onto a high seas adventure program like Oceanics without parental prompting. She was superstitious, apprehensive, and asked what I considered to be strange questions during the worst of times. She made no attempt to hide her fears while living very much in the situational present. But Linda learned to perform her tasks after plenty of hands-on training, and ultimately braved the storms like the rest of us. I enjoyed her friendship. She was a fun girl who laughed and enjoyed life's simple pleasures when things were going well. And found some security in her relationship with Billy K.

Lucy Rogers was from Morgantown, Pennsylvania, just 25 miles east of Lancaster, which made us almost neighbors before coming aboard. She joined Oceanics in the fall of 1972 as a weathered 19-year-old in search of a restart in life. Things had not necessarily gone well during her two previous years. Although Lucy appeared to be outspoken, confident, decisive, and sometimes rough around the edges, she had a soft, unprotected spot deep inside where kindness and compassion found enough fertile soil to take root. She certainly played an interesting role within our diverse community aboard the *Statsraad Lehmkuhl.*

Malcom McGreggor, an 18-year-old boy from the South, couldn't hide his cultural roots even if he tried. His slow, calm demeanor and southern drawl was proof enough. He was a quiet boy, often seen on the fringes of the action, never in the forefront. He seldom talked about himself or his family. Like many of us, he looked like a hippie with shoulder length brown hair, often tied in place with a handkerchief headband. Malcom enjoyed humor and avoided conflict whenever possible, but wasn't without opinions concerning the program or life in general. His boyish grin and shoulder-shrug acceptance of most everything became his trademark. It was difficult not to like Malcom.

Mark Kaiser was a good-looking, independent student with curly but shorter hair than most guys onboard. Self-confidence defined him. He didn't need compliments or encouragement from shipmates to feel good about himself. Mark had a good head on his shoulders as well, not just in appearance, and he had little interest in mincing words or involving himself in needless conversations. He was a student of Zen. That said, he was creatively adventurous and could talk extensively about riding a camel across the Sahara or hitchhiking his way from Europe to India. I believe Mark was well-read, which was to his credit.

Martin Schipper was another shipmate who I never learned to know well. He was quiet, somewhat reserved and shy, maybe because of growing up in an abusive home. He and Lilly were high school friends before joining the program. Martin never cared to be in the limelight. I thought him to be a humble guy. Regardless, he appeared to be level-headed, trustworthy, hardworking, and cooperative, seldom going negative about anything or making waves aboard ship. He left that solely to the sea.

Mitch Handman was one of the younger students in the program who, like Kevin, remained innocently upbeat, eager to learn and participate in the program both above deck and below as directed. He also willingly interacted socially with shipmates, especially within his circle of friends and guarded comfort zone, while sharing his generous smile and cooperative attitude as an inquisitive young teen.

Mitch Handman

Mary Leeder, another girl from Minnesota, sat next to me on the plane from JFK to Bergen. She was one of my first acquaintances before boarding ship. Her initially quiet tone onboard was probably misleading, but she remained low-key throughout the Oceanics experience, at least from my perspective. I heard unsubstantiated stories about her occasional wild side, but I never saw it. Mary found her place of comfort onboard with Charlie, a continuation of their relationship before the ship.

Nancy Mair appeared to be a solid cadet from the start, making efforts to perform her tasks well and do what she was told without questioning authority. As one of only 16 female cadets, also from Minnesota, she extended limited trust to the guys onboard but found her eventual protective security by hooking up with my roommate, Jones. Nancy was friendly but cautiously serious, careful not to share more personal information than necessary.

Nancy Mair

Nancy Graham (Stumpe Ra) was probably one of the most misunderstood female cadets onboard. During sail training she received the nickname Stumpe Ra, named after a Norwegian cartoon character and the storm sail yards on the fore and store masts. She was tall, thin, and embarrassingly innocent when she came onboard, but also inquisitive and curious to the core. Nancy didn't deserve all the ribbing she received from The Brotherhood, as innocence isn't a prosecutable offense. But she endured, built character, and eventually clawed her way to respectability among fellow shipmates by the end of the Oceanics experience.

Nancy Graham

Perry Alexander was a complex character from Miami, Florida. He heard about Oceanics through a friend who had been a cadet aboard the cursed *Antarna* the prior year. Perry was tall (6'6"), thin, outspoken, defiant, and perceived as bullish within the established community aboard ship. He and Tom grew up as childhood buddies and their friendship carried into the Oceanics experience and beyond. Both were enrolled in the program by their parents in hopes of correcting their drug-induced, dead-end teenage behavior on the streets of Miami. Perry joined ranks with several chips, figuratively speaking, on his boney shoulders. His father had abandoned the family years before and I don't believe Perry ever forgave him for that. Regardless, he came aboard the *Statsraad Lehmkuhl* in the fall of 1972 with a sack of unresolved issues from his past. His mother, although sweet and caring, couldn't afford tuition costs, so Perry joined ship with full scholarship funding.

Pisacano (L) and Jones safety training

Pisacano, ethnically Italian, was a handsome, confident, socially adept Florida boy with black wavy shoulder-length hair. He found his way into the center of community life from the get-go with his humor and wit, but also by his willingness to engage most everyone. Unfortunately, Pisacano was cursed with a serious case of motion sickness every time we headed out to sea, worse than anyone else onboard. His cabin was next to mine, so I heard his vomiting and dry heaving on the regular. That was sadly difficult to listen to, both for his sake and mine, but I was encouraged by his character strength to endure. Seasickness is hell.

Randy Smith was a thin, blonde-haired boy who mostly walked the line concerning rules and regulations onboard. He was never a troublemaker from what I saw, and he fit into the majority group of kids behind the scenes who strove to do well amidst discipline, hard work, scholastic expectations, and social chaos. Randy was quietly steady, a hard worker, and had a positive spirit.

Richie Yusem came from affluence, evidenced by his agitating arrogance and expectations of special personal treatment onboard, without an ounce of humility. Richie loved attention and talked incessantly, unable to shut up, even when he should have. The fact that he stuck his foot in his mouth repeatedly without ever learning his lesson made him a funny guy. But it also made him an easy target for The Brotherhood, who renamed him Bitchy Useless. He embraced chaos and conflict. If there was none, he created it.

Rick Goodfriend was another tall Florida boy who joined our community with very long hair. Noticeably a bit quieter and more filtered than the other guys from Florida, he wasn't necessarily less mischievous. Beyond the adventures provided by the program, Rick was an opportunist, always out for a good time. His eventual haircut on deck one day inspired more whooping and hollering from the Norwegian crewmen than any other haircut throughout the course of the year.

Sam Godfrey, at 16 years of age, was another one of the younger kids onboard, but he was philosophically inquisitive and emotionally mature for his age. I loved talking and hanging out with him both on and off the ship. Like me, he played the recorder. We practiced and performed familiar songs together on several occasions. Sam smiled sparingly, but he enjoyed humor. His round wire-rimmed glasses, wavy brown hair, and calm, quiet demeanor portrayed him as a young intellectual. Maybe he was.

Sam Godfrey

Steve Paulus (Rufus), of Asian descent, came aboard from New York sporting long, shoulder-length black hair parted in the middle. Like Sam, he wore round, wire-rimmed glasses. Somehow he acquired the nickname "Rufus T. Firefly"—either from himself or from his peers onboard—and the name "Rufus" stuck. In fact, it followed him for a lifetime among shipmates. He was another positive-minded student-cadet who worked diligently for the good of the ship and the community, steering clear of conflict while making the most of his Oceanics experience. Rufus was an intelligent kid who communicated well, paid attention to details, possessed organizational skills, and humored his friends with dry sarcasm. A successful future surely seemed to be in the cards for him.

Steve Paulus (Rufus)

Susan Nelson, also from Minnesota, joined our community in Bergen the same day as Jim, Janet, and George. Her adorable red hair and freckles stood out among the students, as did her social attributes and spirited personality. Susan played an important role as a female cadet willing to participate in the details pertaining to both ship and community as her positive influence was felt below deck and above.

Tara Dineen, one of the older students onboard, worked in the Oceanics New York office during the summer of 1972 as Stephanie's assistant. It was she who answered the door when my brother, Merv, and I arrived for my interview. And she continued helping Stephanie with small tasks in various ports throughout the year. Tara was privy to things the rest of us were not. However, she wasn't exempt from the rules, work, and discipline onboard, including sail training. She was a full-fledged cadet who stayed quietly upbeat, even in the difficult times onboard.

Susan Nelson

Tim Harris was a mild-mannered kid with a snarky grin and dark brown bangs often hiding his face. He hovered on the social fringes of the community at large but was creatively articulate within the realms of his inner circle of young friends, mostly out of the limelight. Many Oceanics kids' gifts were not discovered until long after our time together onboard ship. I believe Tim was one of those.

Tom Thornton, despite his unorthodox behavior, defiance, and complaints, proved to be a worthy cadet. His thick red hair tied back in a ponytail gave him an elf-like appearance. He came onboard as a full tuition paying student. His adopted father, a successful lawyer, had laid plenty of groundwork for Tom's future. However, Tom was determined to find his way in his own time. I suppose Oceanics played host to some of that. He and Perry were like two peas in a pod, insepa-rable, despite Stephanie's best efforts to keep them apart. Both influenced the other significantly. Tom's dry sense of humor, chronic complaining, and creative sarcasm, unlike anyone else onboard, kept me smiling throughout the year.

Willy Baldwin was an interesting, wiry guy who mostly minded his own business, but without isolating himself. He engaged others without criticism or judgment but didn't seem to feel the need to be loved and accepted by the community at large. Socially independent, articulate, descriptive, and sometimes abstract, he could survive without much support from others. He lived according to whatever made sense to him at the time. Even-keeled and sometimes humorous, Willy seldom displayed anger or exuberance.

Yappi Joseph, a student from the Ivory Coast, had skin that was blacker than black, and large, beautiful teeth that were whiter than white. His broad smile, deep booming voice, and happy spirit characterized him. He was a solid boy with strong arms and broad shoulders, and his appreciation for the program was remarkable. Yappi didn't carry an ounce of rebellion or defiance in his bones and did his best in every class, every task, and every order from the crew and administration alike.

Yappi Joseph, Student from Ivory Coast

Zoe Avery was a 16-year-old New England girl of average height, thin, cute, and adorable, with very long brown hair. Her smile was genuine but soft as she quietly found her place onboard as a supportive cadet, attentive student, and cooperative shipmate. She pulled her own weight in most everything she did without drawing attention to herself. Although socially reserved, she was subtly competitive and covertly adventurous within the parameters of the regulatory expectations onboard. She did as she was told without questioning authority. I found her to be encouraging, accepting, kind, friendly and fun, a realist who seldom complained. By year's end, she had become one of my favorite shipmates. I wished with all my heart I had taken more time to further cultivate our relationship. My feelings for her were confusing, and as fate would have it, they remained unexplored.

Zoe on work duty

52 YEARS LATER – 2025

Reunion after 52 years - (L to R) Kjemptrup, Steve Paulus, me (April 2025)

ABS Christine Thoresen

*Me wearing climbing harness for the
1st time ever w/videographer Andre*

My first climb in 52 years

Lookout bell on the foredeck

Me in Lerwick, Scotland

Christine (Spiderwoman)

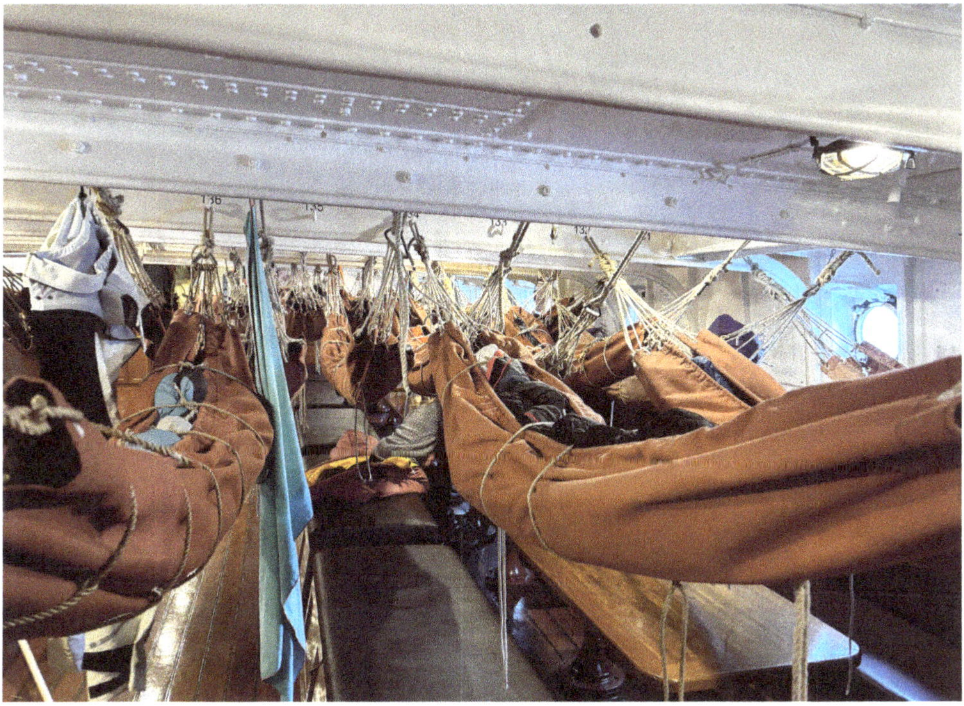

Hammocks in the banjers

Arctic climb (me in center)

Northern lights

Furling sails

Approaching Tromso, Norway

*April 2025 reenactment of 52 years earlier
(see page 232)*

*Me at the helm wearing the same hat as in
1972 (see page 251)*

Me on lookout watch

Shipmate Bryan enduring the cold

Furling the merse

My climb to the royl yard with Tom Grant en route to Greenland

Artic sunset

292

Ice in Nuuk Harbor

My Greenlander shipmates; Pinnaluk and Miriam

First sighting of Greenland

Bracing yards

Sunset

Steve Paulus, Andre Marton Pedersen, me in Nuuk

Nuuk, Greenland

Daughter Jessica and son Ty with me at the wheel in Seattle

Barrels of aged rum in the bottom of the hull

5 year old Greenlander Marley and me

Statsraad Lehmkuhl docked in Nuuk, Greenland

ABOUT THE AUTHOR

Marlie Smucker grew up in a conservative Mennonite family in the small farming community of Bird-in-Hand, Pennsylvania, and has lived in Lancaster County most of his life, despite extensive travels to numerous countries on five continents.

He has been involved in his community as a business owner, volunteer for various groups and charities, and as a mentor to young men. He is a father to three adult children, two stepchildren, and a proud grandpa of eight. He continues to be blessed with a spirit of adventure, plenty of grace, and many friends, but his greatest joy in life is his family.

Marlie has faithfully journaled every day since the age of 15, a span of nearly 60 years. This is his first published book, but it won't be his last.

ACKNOWLEDGEMENTS

I am grateful to everyone who helped bring this project to fruition.

My daughter, Jessica Smucker, proofread the manuscript at various stages, helped with editing, provided tech support, and project managed the final stages of publishing and promotion.

My editor, Lucy Church-Stoltzfus, was sensitive and supportive in her approach, applying a light touch that honored and encouraged my voice as narrator.

Amy Wissing and Lisa Camp at Lancaster Design & Consulting went above and beyond with the layout and book design, bringing my words to life with a lovely visual presentation. They were patient and reassuring at every step, and I am so impressed with their creativity, efficiency, and warmth.

Dan Zdilla created the cover image, a collage based on a 1972 photograph of me up in the rigging, made entirely from *National Geographic* magazine clippings. The original paper collage hangs framed in my office at home.

Joe Feinblatt, former professor and shipmate, took numerous photos during our time with Oceanics and graciously supplied me with many that appear on these pages.

My shipmate, Steve Paulus, has worked hard over the past few years to track down our former shipmates and form an Oceanics alumni community. I am grateful to him for reconnecting me with the *Statsraad Lehmkuhl* after so many years. Getting back in touch with old friends and fellow sailors was the motivation I needed to finish writing this book.

I will never forget Andre Marton Pederson, videographer, and Christine Thoreson, ABS, who climbed with me to the royl yard of the *Statsraad Lehmkuhl* in April 2025, helping me to realize a dream I wasn't sure I could manage as a 72 year-old recovering from rotator cuff surgery.

Finally, I am grateful to all my shipmates from 1972-73, for their individual and collective roles in creating these stories and adventures.